NATIONAL CENTER FOR EDUCATION STATISTICS

Urban Schools
The Challenge of Location and Poverty

Laura Lippman
Shelley Burns
Edith McArthur
National Center for Education Statistics

With contributions by
Robert Burton
Thomas M. Smith
National Center for Education Statistics

Phil Kaufman
MPR Associates, Inc.

U.S. Department of Education
Office of Educational Research and Improvement   NCES 96-184

U.S. Department of Education
Richard W. Riley
Secretary

Office of Educational Research and Improvement
Sharon P. Robinson
Assistant Secretary

National Center for Education Statistics
Jeanne E. Griffith
Acting Commissioner

Data Development and Longitudinal Studies Group
John H. Ralph
Acting Associate Commissioner

The National Center for Education Statistics (NCES) is the primary federal entity for collecting, analyzing, and reporting data related to education in the United States and other nations. It fulfills a congressional mandate to collect, collate, analyze, and report full and complete statistics on the condition of education in the United States; conduct and publish reports and specialized analyses of the meaning and significance of such statistics; assist state and local education agencies in improving their statistical systems; and review and report on education activities in foreign countries.

NCES activities are designed to address high priority education data needs; provide consistent, reliable, complete, and accurate indicators of education status and trends; and report timely, useful, and high quality data to the U.S. Department of Education, the Congress, the states, other education policymakers, practitioners, data users, and the general public.

We strive to make our products available in a variety of formats and in language that is appropriate to a variety of audiences. You, as our customer, are the best judge of our success in communicating information effectively. If you have any comments or suggestions about this or any other NCES product or report, we would like to hear from you. Please direct your comments to:

> National Center for Education Statistics
> Office of Educational Research and Improvement
> U.S. Department of Education
> 555 New Jersey Avenue NW
> Washington, DC 20208–5574

July 1996

Suggested Citation

U.S. Department of Education. National Center for Education Statistics. *Urban Schools: The Challenge of Location and Poverty* , NCES 96–184, by Laura Lippman, Shelley Burns, and Edith McArthur, with contributions by Robert Burton, Thomas M. Smith, and Phil Kaufman, Washington, DC: 1996.

For sale by the U.S. Government Printing Office
Superintendent of Documents, Mail Stop: SSOP, Washington, DC 20402-9328
ISBN 0-16-048669-6

Foreword

In the past, analytic reports prepared by the National Center for Education Statistics (NCES) have used the data available from one of our survey programs to address a variety of issues. In this report, we have attempted to do something different. We have chosen some specific policy-relevant questions and have tried to answer them using data from several of our surveys as well as other federal surveys.

The questions we chose illuminate the condition of education in urban schools compared to schools in other locations. Much attention has been given recently to America's urban schools, which are perceived to be in a state of some deterioration. Critics like Jonathan Kozol (*Savage Inequalities*) have vividly pointed out the problems with run-down facilities, unmotivated teachers, crime, and low expectations in inner city schools based on firsthand observations. Many believe that urban youth are more at risk today than youth living elsewhere. Information on these youths is important to the Department of Education because our mission is to ensure equal access to a high quality education for all.

We thought we could add to the existing information by exploring differences between students from urban schools and students in other locations on a broad spectrum of student and school characteristics. In particular, we explored how the concentration of student poverty in schools is related to these differences. To do this, we used sophisticated analytical methodologies, but we hope the results are still easy to understand. Our goal was to provide useful information for people interested in the relationship of poverty and urbanicity to student outcomes and background characteristics, as well as school and teacher characteristics.

To help us in planning for future analyses, we would welcome your reaction to this report. Did it answer some important questions about urban schools for you? Were the results easy to understand? Did it provide a "big picture" of urban schools? Did it suggest other issues or topics that could be addressed in a similar manner? The answers to these questions will help us to gauge the success of our effort to produce a new type of report, analyzing a particular topic with relevant data from various sources. We are continually striving to improve our reports to make them more relevant, accessible, and thought provoking.

Jeanne E. Griffith
Acting Commissioner

Acknowledgments

The authors wish to acknowledge the contributions made by the many people involved with this project at every stage of its development.

The analysis of data from many surveys could not have been accomplished without the help and expertise of NCES survey directors and staff and our colleagues at MPR Associates and Pinkerton Computer Consultants. We wish to thank Jeff Owens, Jerry West, Sharon Bobbitt, and Alex Sedlecek of NCES for their willingness to take the time to share their expertise with us, and John Tuma and Phil Kaufman of MPR Associates for their analytical work. Bruce Daniel of Pinkerton Computer Consultants efficiently and cheerfully provided endless tabulations of data from multiple surveys.

Mary Frase, John Ralph, and Bob Burton offered helpful suggestions to the write-up and formatting of the indicators, which markedly improved the presentation. Jenny Manlove helped write a section of the report in chapter 1 on community level background characteristics.

The report was reviewed by very thoughtful and generous people both within and outside of NCES, who improved the report immeasurably. Our NCES reviewers included Mary Frase, Bob Burton, John Ralph, Jeanne Griffith, Jerry West, Paula Knepper, Sharon Bobbitt, and Kerry Gruber. Our external reviewers included Michael Casserly, Gary Natriello, Floraline Stevens, and Donald Hernandez. Their contributions were innumerable, but any remaining flaws are ours alone.

The project generated many activities at MPR Associates that were orchestrated by the conscientious work of Fena Neustaedter, Patty Holmes, and Susie Kagehiro. Andrea Livingston expertly edited the report, and Leslie Retallick's design for the layout and graphics greatly enhanced the report. Elliott Medrich provided helpful editorial suggestions and took on the task of orchestrating the final editing and layout. Dawn Nelson at NCES handled the administrative aspects of contracting with MPR Associates and provided last-minute assistance with writing. Suellen Mauchamer orchestrated the production of the report.

The authors particularly wish to thank John Ralph for his inspiration, enthusiasm and support throughout the project, and Jeanne Griffith for her insights, support, and patience. This project took on many challenges, and its success was directly due to the willingness of Emerson Elliott, while Commissioner, and Jeanne Griffith, currently Acting Commissioner, to allow the authors to pursue the paths where the analysis led.

Executive Summary

Many Americans believe that urban schools are failing to educate the students they serve. Even among people who think that schools are doing a good job overall are those who believe that in certain schools, conditions are abysmal. Their perception, fed by numerous reports and observations, is that urban students achieve less in school, attain less education, and encounter less success in the labor market later in life.

Researchers and educators often link this perceived performance of urban youth to home and school environments that do not foster educational and economic success. Moreover, urban educators report the growing challenges of educating urban youth who are increasingly presenting problems such as poverty, limited English proficiency, family instability, and poor health. Finally, testimony and reports on the condition of urban schools feed the perception that urban students flounder in decaying, violent environments with poor resources, teachers, and curricula, and with limited opportunities.

This report addresses these widespread beliefs about the performance of urban students, and their family and school environments. Using data from several national surveys, it compares urban students and schools with their suburban and rural counterparts on a broad range of factors, including student population and background characteristics, afterschool activities, school experiences, and student outcomes.

A specific focus of this report is how poverty relates to the characteristics of the students and schools studied. Since, on average, urban public schools are more likely to serve low income students, it is possible that any differences between urban and non-urban schools and students are due to this higher concentration of low income students. In this study, the methodology used to explore differences between urban, suburban, and rural students and schools incorporates a control for the concentration of poverty in the school. Thus, this study allows comparisons to be made between urban and other schools and students, after factoring out

one major characteristic of urban schools that is often related to differences between schools—the higher concentration of low income students.

In addition, this report focuses on those urban schools that serve the highest concentrations of low income students, in light of national concern over these schools. Previous research has suggested that students from schools with high concentrations of low income students and students from urban schools would be expected to have less successful educational outcomes, less supportive home environments, and less positive school experiences than students from other schools. In fact, this study finds large differences between urban and non-urban schools and between high poverty and low poverty schools on most of the indicators of student background, school experiences, and student outcomes studied.

Students attending schools with both an urban location *and* a high poverty concentration were expected, therefore, to have particularly unfavorable circumstances. This report documents how urban high poverty schools and their students compare with their counterparts in other locations across many areas of concern, according to national surveys. Furthermore, the analysis specifically examines whether these schools and students compare less favorably than predicted, when considering together the effects of poverty concentration and an urban location. If the differences between urban high poverty schools and others are no greater than predicted, it indicates that the circumstances in these schools are related in predicted ways to the effects of poverty concentration and an urban location added together. However, if the differences are greater than predicted, it indicates that the effects of poverty concentration and location interact, and that the level for that particular measure exceeds the level that was predicted from these two effects alone. When this occurs, urban high poverty schools and their students are said to compare particularly unfavorably (or favorably, as the case may be) to other schools on that measure.

Student Characteristics

This study describes students who attended public schools primarily in the 1980s and examines their outcomes through 1990. Although the number of students in urban schools remained stable at about 11 million between 1980 and 1990, the proportion of those students who were living in poverty or who had difficulty speaking English increased over the decade. The proportion of students in urban schools who belonged to an Hispanic or "other" minority group (which includes Asians and Pacific Islanders) increased over the decade, while the proportion who were white declined and the proportion who were black stayed about the same. The increasing proportion of children with non-English backgrounds in urban locations has led to a greater proportion of children with difficulty speaking English in those locations.

Urban children were more than twice as likely to be living in poverty than those in suburban locations (30 percent compared with 13 percent in 1990), while 22 percent of rural children were poor in 1990 (figure A). Likewise, urban students were more likely than suburban or rural students to receive free or reduced price lunch (38 percent compared with 16 and 28 percent,

respectively). It follows then, that urban students were more likely to be attending schools with high concentrations of low income students. Forty percent of urban students attended these high poverty schools (defined as schools with more than 40 percent of students receiving free or reduced price lunch), whereas 10 percent of suburban students and 25 percent of rural students did so (figure B). Previous research suggests that a high concentration of low income students in a school is related to less desirable student performance.

Figure B
Percentage distribution of students, by school poverty concentration within urbanicity categories: 1987–88

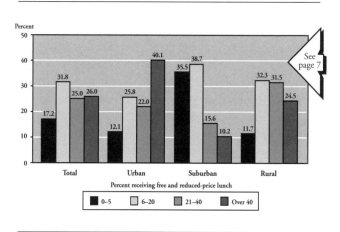

See page 7

SOURCE: U.S. Department of Education, National Center for Education Statistics, Schools and Staffing Survey, 1987–88.

Figure A
Poverty rates for children under 18, by urbanicity: 1980 and 1990

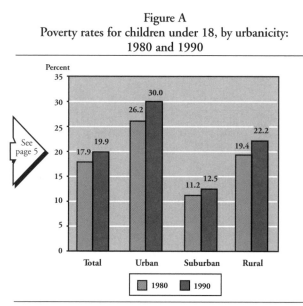

See page 5

SOURCE: U.S. Bureau of the Census, Current Population Reports, Series P-60, Nos. 181 and 133.

Aside from the greater likelihood of being poor and having difficulty speaking English, urban students were more likely than suburban students to be exposed to risks that research has associated with less desirable outcomes. Urban students were more likely to be exposed to safety and health risks that place their health and well-being in jeopardy, and were less likely to have access to regular medical care. They were also more likely to engage in risk-taking behavior, such as teenage pregnancy, that can make desirable outcomes more difficult to reach.

Student Background Characteristics and Afterschool Activities

Urban students were equally or more likely than other students to have families with certain characteristics that have been found to support desirable education outcomes, including high parental educational attainment, high expectations for their children's education, and frequent communication about school. However, there were some important exceptions. They were less likely to have the family structure, economic security, and stability that are most associated with desirable educational outcomes.

This section and those that follow use the analysis methodology described above to compare urban students with students in other locations while accounting for differences in school poverty concentration, and to compare students in urban high poverty schools with those in other high poverty schools. When compared to their suburban and rural counterparts, students in urban and urban high poverty schools were

• at least as likely to have a parent who completed college (figure C);

Figure C
Percentage of 8th-grade students with a parent in the household who had completed 4 years of college, by urbanicity and school poverty concentration: 1988

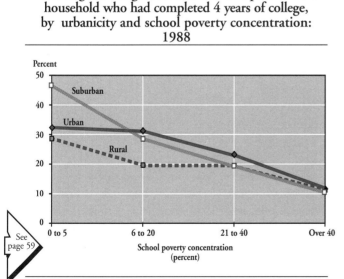

See page 59

SOURCE: U.S. Department of Education, National Center for Education Statistics, National Education Longitudinal Study of 1988, Base Year Survey.

• at least as likely to have parents with high expectations for their education; and

• as likely to have parents who talked with them about school.

However, they were

• less likely to live in two-parent families (figure D);

Figure D
Percentage of 8th-grade students living in a two-parent family, by urbanicity and school poverty concentration: 1988

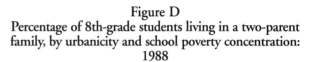
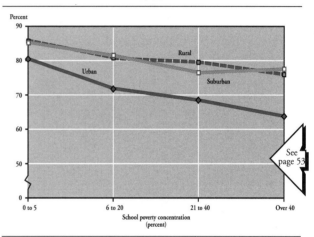

See page 53

SOURCE: U.S. Department of Education, National Center for Education Statistics, National Education Longitudinal Study of 1988, Base Year Survey.

• more likely to have changed schools frequently; and

• less likely than some but not all other groups to have at least one parent in a two-parent family working.

When examining their afterschool activities, students in urban schools, overall, were just as likely to be offered school sports activities and to work after school as students in schools elsewhere, but were less likely to participate in school-sponsored sports activities, even after accounting for poverty concentration. The afterschool experiences of students in urban high poverty schools were similar to those of students in high poverty schools in other locations.

In all of the student background and afterschool characteristics studied, students in urban high poverty schools compared in predicted ways to those in other schools. The differences between these students and students in other schools were related to the effects of poverty concentration and an urban location added together.

School Experiences

This report examines a wide range of school experiences, including: school staffing and resources, school program offerings, and student behavior. It finds that students and teachers in urban schools had greater challenges to overcome in a number of areas compared to their suburban and rural counterparts, even when the higher concentration of poverty in urban schools is considered. For example:

• Urban schools had larger enrollments, on average, than suburban or rural schools at both the elementary and secondary levels.

• Urban teachers had fewer resources available to them and less control over their curriculum than teachers in other locations, as did teachers in urban high poverty schools compared with those in rural high poverty schools (figure E).

Figure E
Percentage of teachers who think that teachers have a great deal of influence on establishing curriculum, by urbanicity and school poverty concentration: 1987–88

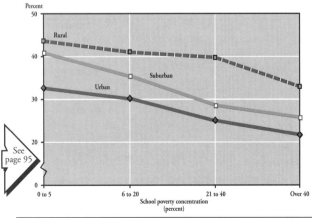

SOURCE: U.S. Department of Education, National Center for Education Statistics, Schools and Staffing Survey, 1987–88, Teacher File.

• Teachers in urban and urban high poverty schools had comparable levels of experience and salaries as their suburban counterparts, but they had more experience and higher salaries than most of their rural counterparts. However, administrators of urban and urban high poverty schools had more difficulty hiring teachers than their counterparts in most other schools (figure F).

Figure F
Percentage of principals who report difficulty hiring teachers, by urbanicity and school poverty concentration: 1987–88

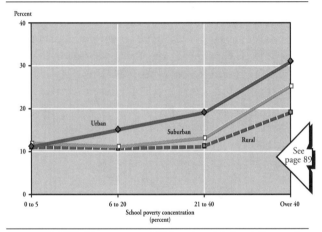

SOURCE: U.S. Department of Education, National Center for Education Statistics, Schools and Staffing Survey, 1987–88, Administrator File.

• Teacher absenteeism, an indicator of morale, was more of a problem in urban schools than in suburban or rural schools, and in urban high poverty schools compared with rural high poverty schools.

• Students in urban and urban high poverty schools were just as likely as their non-urban counterparts to be offered and to participate in certain programs and courses, with the following exceptions: they were more likely than their rural counterparts to have attended preschool, and they were less likely than most other groups to have attended schools with gifted and talented programs.

- Student behavior problems were more common in urban schools than in other schools, particularly in the areas of student absenteeism, classroom discipline (figure G), weapons possession, and student pregnancy. However, the use of alcohol was less of a problem in urban schools than in rural schools.

Figure G
Percentage of teachers of 8th-grade students who spend at least 1 hour per week maintaining classroom order and discipline, by urbanicity and school poverty concentration: 1988

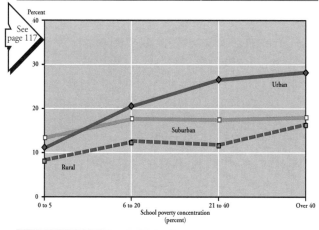

See page 117

SOURCE: U.S. Department of Education, National Center for Education Statistics, National Education Longitudinal Study of 1988, Base Year Teacher File.

- Students in high poverty schools regardless of location were less likely to feel safe in school, or to spend much time on homework than those in low poverty schools. However, students in urban high poverty schools were much more likely to watch television excessively (figure H) and to require more discipline by teachers in class compared with their counterparts in other locations; they were also more likely to be absent and possess weapons than those in rural high poverty schools.

Among the school experiences studied, urban high poverty schools and their students exceeded the levels predicted when considering the effects of urbanicity and poverty concentration in three areas: students

Figure H
Percentage of 10th-grade students who watch 3 or more hours of television on weekdays, by urbanicity and school poverty concentration: 1990

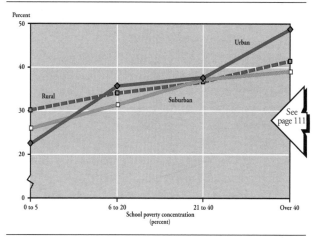

See page 111

SOURCE: U.S. Department of Education, National Center for Education Statistics, National Education Longitudinal Study of 1988, First Follow-up Student File.

were more likely to watch television excessively, less likely to have access to gifted and talented programs, and were more likely to have minority teachers (considered by many to be a favorable circumstance). The levels of these indicators were unusual when compared with non-urban schools, and were not explained solely by the effects of poverty concentration and location added together.

Urban high poverty schools often compared unfavorably to rural high poverty schools on measures of school experiences, but were often similar to suburban high poverty schools on these measures. Further analysis suggested that high poverty concentration in rural schools was not as strongly related to students' school experiences as it was in urban or suburban schools.

Student Outcomes

Many of the student background characteristics and school experiences of urban students outlined above would suggest that students in urban and particularly urban high poverty schools had greater challenges to overcome than did suburban or rural students in achieving academically, attaining education, and encountering success in the labor market. This study finds important differences in the achievement, attainment, and economic outcomes of urban students compared with those in other locations. These differences were more pronounced at younger ages and many diminish with age. However, for a minority of students who attended urban schools, the likelihood of long-term poverty and unemployment was much greater than for those who attended school in other locations.

When urban students were compared with suburban and rural students, while accounting for the higher concentration of poverty in urban schools, and when students in urban high poverty schools were compared with those in other high poverty schools:

- 8th graders in urban and urban high poverty schools scored lower on achievement tests, but their 10th-grade counterparts scored about the same as those in other locations.

- Students in urban and urban high poverty schools were less likely to complete high school on time (figure I), but they completed postsecondary degrees at the same rate as others.

Figure I
Percentage graduating on time among the sophomore class of 1980, by urbanicity and percent disadvantaged in school

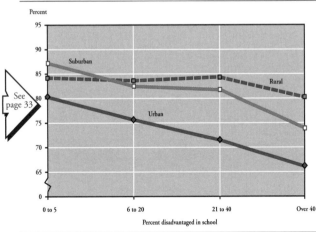
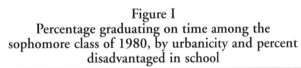

See page 33

SOURCE: U.S. Department of Education, National Center for Education Statistics, High School and Beyond Study, Third Follow-up Survey, 1986.

- Young adults who had attended urban schools had lower rates of participation in full-time work or school 4 years after most of them would have left high school, but had similar participation rates 7 to 15 years after high school; those from urban high poverty schools had levels of activity that were similar to those from other high poverty schools.

- Young adults who had attended urban and urban high poverty schools had much higher poverty and unemployment rates later in life than those who had attended other schools (figures J and K).

Figure J
Percentage of young adults living in poverty, by high school urbanicity and percent disadvantaged in high school: 1990

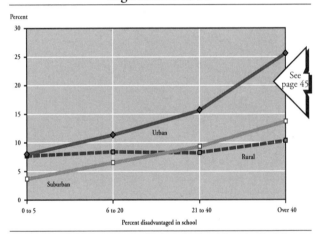

See page 45

SOURCE: U.S. Department of Labor, National Longitudinal Survey of Youth, 1990.

Although students in urban high poverty schools compared less favorably than students in high poverty schools located elsewhere on many measures, it is important to keep their absolute levels of performance in mind. Despite the challenges that students from urban high poverty schools face, the great majority of these students graduated from high school on time (66 percent), and during their young adult years, were more likely than not to be employed or to be in school full time (73 percent), and were living above the poverty line (74 percent).

The levels of the outcomes measured for students from urban high poverty schools would have been

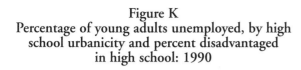

Figure K
**Percentage of young adults unemployed, by high
school urbanicity and percent disadvantaged
in high school: 1990**

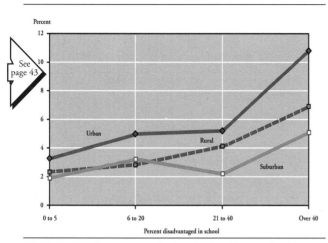

SOURCE: U.S. Department of Labor, National Longitudinal Survey
of Youth, 1990.

predicted from the effects of poverty concentration
and an urban location added together. Given the large
overall variation on these measures by urbanicity and
poverty concentration, the outcomes for these students were not unusual.

Discussion

Looking across all of the measures of student background, school experiences, and student outcomes
studied, some general findings emerge:

• Urban students and schools compared less favorably to their non-urban counterparts on many
measures even after accounting for the higher
concentration of low income students in urban
schools.

• Urban high poverty schools and their students
performed similarly or more favorably than
other high poverty schools and students on half
of the measures studied. On these measures,
large differences were found by school poverty
concentration, so that high poverty concentra-

tion seemed to present equally challenging circumstances in all locations.

• On the other half of the measures studied, urban
high poverty schools and their students compared unfavorably to other high poverty schools.
These measures tended to show consistent differences by location across the levels of poverty
concentration.

• When considering the large overall variations by
location and poverty concentration, urban high
poverty schools and their students, with few
exceptions, were no different than the effects of
location and poverty concentration added
together would have predicted.

Previous research has suggested that students from
schools with high concentrations of low income students, and students from urban schools would have
less supportive family backgrounds, less favorable
school experiences, and less successful educational
outcomes than students from other schools. This
study provides evidence that students in urban
schools are more likely than those in other locations
to have characteristics such as poverty, difficulty
speaking English, and numerous health and safety
risks that present greater challenges to them and their
educators. This study also provides evidence that
important differences do exist between the student
background characteristics, school experiences, and
outcomes of urban and other students, and that these
differences represent more than that which can be
attributed to differences in the school concentration
of low income students. When these differences
remain after accounting for poverty concentration, it
is possible that the above-cited differences between
urban and non-urban student characteristics, or other
differences between urban, suburban, and rural locations come into play.

However, in every domain of students' lives studied—
student background characteristics, school experiences,
and student outcomes—there were instances where
urban students and schools were similar to their non-

urban counterparts after accounting for poverty concentration, suggesting that some of the often-cited bleak perceptions of urban schools and students may be overstated. Given the greater challenges that urban students and schools face, the fact that they were similar to their non-urban counterparts on these measures suggests that they may not only be meeting the challenges, but performing above expectations in these areas.

Moreover, this report provides evidence that challenges the perception that urban schools with the highest poverty concentrations are always much worse off than other schools. The report documents large variations in schools and students in all of the important areas considered when assessing school performance—student background, school experiences, and student outcomes. Within this overall variation, differences between urban high poverty schools and other high poverty schools did not usually exceed differences between urban and other schools at other levels of poverty concentration. On half of the measures, urban high poverty schools did compare unfavorably to high poverty schools in other locations; however, in an equal number of cases, urban high poverty schools were similar or even compared favorably.

The findings from this study suggest certain areas where the differences between the student background, school experiences, and outcomes of students in urban and other schools—particularly in urban high poverty schools compared with other high poverty schools—are

most pronounced. These areas could benefit from further research:

Student Background

- Single-parent families

- School mobility

School Experiences

- Difficulty hiring teachers

- Teacher control over curriculum

- Weekday television watching

- Student absenteeism

- Classroom discipline

- Weapons possession

- Student pregnancy

Student Outcomes

- High school completion

- Poverty and unemployment of young adults

Contents

Contents—Continued

List of Figures

Figure   Page

Chapter 3   Student Background Characteristics and Afterschool Activities

List of Charts and Tables

Chapter 1

Introduction

Many Americans believe that urban schools are failing to educate the students they serve. Their perception is that urban students are floundering in an environment of disruption, violence, decaying buildings, poor quality teaching, and scant resources. This perception has been fueled by various reports and testimony about conditions in urban schools, which have based their findings on data and observations gathered from selected urban schools. According to these reports, students in urban schools have lower levels of achievement, completion of high school and higher education, and employment (Carnegie Foundation 1988; Louis and Miles 1990). Moreover, from the view of city school administrators, the challenges of educating today's urban youth are daunting, with more and more students presenting problems such as "poverty, limited-English proficiency, family instability, discrimination, disability, malnutrition, and poor health" (Council of the Great City Schools 1994, p. viii). Lack of parental support and unsafe communities are also cited as detrimental to urban students (Carnegie Foundation 1988). Urban schools themselves are often portrayed as decaying and crowded facilities that are inadequately staffed with overworked teachers lacking the basic tools of teaching, who must function under poor leadership in an overly bureaucratic and anonymous environment (Louis and Miles 1990; Walker 1989; Carnegie Foundation 1988).

This study addresses these perceptions about urban students, families, and schools using nationally representative survey data to compare students and schools in urban areas to those in suburban and rural areas on a broad range of indicators. These indicators characterize students (chapter 1), their education outcomes (chapter 2), their family background and afterschool activities (chapter 3), and school experiences (chapter 4).

This report goes beyond providing simple comparisons between urban and suburban or rural schools, however. Since urban public schools are more likely to have higher concentrations of students from low income families, it is possible that any differences between urban and other public schools are actually due to the higher concentration of low income students in urban public schools. This study examines whether urban schools, overall, would still look different from other schools if the concentration of low income students in urban schools did not differ from that at other schools. One contribution of this report to existing research, then, is to identify which education outcomes, family background characteristics, and school experiences are different in urban schools, after factoring out one major characteristic that is often related to these differences—high concentrations of low income students.

The quality of education in those urban public schools that serve the highest concentrations of low income students is a primary focus of this report, since the commonly held perception is that conditions are much worse in these schools than in others. This study analyzes these *high poverty urban schools* separately, and determines whether the conditions and outcomes for students in these schools are even less favorable than an urban location and high poverty concentration added together would predict. That is, do these two characteristics, each with known and measurable negative effects, interact, providing evidence of unusual circumstances in these schools compared to those at other locations and levels of poverty concentration? For each indicator studied, urban high poverty schools are compared to high poverty schools in other locations, and the size of this gap is compared to that between urban and other schools at lower levels of poverty concentration. This suggests whether, given overall variations by location and poverty concentration, urban high poverty schools are *different than predicted* when compared to other schools.

There are four research questions asked, then, across a wide spectrum of data on student outcomes, family background and afterschool experiences, and school experiences. The word "schools" is meant to refer to students in the schools as well. They are as follows:

1) Are urban schools different from suburban or rural schools?

2) Are schools with high poverty concentrations different from those with lower poverty concentrations?

3) When taking school poverty concentration into account, are urban schools different from other schools?

4) Are the indicators in urban high poverty schools at unexpected levels compared to other schools, when considering overall variations by location and poverty concentration? And, are urban high poverty schools different from other high poverty schools?

Chapter 2 presents the results of the analysis for indicators of education outcomes, chapter 3 for indicators of student background and afterschool activities, and chapter 4 for school experience indicators. Each chapter begins with a chart that lists the indicators to be discussed and the essential results of the analysis in a condensed format—charts 2.1, 3.1, and 4.1. The information presented in this report is grouped to the school level, so that schools and students attending schools in each location and level of poverty concentration are compared to each other.

The remainder of this chapter provides the background and context for the three analytical chapters that follow. Previous research is reviewed; then, urban public schools and their students are compared with their suburban and rural counterparts on various demographic, health, and community characteristics. Finally, the analytical approach, sources of data, and definitions used in this report are detailed.

Previous Research on School Location and Poverty Concentration

Explaining differences between schools has been a longstanding topic of educational research. This report not only focuses on differences between urban and other schools but also considers how the socioeconomic status (SES) of urban students is related to these differences. Past research has suggested that the SES of students, and the socioeconomic composition of schools and neighborhoods are strongly linked to differences between

urban and other schools. This section reviews research that has focused on socioeconomic as well as other factors at the student, school, and neighborhood level and their relationship to education outcomes.

Student Level

Coleman and associates (1966) found that differences between schools in average achievement were largely related to differences in the socioeconomic backgrounds of the students. Moreover, they found that when these differences were held constant, variations in facilities, curricula, and teacher quality among schools accounted for only a small fraction of the difference in student achievement. Researchers have tested and retested this finding, and have agreed, in general, that schools have only small effects on student learning or on the probability of attending college, once individual background is held constant (Armor 1972; Mayer and Jencks 1989).

Urban schools are more likely to have low income students attending than other schools. For example, 44 percent of urban public school students are eligible to receive free or reduced price school lunch, compared with 23 percent of suburban students and 30 percent of rural students (U.S. Department of Education 1994). Furthermore, urban students are more likely to be disadvantaged by having only one parent; having less educated and/or unemployed parents; having handicapping conditions or learning, emotional, or health disabilities; having difficulty speaking English; or by being homeless (Peng et al. 1992; Hodgkinson 1989). (See the following section for a full discussion of the prevalence of many of these and other conditions in urban versus suburban or rural areas.) Finally, urban children are more likely to have more than one of these attributes, thereby compounding their disadvantage (Peng et al. 1992).

School Level

The Coleman study also found that a student's family background was not the only "outside school" determinant of achievement. According to Coleman et al. (1966, 22), achievement is strongly related to the educational backgrounds and aspirations of other students in the school. "Children from a given family background, when put in schools of different social composition, will achieve at quite different levels." This composition effect has been corroborated by other researchers, and is found to be particularly strong for low income students. In their assessment of the Chapter 1 compensatory education services program, Kennedy, Jung, and Orland (1986, 22) found that

> . . . the relationship between family poverty status and student achievement is not as strong as the relationship between school poverty concentrations and school achievement averages. Non-poor students attending schools with high concentrations of poor students were found to be more likely to fall behind than poor students who attend schools with small proportions of poor students.

A later assessment of the Chapter 1 program, the Prospects study, found that average achievement declines as school poverty concentration increases. On average, students in high poverty schools scored significantly below those who attended low poverty schools (Abt Associates 1993). Pelavin Associates (1993) using a multilevel analysis model (to account for the fact that average correlations are always higher than individual level correlations), with the National Education Longitudinal Study of 1988 (NELS:88), still found a negative effect of poverty concentration on average achievement, above and beyond the effect of family income and prior achievement. In this analysis, each 10 percent increase in school poverty concentration resulted in a small, but significant, decrease in math achievement for the average student. Also using NELS:88, Anderson et al. (1992) found that low income students in schools with small concentrations of such students score higher than their counterparts in schools with high concentrations of low income students. In another analysis, using the High School and Beyond Study, Myers (1985) found that students in high poverty schools had lower achievement than did students in low poverty schools, even after holding family SES constant. Moreover, in a review of research on the effects of school-level SES, Jencks and Mayer (1990) found that school-level SES affects students' chances of graduating as well as how much they learn, after controlling for family background. This research has demonstrated, then, that school poverty concentration has an important relationship to levels of achievement, which

remains even after controlling for individual student family background.

Research on *urban* schools offers further evidence of the importance of the student composition of schools. Some studies have shown no urban effects once student background is held constant (Gamoran 1987; Barro and Kolstad 1987). Others have found that differences in family background did not sufficiently explain gaps in achievement between urban and suburban schools; rather, these gaps were explained by differences in student composition. Urban schools were different, because they were more likely to have concentrations of less advantaged students, which in itself produces special problems (Hoffer 1992). Research suggests that such concentrations may lower the level of engagement, effort, and aspirations of all students (Hoffer 1992; Ralph 1990), and that some peer groups in inner cities may even develop an aversion to academic work and learning (Fordham and Ogbu 1987).

Other characteristics of urban schools besides the SES of their students are often identified as related to urban school problems and poorer student outcomes. For instance, because urban schools are likely to have fewer resources than suburban schools, school level achievement differences may reflect inequities in resources (Panel on High-Risk Youth 1993; Orland 1990). Researchers also suggest that the larger size and often burdensome centralized bureaucracy of urban schools can restrict the independence and collegial support among school staff and create a more impersonal environment for students (Hoffer 1992; Glazer 1992). Finally, it is perceived that violence and disruptions are more prevalent in urban schools. All of these location-specific school characteristics help to reinforce the view that a school's location can influence a student's likelihood of being undereducated (Waggoner 1991).

Neighborhood Level

Research suggests that differences between schools and student outcomes are related to differences in the composition of neighborhoods, even after controlling for family background. Poor neighborhoods, in particular, have been found to negatively affect students' education outcomes. While living in affluent neighborhoods increases IQ at age 5 for both poor and non-poor children, living in poor neighborhoods raises the odds of a child developing behavior problems, becoming pregnant as a teenager, and dropping out of school (Brooks-Gunn et al. 1993; Duncan et al. 1994; Clarke 1992; Crane 1991; Jencks and Mayer 1990). Most researchers have found that neighborhood characteristics have a smaller effect on school outcomes than do family and school characteristics (Clarke 1992; Coulton and Pandey 1992; Mayer and Jencks 1989).

Urban schools are more likely to serve neighborhoods in which there are high concentrations of poverty (Wilson 1987). The geographic concentration of poverty in cities during the 1970s and 1980s was accompanied by the concentration of undesirable conditions to which children were exposed, such as education failure, violence, crime, welfare dependency, and family disruption (Massey et al. 1994). Moreover, those who live in urban neighborhoods with high proportions of welfare recipients have lower chances of finding well-paying jobs (Jencks and Mayer 1990). Parents in urban high poverty neighborhoods are less likely to be employed or married, and community ties are weaker, negatively affecting parent involvement in the school (Wilson 1987). Researchers have also noted the lack of positive role models and social institutions in these communities to support and encourage positive behaviors in children (Sawhill et al. 1992).

Thus, previous research suggests that both students from schools with high concentrations of low income students and those from urban schools would be expected to have less successful education outcomes, home environments that are less supportive, and less positive school experiences than students from other schools. This report will continue this vein of research by testing whether data from several nationally representative surveys of schools, students, and young adults replicate these results from smaller, more specialized studies.

The Setting: Urban Schools and Communities

The analysis in the following chapters focuses on students who attended public school during the late 1980s to 1990 (with the exception of a few long-term outcomes

of students who were in school during the late 1970s and early 1980s). This section describes urban public schools and urban communities in comparative perspective during this same time period, drawing from several national surveys.[1]

Urban Schools

Between 1980 and 1990, the total number of students enrolled in public schools fell from about 40 million to 38 million (figure 1.1). However, the number of students in urban schools and suburban schools stayed about the same, at about 11 million and 17 million, respectively. The number of students in rural schools declined from about 13 million to less than 11 million.

Figure 1.1
Number of students enrolled in public schools, by urbanicity: 1980 and 1990

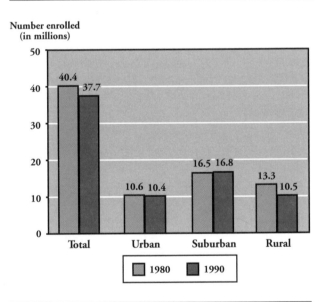

SOURCE: U.S. Bureau of the Census, Current Population Survey, October 1980 and October 1990.

---

[1]This section uses data from the surveys conducted by the National Center for Education Statistics (NCES), the Bureau of the Census, Bureau of Justice Statistics, and the National Center for Health Statistics. This report uses the terms *urban, suburban,* and *rural* to denote urbanicity categories for all surveys. These categories correspond to the Bureau of the Census definitions of central city metropolitan, other metropolitan, and nonmetropolitan with the exception of the NCES Schools and Staffing Survey. See the section on definitions and the appendix for a full discussion.

Thus, the percentage distribution of all public school students changed over the decade, with an increase in the proportion attending both urban and suburban schools, and a decrease in the proportion in rural schools (figure 1.2). The proportion of students in urban schools increased from 26 to 28 percent (see appendix table 1.1).

Figure 1.2
Percentage distribution of students enrolled in public schools, by urbanicity: 1980 and 1990

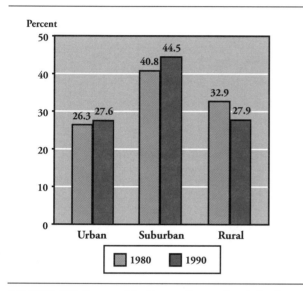

SOURCE: U.S. Bureau of the Census, Current Population Survey, October 1980 and October 1990.

Among students living in urban, suburban, and rural areas, there are differences in the proportions who attend private schools. Since this report presents information only on public school students, the extent to which the data are representative of all students in each area varies. While nationally about 12 percent of all students were in private schools during the 1987–88 school year, in urban areas that percentage approached 17. Thirteen percent of suburban students and 7 percent of rural students attended private schools (see appendix table 1.2).

Urban public schools are larger, on average, than suburban or rural schools at every level. The average size of urban elementary schools is 528 students, while that of suburban schools is 492, followed by rural schools with

354 students. At the middle or junior high school level, urban schools enroll 735 students on average, while the average enrollments for suburban and rural schools are 662 and 463, respectively. At the secondary or high school level, the average size of urban schools is more than twice that of rural schools, with 1,313 students compared with 577 students, and it is slightly larger than suburban schools, which have an average of 1,197 students (see appendix table 1.3).

School Poverty Concentration

Poverty rates among children are higher in urban locations than in the surrounding suburban or rural areas, which translates into higher concentrations of poor students in urban public schools. In 1990, 20 percent of children were living in poverty nationwide. However, 30 percent of children in urban locations were living in poverty, more than twice the rate for children living in the surrounding suburbs (13 percent). Among children living in rural areas, 22 percent were poor (see figure 1.3 and appendix table 1.4). Further, the poverty rate among children increased in all three

Figure 1.3
Poverty rates for children under age 18, by urbanicity: 1980 and 1990

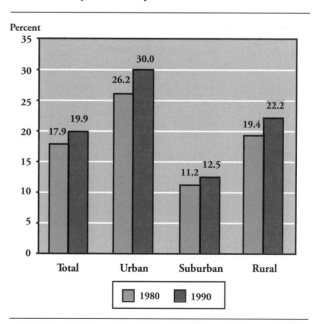

SOURCE: U.S. Bureau of the Census, Current Population Reports, Series P-60, Nos. 181 and 133.

localities between 1980 and 1990, increasing in urban areas from 26 percent in 1980 to 30 percent in 1990.

Another measure of the economic well-being of children is the socioeconomic status (SES) of their families. This is usually a composite measure of the parents' education, occupation, as well as income, and is therefore considered a more complete measure of the resources that a family can contribute to their child. Thirty-three percent of urban 8th graders came from families whose SES was in the lowest quarter nationally in 1988, while this was true for 19 percent of suburban students (see figure 1.4 and appendix table 1.5). In other words, one out of three urban students came from families whose estimated ability to contribute to their child's development was among the poorest in the nation. Rural students were just as likely as urban students to have families whose SES was in the lowest quartile.

Federal programs exist that support low income students by funding their schools to provide them free and reduced price lunches and supplemental education services. The National School Lunch Program administered by the U.S. Department of Agriculture's Food and Consumer Service provides free or reduced price lunches for children from families whose income is below 185 percent of the poverty line for that year (see section below on definitions of poverty). Overall, 28 percent of public students nationally received this service during the 1987–88 school year. In urban schools, 38 percent received free or reduced price lunches (see figure 1.5 and appendix table 1.6), and in suburban and rural schools the percentages were 16 and 28, respectively. More students are eligible to receive school lunches than actually receive them, however, particularly in secondary schools where participation in the program is a source of embarrassment for some students. For the same year, it was estimated that 42 percent of urban students, 18 percent of suburban students, and 31 percent of rural students were eligible for this service (see appendix table 1.6). Thus, higher proportions of urban students are eligible for and receive school lunches than in other locations.

Figure 1.5
Percentage of students in poverty-related programs, by urbanicity: 1987–88

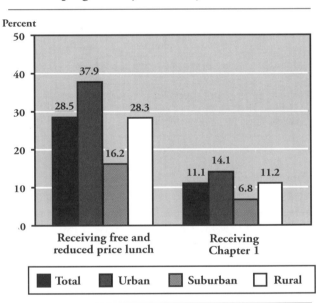

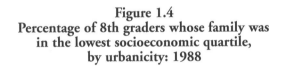

SOURCE: U.S. Department of Education, National Center for Education Statistics, School and Staffing Survey, 1987–88.

Figure 1.4
Percentage of 8th graders whose family was in the lowest socioeconomic quartile, by urbanicity: 1988

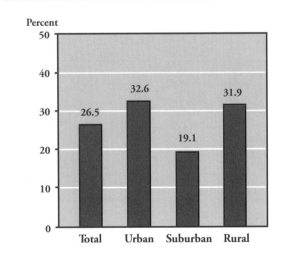

SOURCE: U.S. Department of Education, National Center for Education Statistics, National Education Longitudinal Study of 1988, Base Year Survey.

Chapter 1 of the Elementary and Secondary Education Act (renamed Title 1 under the 1994 Elementary and Secondary Education Act) provides federal funds for education services for disadvantaged students who are performing below grade level. Figure 1.5 shows the proportion of students in each locale that participated in the Chapter 1 program during the 1987–88 school year. Fourteen percent of urban students participated, as did about 7 percent of suburban students and 11 percent of rural students. The levels of participation varied by location similarly for both the school lunch and Chapter 1 programs, with participation in the Chapter 1 program lower than participation in the school lunch program in every location.

The percentage of students receiving free or reduced price lunch in school is the measure of school poverty concentration that is used in this report, since it is most widely available and comparable nationwide. This measure is not a precise measure of the extent of poverty in schools, however. (See the section on definitions for a full description of this measure.) In this report, students are grouped into four categories corresponding to the approximate quartiles of poverty concentration of a nationally representative sample of public schools. The categories of school poverty concentration are 0–5 percent, 6–20 percent, 21–40 percent, and more than 40 percent of students in poverty. Figure 1.6 and appendix table 1.7

show the distribution of public school students by these four categories of school poverty concentration.

Urban students are more likely than suburban or rural students to be in high poverty schools, those with poverty concentrations of more than 40 percent. In fact, 40 percent of urban students attend these schools, compared with 10 percent of suburban students and 25 percent of rural students. Urban students are much less likely than suburban students to be in low poverty schools, those with 0–5 percent of students in poverty. Only 12 percent of urban students attend low poverty schools, compared with 36 percent of suburban students. Rural students are about as likely as urban students to be in low poverty schools (12 percent).

In suburban areas, three out of four students attend schools with a poverty concentration of 20 percent or less. This striking difference between suburban and other schools is illustrated in figure 1.7 and appendix table 1.8: 38 percent of urban students and 44 percent of rural students attend such schools. The distribution of urban students by school poverty concentration is more similar to that of rural students than suburban students.

Figure 1.6
Percentage distribution of students, by school poverty concentration within urbanicity categories: 1987–88

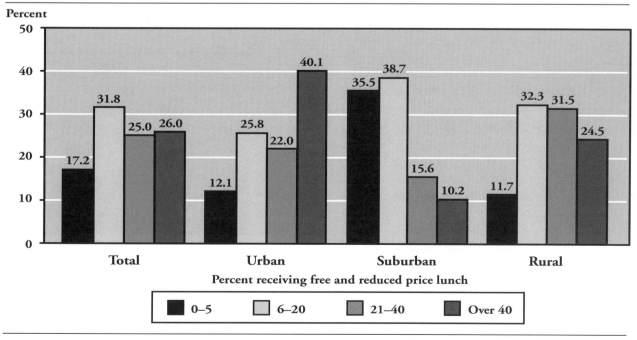

SOURCE: U.S. Department of Education, National Center for Education Statistics, School and Staffing Survey, 1987–88.

Figure 1.7
Percentage distribution of students by school poverty concentration deciles, by urbanicity: 1987–88

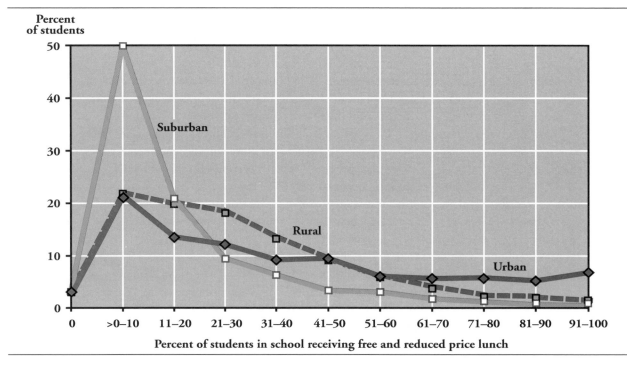

SOURCE: U.S. Department of Education, National Center for Education Statistics, School and Staffing Survey, 1987–88.

Student Minority Status

Urban public schools are more likely to serve students who have difficulty speaking English or who belong to a racial or ethnic minority.

During the 1980s, the proportion of public school students nationwide who had difficulty speaking English increased from about 3 to 5 percent (see figure 1.8 and appendix table 1.4). In urban schools, this percentage rose from twice the national level in 1979 (6 percent) to 9 percent by 1989. Suburban schools and rural schools had smaller percentages of students who had difficulty speaking English in 1989, 4 percent and 2 percent, respectively.

Similarly, the percentage of students in urban public schools who are classified as Hispanic or "other" (which includes Asians and Pacific Islanders) increased over the decade (see figure 1.9 and appendix table 1.9). Hispanics and "other" minorities made up 19 percent

Figure 1.8
Percentage of students with difficulty speaking English, by urbanicity: 1979 and 1989

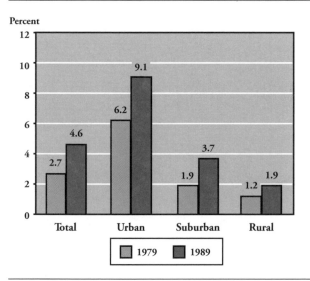

SOURCE: U.S. Bureau of the Census, Current Population Survey, November 1979 and 1989.

Figure 1.9
Trends in the racial-ethnic distribution of urban students: 1980 and 1990

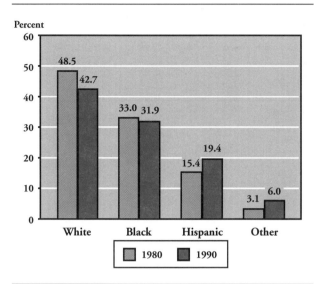

Percent

■ 1980   ■ 1990

NOTE: White refers to white, non-Hispanic students. Black refers to black, non-Hispanic students.

SOURCE: U.S. Bureau of the Census, Current Population Survey, October 1980 and October 1990.

of urban students in 1980, increasing to 25 percent of urban students by 1990. Non-Hispanic whites (henceforth, whites) declined as a percentage of urban students over the decade, while the percentage of students who were black, non-Hispanic (henceforth, blacks) stayed about the same.

During the 1987–88 school year, when the students profiled in this report were in school, urban public schools had markedly smaller percentages of white students and higher percentages of black and Hispanic students than suburban or rural schools (see figure 1.10 and appendix table 1.10). Urban schools had a higher percentage of "other" minorities (including Asian and Pacific Islanders) than rural schools, but about the same proportion as suburban schools. Almost half (49 percent) of urban students belonged to a racial or ethnic minority (black, Hispanic, or "other") compared with 20 percent of suburban students and 16 percent of rural students (see appendix table 1.11).

This difference in the racial-ethnic composition of schools is particularly noticeable between high and low

Figure 1.10
Racial-ethnic distribution of students, by urbanicity: 1987–88

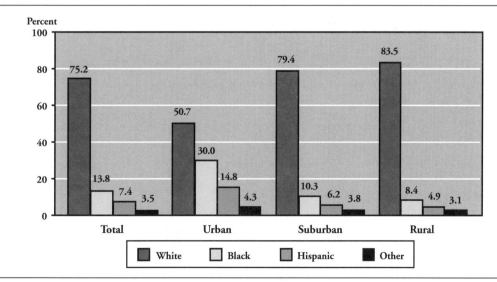

Percent

■ White   □ Black   ■ Hispanic   ■ Other

NOTE: Percentages do not add to 100 because of missing data. White refers to white, non-Hispanic students. Black refers to black, non-Hispanic students.

SOURCE: U.S. Department of Education, National Center for Education Statistics, School and Staffing Survey, 1987–88.

Figure 1.11
Racial-ethnic distribution of students in schools, by urbanicity and school poverty concentration: 1987–88

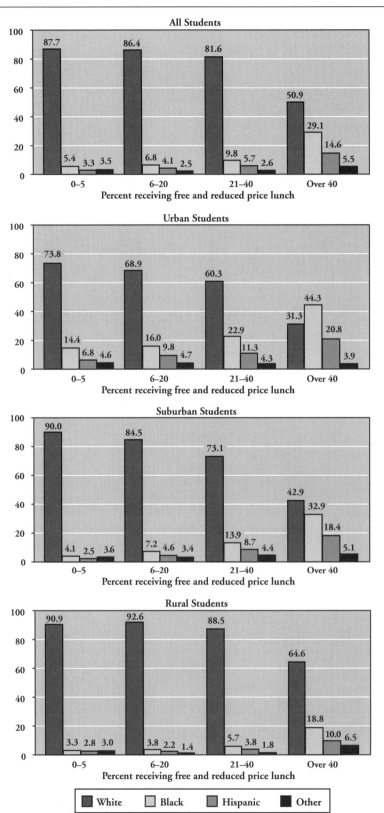

NOTE: Percentages do not add to 100 because of missing data. White refers to white, non-Hispanic students. Black refers to black, non-Hispanic students.

SOURCE: U.S. Department of Education, National Center for Education Statistics, School and Staffing Survey, 1987–88.

poverty schools (see figure 1.11 and appendix tables 1.10 and 1.11). High poverty schools in every location have higher enrollments of minorities than low poverty schools, but urban high poverty schools are more likely to enroll minority students than high poverty schools in suburban or rural areas. Among urban schools, 69 percent of students in high poverty schools belonged to a racial or ethnic minority, compared with 26 percent in low poverty schools. Among suburban schools, 56 percent of students in high poverty schools belonged to a minority group compared with 10 percent in low poverty schools. In rural schools, 35 percent of students in high poverty schools belonged to a minority group compared with 9 percent in low poverty schools.

Community Risk Factors

Children who grow up in urban areas are more likely to be exposed to risks that place their health and well-being in jeopardy. These factors may be related to poorer outcomes for students from urban schools.

In particular, urban children face greater risks of living in poverty and being surrounded by poverty, with all its attendant risks. In addition, they are more likely to be exposed to safety and health risks, and have less access to regular medical care than do other children. They are also more likely to engage in risk-taking behavior that can lead to undesirable outcomes, such as teenage pregnancy, which limit their opportunities for education and economic success. The following is a discussion of selected risk factors that indicate some of the areas in which urban students are at a disadvantage compared to other students and that are related to their performance in school. The data refer to circa 1990 to be consistent with data on urban schools and students analyzed in the subsequent chapters.

Youth living in urban communities are more likely to be victimized by crime than those living in other community types (see figure 1.12 and appendix table 1.12). This is true both for crimes of violence and crimes of theft. The rate of victimization from violent crimes for persons ages 12 and above was 41 per 1,000 in urban communities in 1990, compared with 25 per 1,000 in suburban communities and 23 per 1,000 in rural com-

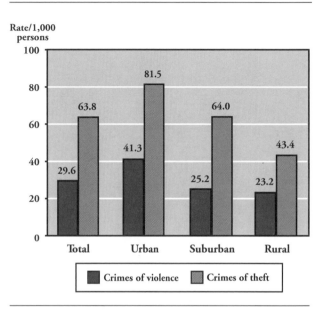

Figure 1.12
Victimization rates for persons ages 12 and over, by type of crime and urbanicity: 1990

Rate/1,000 persons

SOURCE: U.S. Department of Justice, Bureau of Justice Statistics, Criminal Victimization in the United States, 1990.

munities. The urban rates of victimization from theft were also higher (82 per 1,000) than suburban (64 per 1,000) or rural areas (43 per 1,000).

Children's health can affect their overall development and education performance. Children who live in urban locations are at higher risk for health problems than other children. The infant mortality rate is considered to be a sensitive summary indicator of neonatal, infant, and child health conditions, since it is highly correlated with other child health indicators. In urban locations, infants have higher mortality rates than in both suburban and rural locations (about 10 per 1,000 compared with about 8 per 1,000 for suburban areas and 9 per 1,000 for rural) (see figure 1.13 and appendix table 1.12).

Access to medical care is more limited for children in urban areas, and is more likely to be on an emergency basis compared with other areas. Urban children are less likely than other children to receive regular attention by a private physician, and instead use a clinic,

Figure 1.13
Infant mortality rates, by urbanicity: 1990

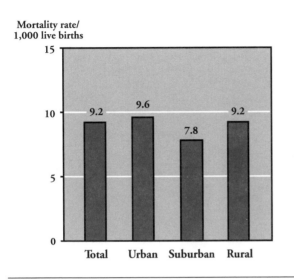

Mortality rate/
1,000 live births

SOURCE: National Center for Health Statistics, Vital Statistics of the United States, 1990, Vol. 2, Mortality, Public Health Service, Washington, D.C., Government Printing Office, 1993.

health center, or hospital emergency room as a regular source of health care (see figure 1.14 and appendix table 1.12). Fully 23 percent of children in urban areas—over twice the proportion of suburban children (11 percent)—receive regular care from these sources. About 16 percent of children in rural areas receive their health care from a clinic, health center, or hospital emergency room.

Urban children are also less likely to be covered by health insurance or Medicaid than children in suburban areas, but they are no different from rural children on this measure. Eighty-two percent of urban and rural children are covered, compared with 85 percent of suburban children (appendix table 1.12).

Teenage motherhood can have direct consequences on girls' educational attainment and lifelong earnings potential (Panel on High-Risk Youth 1993). Urban teenage girls are more likely than suburban girls, but not rural girls, to become teenage mothers (see appendix table 1.13). In a survey of girls scheduled to be 12th graders in 1992, about 17 percent either had or were expecting a child in urban areas, compared

with 10 percent in suburban areas and 14 percent in rural areas.

The data presented in this section on urban schools and their settings support the commonly held view that urban public schools either have or are located in areas with a higher incidence of conditions frequently associated with poorer educational outcomes than suburban or rural public schools. Such conditions include larger school size, higher concentrations of poor students and students with difficulty speaking English, and higher levels of risk factors affecting children's health and well-being. These conditions are presented as examples illustrating the different circumstances that face students and educators in urban, suburban, and rural schools as a context from which to consider the results of the analyses that follow. In fact, these conditions are among the many non-poverty attributes of urban locations that contribute to the differences observed between urban and non-urban schools, though they are not explicitly tested for in the analysis. Rather, the analysis tests the effects of two major characteristics of schools—poverty concentration and urbanicity—and the latter

Figure 1.14
Percentage of children 17 years of age and under whose regular source of health care is a clinic, health center, or hospital emergency room, by urbanicity: 1988

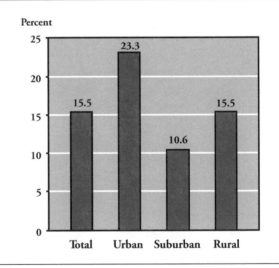

Percent

SOURCE: U.S. Department of Health and Human Services, National Center for Health Statistics, Vital and Health Statistics, Advance Data, No. 188, October 1, 1990.

can be said to serve as a proxy for all of the attributes of urban settings.

The data presented in this section and the research reviewed in this chapter lead one to expect that urban students would indeed have poorer education outcomes than the students in other schools. Chapter 2 examines this question using the analytical approach, data sources, and definitions described below.

Approach

In addressing the question: Are urban schools different? one might simply report the differences observed between urban and other schools. But since urban schools have higher concentrations of low income students and the relationship between such concentrations and less desirable education outcomes is well-documented (see section on previous research), the question becomes: Are urban schools different after accounting for differences in the concentration of poverty between schools in different locations? Further, if there is a relationship between an urban location and the outcomes separate from the effect of higher poverty concentration, do these two characteristics combine to produce an additional effect, or interaction, for urban schools with the highest poverty concentrations? That is, are conditions and outcomes for students in these schools compared to other schools different than predicted because of a compounding effect of an urban location and high concentrations of low income students in the school?

The basic approach, then, is to take two salient characteristics of schools—location and poverty concentration—and test their independent and joint relationship to indicators of education outcomes in chapter 2, family background and afterschool experiences in chapter 3, and school experiences in chapter 4.

The first area in which urban schools are compared with other schools is education outcomes. This analysis establishes whether there are, in fact, differences between the academic achievement, educational attainment, and economic outcomes of students who attended urban

public schools and other students. Differences in school experiences are believed to have long-term effects on the students' postsecondary and career opportunities, and their ability to maintain a livelihood. In order to capture these effects, longitudinal data are used that follow students who attended secondary school in different locations through their postsecondary and labor market experiences. The outcomes of students are compared not only while they are in school but also at several milestones thereafter. Then, the family background factors and school experiences that might be related to the different outcomes are analyzed, and reported on at the time the students were in school, which for most was during the 1980s.

In conducting the analysis for this report, four basic steps were used, each of which answers a specific question:

1) Are urban schools different from other schools? That is, do urban students have different outcomes and experiences than suburban or rural students?

2) Are schools with high poverty concentrations different from those with lower poverty concentrations? That is, do students from schools with high poverty concentrations have different outcomes and experiences than students from other schools?

3) Are urban schools different from other schools after taking into account the poverty concentration of the school? That is, is an urban school location related to the different outcomes and experiences of students in urban schools, above and beyond the fact that they have higher concentrations of poor students?

4) Are urban high poverty schools different than the combination of the effects of an urban location and a high poverty concentration would predict? That is, does the combination of an urban and high poverty setting interact so that the outcomes and experiences of students in those settings are different than predicted? And, are urban high poverty schools different from

other high poverty schools? Is high poverty concentration in an urban setting different than it is in other settings?

Analysis of variance is the primary statistical test used to answer these questions. Although hierarchical linear modeling was considered as a possible basic analytical tool because it has some technical advantages when analyzing data from two levels (student-level and school-level, in the present case), it was decided that analysis of variance was preferable for two reasons. First, results from analysis of variance are more directly linked to the research questions and can be more easily presented to a general audience. Second, even if hierarchical linear modeling had been the analysis of choice, it would have been applicable to some, but not all, of the data sets that are used in the report. It seemed preferable to use a single analytical method throughout the report.

There are four models that correspond to the four research questions stated above (see Appendix B for formulas and notation for the models). Data are presented in three figures for each indicator in the report.

1) Model 1 tests the overall effect of urbanicity. If the overall test is statistically significant, it tests the difference between urban and suburban schools, and between urban and rural schools. The data by urbanicity are presented in a bar graph in the first figure of each indicator.

2) Model 2 tests the overall effect of poverty concentration. If the overall test is statistically significant, model 2 tests the difference between students in schools with the highest poverty concentration and students in schools at the three other levels of poverty concentration. Data by poverty concentration are presented in a line graph in the second figure for each indicator.

3) Model 3 tests the overall effect of urbanicity, controlling for differences in poverty concentration. If the overall test is statistically significant, model 3 tests the difference between urban and

suburban students, controlling for poverty concentration, and the difference between urban and rural students, controlling for poverty concentration.

4) Model 4 tests the overall effect of the interaction between urbanicity and poverty concentration. If the overall test is statistically significant, model 4 tests whether the difference between urban and other schools at the highest poverty concentration is the same as the difference between urban and other schools at lower levels of poverty concentration. In addition, the difference between urban high poverty schools and other high poverty schools is tested for significance.

The data on urbanicity by poverty concentration related to models 3 and 4 are represented in the third figure of each indicator. Although there are many possible patterns for this figure, the following sample figures illustrate in simplified terms the way the data would appear if they perfectly represented the effects that this analysis tests. The reader may compare these figures with the actual data presented in the figures of the report.

Figure 1 indicates an effect of poverty concentration but no urbanicity effect when poverty concentration is held constant. That is, the differences between urban and other schools for variable Y are explained by the higher concentration of poor students in urban schools. The difference between urban and other schools with

Figure 1

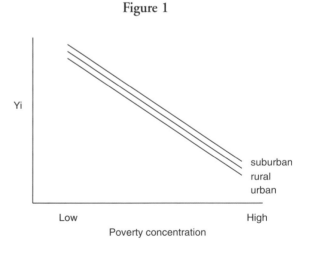

high poverty concentrations is the same as it is at lower poverty concentrations; therefore urban high poverty schools are no different than predicted.

Figure 2 indicates both the effects of poverty concentration and of urbanicity above and beyond the effect of poverty concentration. That is, significant differences between urban and other schools remain after accounting for the higher concentration of poverty in urban schools. The difference between urban high poverty schools and other high poverty schools is similar to the difference

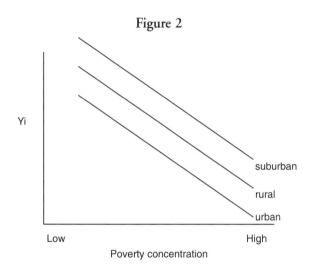

Figure 2

between urban and other schools with lower poverty concentrations; therefore, urban high poverty schools are no different than predicted.

Figure 3 displays an instance in which students in urban schools with a high poverty concentration are at particular risk for less desirable experiences or outcomes. The difference between urban and other schools is wider at higher poverty concentrations than it is at lower poverty concentrations; therefore, urban high poverty schools are different on this indicator than predicted. The combination of an urban and high poverty setting interact to produce unexpectedly high or low levels of the indicator for students in those settings. And, students in urban high poverty schools are different from students in other high poverty schools.

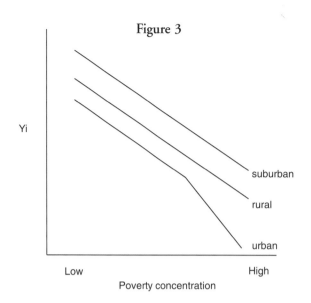

Figure 3

Of course, the actual data do not behave as simply as the data in figures 1, 2, and 3, and the patterns can be quite complicated.

In addition, there is another simple pattern that occurs in the data—one that is not explicitly tested by models 1 through 4. This pattern is shown in figure 4.

In this case, there is an interaction between urbanicity and poverty concentration, but not the one we were

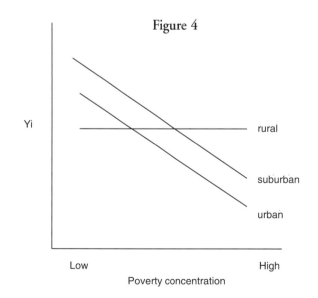

Figure 4

explicitly looking for in model 4. In fact, what is interesting is the lack of an overall effect of poverty concentration on rural schools compared with a quite marked effect for urban and suburban schools. That is, what is of interest here is the overall effect of poverty concentration for rural schools, rather than the simple contrast between high poverty concentration and low poverty concentration schools. A model was developed to test whether the slopes of the lines relating the poverty concentration with the measure of interest in urban, suburban, and rural schools differed from one another, and for rural schools, to test whether it differs from zero.

The above discussion describes the research questions posed in this report and the methodology used to supply the answers. It is important to alert the reader to the limitations of the analysis in this report.

- This report does not control for individual student-level background. Research has often shown that effects attributed to social composition or context often diminish when controls for individual background are added. The measure of school poverty concentration (the percentage of students in the school receiving free or reduced price lunch) is intertwined with a measure of student background, since it is the aggregation of individual students' poverty status. Indicators of family background of students that are related to education outcomes are presented in chapter 3.

- The analysis in this report does not determine the relative strength of the relationship of urbanicity or school poverty concentration to the indicators; it simply tests whether differences by urbanicity remain after taking into account differences in poverty concentration. Further, the analysis does not determine how much of the difference between urban and other schools can be attributed to urbanicity or poverty concentration.

- A finding that school urbanicity or poverty concentration is related to a particular student outcome or experience does not suggest that

these school characteristics caused that outcome or experience. It only suggests that there is a statistical association between urbanicity or poverty concentration and the outcome or experience. If it is found that an urban school location matters, this suggests that the constellation of characteristics that are currently found in urban areas is related to the outcome or experience, not necessarily location itself. "Urban" in this context stands for all the characteristics of urban areas, as is the case for "suburban" and "rural." If it is found that an urban location matters even when accounting for higher urban poverty concentrations, this suggests that there are additional non-poverty attributes of urban areas that are related to the indicator.

- The analysis does not estimate causal relationships between the family background and school experiences of students and their education outcomes. However, the student background and school experiences indicators presented were considered important, both in the research literature and in initial analyses demonstrating important differences by school urbanicity and poverty concentration (see technical notes, appendix C). Further, the analysis does not determine the relative importance of family background compared with school-level factors in affecting student outcomes. Rather, the analysis is primarily descriptive of student outcomes, family background, and school experiences, and how they vary across school locations and levels of school poverty concentration.

Sources

This report describes public school students and their environments, and their educational and economic outcomes in the late 1980s to 1990. The data sources and definitions of poverty and urbanicity for each data set used in this report are described in detail in the appendices and in the introductions to each chapter. The following provides a summary.

The contextual data provided in the section of this chapter entitled "The Setting: Urban Schools and Communities" have been calculated by the authors from the U.S Bureau of the Census' Current Population Surveys of March and October 1980 and 1990, and November 1979 and 1989; the National Center for Education Statistics' 1987–88 Schools and Staffing Survey (SASS), and the National Education Longitudinal Study of 1988 (NELS:88); the U.S. Department of Justice, Bureau of Justice Statistics, National Crime Victimization Survey; and the National Center for Health Statistics, Vital Statistics of the United States 1990, and the 1988 National Health Interview Survey.

The indicators of education outcomes described in chapter 2 are derived from three nationally representative data sets. Achievement data for 8th and 10th graders come from NELS:88, which assessed a sample of 8th graders in 1988 and reassessed them in 1990 when most of them were in the 10th grade. The achievement of 10th graders in 1990 is compared with those in 1980 using a comparable assessment that was part of the High School and Beyond Study (HS&B). The third follow-up survey of HS&B, which surveyed 1980 sophomores in 1986 (4 years after most would have finished high school), is the source of data on high school completion; the 1990 follow-up of the National Longitudinal Survey of Youth (NLSY), which surveyed young adults ages 25-32, is the source of data for post-secondary completion and for all the measures of economic outcomes. Thus, the student outcomes described in chapter 2 refer to data gathered from 1980 to 1990.

Chapters 3 and 4 describe the family, afterschool, and school experiences of students during the same time period. The indicators of family background and after-school activities that are presented in chapter 3 are derived from the NELS:88 base year survey of 8th graders in 1988 and the first follow-up survey of 10th graders in 1990. The data sources for school experiences in chapter 4 are the same two NELS:88 surveys, as well as the 1987–88 Schools and Staffing Survey. High school transcript data are from the National

Assessment of Educational Progress (NAEP) High School Transcript Study of 1990.

Definitions of Urbanicity and Poverty Concentration

The definitions of urbanicity and poverty concentration vary somewhat across the sources of data. Although every effort was made to use comparable data when possible, some differences should be noted.

The categories used in this report to denote the urbanicity of a school are urban, suburban, and rural. For all surveys except SASS, these correspond to U.S. Bureau of the Census classifications of the school location. Schools classified as urban are located in central cities of Metropolitan Statistical Areas (MSAs); schools classified as suburban are located within the area surrounding a central city within the MSA; and schools classified as rural are outside of an MSA. Urban schools were located in central cities of all sizes, as defined by the Census Bureau. For the 1987–88 SASS, the school administrator was asked to assign one of ten residence categories to his or her school, and these have been collapsed into three categories for this report as follows: urban schools located in cities of 50,000 people or more; suburban schools located in the suburbs of cities of 50,000 or more; and rural schools, including rural or farming communities, towns of less than 50,000 people that are not suburbs of a larger city, and Indian reservations.

Information on school poverty concentration for each survey is obtained from school administrators in which they report the percentage of students in the school who receive free or reduced price lunch (for the NELS, SASS, and NAEP surveys), or report the percentage in the school who are classified as disadvantaged (for the HS&B and NLSY surveys). The term "disadvantaged" was more commonly used at the time students were in high school in the late 1970s and early 1980s when they were surveyed as part of the HS&B and NLSY studies, and can have several interpretations (Natriello et al. 1990; Ralph 1992). School administrators were likely to have interpreted "disadvantaged" to mean students who would be eligible for services under Chapter

1 of the Elementary Secondary Education Act—i.e., students who are economically disadvantaged as well as performing below grade level.

In the more recent surveys used in this report (NELS, SASS, and NAEP), the measure of poverty concentration that is available is the proportion of students receiving free and reduced price lunch. Unlike the concept of disadvantaged discussed above, school performance does not affect eligibility for free or reduced price lunch. Students are eligible to receive free or reduced price school lunch if their family's income is below 185 percent of the poverty guidelines issued by the U.S. Department of Health and Human Services (HHS). These HHS poverty guidelines are based on the poverty thresholds determined annually by the U.S. Bureau of the Census, which are rounded and adjusted for differences in family size. The Census Bureau poverty thresholds, first developed by Mollie Orshansky in 1964 for the Social Security Administration, are based on a multiple (about three times) of the cost of a nutritionally adequate diet for an individual's family. Poverty thresholds differ by family size, number of related children in the family under 18 years old, and by age of householder in one- and two-person households. The thresholds are adjusted annually to the Consumer Price Index (U.S. Bureau of the Census 1993).

When the proportion of students receiving free or reduced price lunch is used as a measure of poverty concentration, the estimates produced of the relationship of poverty to the indicators are conservative, since the student's family can have an income of up to 185 percent of the poverty line to qualify for free or reduced price lunch. Therefore, a portion of these students are actually living above the poverty line. A more accurate measure of poverty may have resulted in sharper differences between low and high poverty schools. Furthermore, the proportion of students who actually receive free or reduced price lunch is less than the proportion who are actually eligible, particularly in middle and high schools, because older students are often embarrassed to sign up for the program. Consequently,

the proportion of students participating in this program is often an underestimation of poverty concentration in the schools in which middle and high school students were surveyed.

As mentioned earlier in this report, schools are grouped into four levels of poverty concentration that correspond to the approximate quartiles of students receiving free or reduced price lunch in a national representative sample of public schools: 0–5 percent, 6–20 percent, 21–40 percent, and more than 40 percent. Throughout the report, the term *low poverty* refers to schools with 0–5 percent poverty concentration, and *high poverty* refers to schools with more than 40 percent poverty concentration.

The Bureau of the Census defines a poverty area in a metropolitan area as a census tract with a poverty rate of 20 percent of more. But evidence from the research literature suggests that a more accurate definition of an area with the type of poverty concentration associated with large metropolitan areas, or ghetto poverty areas, is a neighborhood in a mid- to large-sized city with a poverty rate of 40 percent or more (Ellwood 1988; Sawhill et al. 1992).

The high poverty category has a wide range, from a poverty concentration of more than 40 percent to 100 percent, and also includes a variety of settings. For instance, in the average school included in the high poverty category, 64 percent of the students receive free or reduced price lunch, while urban high poverty schools average 69 percent, suburban high poverty schools 60 percent, and rural high poverty schools 61 percent (1987–88 SASS). In other words, high poverty schools in urban areas have higher average levels of poverty than those in suburban and rural areas. To ensure that categorizing the data in this way did not exaggerate the findings on urban schools, analyses for the indicators were also performed with poverty as a continuous variable in order to confirm the results obtained using poverty concentration categories.

Chapter 2

Education Outcomes

There is a commonly held perception that children in urban public schools exhibit a pattern of academic failure that leads to dropping out of school and later, failure to obtain and maintain a livelihood. This chapter uses nationally representative data and statistical analyses to test this perception.

Chapter 1 reviewed previous research and contextual data suggesting that students in urban public schools—and especially those in urban schools with high concentrations of disadvantaged students—would be expected to compare less favorably on achievement, educational attainment, and on indicators of economic status than students from other schools. This chapter examines the available data for each of these three areas. Further, given that urbanicity is confounded with poverty, it explores whether the urbanicity of a school continues to be related to student outcomes when the higher concentration of poverty in urban schools is considered. The analysis uses data on a battery of indicators of achievement, attainment, and economic outcomes, and these data are subjected to statistical tests to determine the relationship between these outcomes and urbanicity, controlling for poverty and in combination with poverty.

The approach used for the analysis in this chapter will serve as a model for the chapters that follow. Students in national surveys are grouped according to the urbanicity and the level of poverty concentration in the schools they attended, using comparable definitions of urbanicity and poverty concentration. In the achievement section, poverty is measured as the percent of students receiving free and reduced price lunch, while in the attainment and economic outcomes sections, which use data from older surveys, it is measured as the percentage identified as "disadvantaged" by a school administrator.

The data for each outcome measure were subjected to a series of statistical tests using analysis of variance

(see chapter 1 and appendix B) to determine specifically:

1) how the performance of urban students, overall, compared to suburban or rural students;

2) how the performance of students in schools with higher poverty concentrations compared to students in schools with lower poverty concentrations;

3) how the performance of students from urban schools compared if the concentration of poverty in their schools was considered; and finally

4) how the performance of students in urban schools with the highest poverty concentrations compared to those in similar schools in suburban and rural areas, and whether they suffered any additional penalty on achievement tests, in attaining education, and in achieving economic well-being that was related to the interaction, or compounding effect, of an urban and a high poverty setting.

The results of this last test are expressed by the phrase *greater than predicted* when the difference between urban high poverty and other high poverty schools is larger than would be predicted from the combined effects of urbanicity and poverty concentration, or *no different than predicted* when the difference can be explained by these two main effects.

Chart 2.1 summarizes the results of the analyses of education outcomes, grouped into three sections—student achievement, educational attainment, and economic outcomes. The indicators of student achievement are mathematics and reading test composite scores for 8th- and 10th-grade students, and the overall change in 10th graders' mathematics scores from 1980 to 1990. Rates of on-time high school completion and postsecondary degree attainment are presented as milestones of educational attainment. The economic outcomes selected include the extent of engagement in economic activities (work or school) 4 years after graduating high school; and the economic activities and unemployment and poverty rates of young adults 7 to 15 years after graduating high school at ages 25-32, a time that is crucial to developing their careers.

Summary of This Chapter's Findings

- Students in urban public schools compared less favorably than students in suburban schools on all education outcomes, and they compared less favorably than students in rural schools on about half of the indicators of academic achievement, educational attainment, and economic status.

- After accounting for differences in school poverty concentration, the outcomes of urban students compared unfavorably to those in one or both other locations on the following: 8th-grade achievement, high school completion, early engagement in productive activities, unemployment, and living in poverty. Their outcomes were the same as suburban and rural students on 10th-grade achievement, postsecondary completion, and on engagement in productive activities later in their careers.

- Students from high poverty urban schools performed less favorably than those from high poverty rural schools on 8th-grade achievement and high school completion rates. They had higher unemployment rates than did those from suburban high poverty schools. However, the great majority of students from urban high poverty schools still graduated high school on time (66 percent), and were more likely than not to be employed or attending school full time (73 percent) several years after graduating.

- Young adults who had attended high poverty urban schools were much more likely to be living in poverty later in life than those who had attended high poverty schools in other locations.

Even so, the vast majority of these students were living above the poverty line (74 percent).

- School poverty concentration is consistently related to lower performance on every education outcome measured.

Students from urban public schools have less favorable outcomes on most of the areas examined, compared with students attending public schools elsewhere. Yet when achievement, educational attainment, and engagement in productive activities are examined at two points in time, urban students generally compare less favorably relative to suburban and rural students at the earlier point in time, but perform the same as other students at the later point. When differences in poverty concentration are taken into account, urban 8th graders score lower than suburban or rural 8th graders on achievement tests, but by 10th grade, they score the same as their peers in other locations. Similarly, urban students are less likely to finish high school on time, but they complete postsecondary degrees at the same rate as others, when poverty concentration is considered. Urban students are also less likely than suburban students to be working or in school 4 years after graduating high school, but by 7 to 15 years later—a key period in their career development—are just as economically active as others.

Some measurement and selection issues may affect these results. For instance, high schools are larger than middle schools and draw from larger, more heterogeneous catchment areas, which may dilute relationships between school location and student outcomes. Furthermore, 8th-grade students who have dropped out of school by 10th grade are not in the pool of students tested in 10th grade. Finally, the cohort of young adults for whom economic activity and completion of higher education is measured includes those who obtained their high school degrees later than scheduled, which may have allowed them to catch up, thereby reducing differences observed at the earlier points in time.

The higher poverty and unemployment rates of young adults who had attended urban schools, measured after they had a chance to establish themselves 7 to 15 years after they would normally have graduated from high school, does suggest that urban students are more likely to have periods of marginal economic existence than students from schools in other locations. The size of the gap between students from urban schools and others on these two indicators is large. It should be noted that this study did not account for differences by location in labor markets at the time of the surveys. If the survey respondents were living in areas with higher poverty and unemployment rates at the time their progress was measured, these factors would also affect the respondents' status.

Students who attended schools that were both urban **and** had a high concentration of poor or disadvantaged students were at a much higher risk of living in poverty later in life than others. Compared with students from schools in rural areas with similarly high proportions of poor or disadvantaged students, they performed less well on 8th-grade achievement tests and were less likely to complete high school. Moreover, they had higher unemployment rates than those from similar suburban schools. But on the other indicators of achievement, attainment, and economic success, students from urban high poverty schools performed comparably to those from high poverty schools in other locations. In fact, high poverty schools in all locations were similar on half of the indicators, including again,

those at a later point in the life course. This suggests the possibility that the effects of high poverty concentration may diminish over time for certain aspects of these students' lives. The relationship between poverty and the outcomes presented here may be underestimated by the less accurate measure of poverty used in older surveys from which some of the data were drawn.

In no case were the outcomes of students in urban high poverty schools different than predicted: the less favorable outcomes observed for these students could be predicted from the combined effects of an urban setting and a high poverty setting. Thus, there was no evidence that they may have suffered any additional penalty related to the interaction, or compounding effect, of the two.

This chapter focuses on how the outcomes of students from urban high poverty schools differed from those of their counterparts in other locations. The evidence that these students achieve less, attain less education, and fare less well economically than other students is consistent with prior research and the demographic, health, and community risk factors outlined in chapter 1. However, as mentioned previously, the great majority of these students still graduated high school on time (66 percent) and, several years later, were more likely than not to be employed or in school (73 percent) and living above the poverty line (74 percent).

CHART 2.1—SUMMARY OF RESULTS: EDUCATION OUTCOMES

INDICATOR	Are Urban Schools Different?	Are High Poverty Schools Different?*	Are Urban Schools Different after Accounting for Poverty Concentration?	Are Urban High Poverty Schools Different from Other High Poverty Schools? Are Urban High Poverty Schools Different than Predicted?
I. STUDENT ACHIEVEMENT				
8th-Grade Composite Score	Yes, urban lower than suburban and rural	Yes, high poverty lower than most others	Yes, urban lower than others	Yes, same as suburban, lower than rural high poverty No different than predicted
10th-Grade Composite Score	Yes, urban lower than suburban, same as rural	Yes, high poverty lower than all others	No, urban same as others	No, same as other high poverty No different than predicted
1980-1990 Change in 10th-Grade Math Score	Yes, urban lower than others in 1980, lower than suburban in 1990	NA	NA	NA
II. EDUCATIONAL ATTAINMENT				
High School Completion	Yes, urban lower than suburban and rural	Yes, high poverty lower than all others	Yes, urban lower than others	Yes, lower than rural, same as suburban high poverty No different than predicted

INDICATOR	Are Urban Schools Different?	Are High Poverty Schools Different?*	Are Urban Schools Different After Accounting for Poverty Concentration?	Are Urban High Poverty Schools Different From Other High Poverty Schools? Are Urban High Poverty Schools Different Than Predicted?
Postsecondary Degree Attainment	Yes, urban lower than suburban, same as rural	Yes, high poverty lower than most others	No, urban same as others	No, same as other high poverty No different than predicted
III. Economic Outcomes				
Early Productive Activity	Yes, urban lower than suburban, same as rural	Yes, high poverty lower than all others	Yes, urban lower than suburban	No, same as other high poverty No different than predicted
Later Productive Activity	Yes, urban lower than suburban, same as rural	Yes, high poverty lower than most others	No, urban same as others	No, same as other high poverty No different than predicted
Unemployment	Yes, urban higher than suburban and rural	Yes, high poverty lower than all others	Yes, urban higher than others	Yes, higher than suburban, same as rural high poverty No different than predicted
Poverty	Yes, urban higher than suburban and rural	Yes, high poverty higher than all others	Yes, urban higher than others	Yes, higher than other high poverty No different than predicted

*Poverty at the school level is measured by the percentage of students receiving free or reduced-price lunch in the student achievement section and the percentage identified as "disadvantaged" by school administrators in the educational attainment and economic outcomes section.

Student Achievement

Student achievement is a primary measure of school success. Parents and school officials alike interpret test scores as a reflection of whether students, as well as the educational system, are performing satisfactorily (Special Study Panel on Education Indicators 1991).

The challenge in measuring educational achievement nationally is to measure achievement consistently across diverse populations of students throughout the country, who are exposed to a wide range of teaching quality and practices, school resources, and curricula. National assessments have been developed to enable nationwide comparisons of the performance of students who are educated in widely different circumstances.

This section discusses the findings from two such longitudinal surveys (surveys that follow the same individuals over time), which contain national assessments as part of the survey. First, the mathematics and reading test scores of 8th graders in 1988 and 10th graders in 1990 are presented from an assessment administered as part of the National Education Longitudinal Study of 1988 (NELS:88). Then, the performance of the same 10th graders in math in 1990 is compared to that of 10th graders in 1980, who were assessed in a comparable test as part of the High School and Beyond Study (HS&B), to determine if the performance of students in urban, suburban, and rural schools has changed over the decade.

The analysis of the measures of student achievement addressed in this section will be presented in a standard order. First, the average scores of public school students in urban locations will be compared to their counterparts in suburban and rural locations. Second, the average scores of students who attended schools with high concentrations of poverty will be compared to those who attended schools with lower concentrations of poverty. Third, the students are grouped according to the urbanicity and the level of

poverty in their schools, in order to make comparisons between students attending schools with similar concentrations of poor students (measured as those receiving free or reduced price lunch). Finally, students from urban high poverty schools are compared to students from high poverty schools in other locations.

In this analysis, statistical tests are performed to determine whether the differences in the average scores of the groups being compared are statistically significant, rather than due to chance. All differences that are reported are statistically significant.

Findings

- Urban 8th graders scored lower on achievement tests than suburban or rural 8th graders, even when the higher poverty concentration of urban public schools was taken into account.

- Urban 10th graders scored the same as rural 10th graders, but scored lower than suburban 10th graders. However, this was not related to an urban location; rather, it was due to the higher poverty concentration in urban areas.

- Students in urban high poverty schools achieved at about the same level as would be predicted from the combination of an urban and high poverty setting. In fact, in urban high poverty schools, 8th graders scored about the same as those in suburban high poverty schools, and 10th graders scored about the same as those in rural high poverty schools and suburban schools with the highest and next to highest levels of poverty concentration. However, 8th graders in urban high poverty schools scored lower than those in rural locations.

- The concentration of poverty in a school had an important relationship to achievement—as the proportion of poor students in a school increased, student performance on achievement tests in both 8th and 10th grades and in every location generally decreased.

- Between 1980 and 1990, the mathematics achievement of students in public schools in every location increased moderately. However, there were no meaningful differences in the amount of increase across locations. Urban students scored lower in mathematics than both suburban and rural students in 1980, but lower than only suburban students in 1990.

Academic Achievement of 8th Graders

Are urban schools different? In 1988, the academic achievement of 8th graders in urban public schools lagged behind that of their peers in suburban and rural schools (figure 2.1). In a national test of math and reading achievement, students scored a mean of 49.5 overall, but urban 8th graders scored 47, or at the 38th percentile, while suburban students scored 51 (at the 54th percentile), and rural students scored 49 (at the 46th percentile).[2]

Are high poverty schools different? Students in schools with high poverty concentrations also achieved at lower levels than students in most other schools. Students in schools with the highest concentration of poverty scored an average of 45 (at the 31st percentile), while

students in schools with the lowest concentration of poverty scored 53 (at the 62nd percentile) (figure 2.2).

Are urban schools different after accounting for poverty concentration? The low performance of urban students cannot be attributed to the poverty concentration of their schools alone. They still would have performed less well, on average, than students in other areas, even if their school had the same level of poverty concentration as schools in other areas.

Is 8th-grade student achievement in urban high poverty schools lower than predicted? Students in urban schools with high concentrations of poverty had lower composite scores than students in similar schools in rural

Figure 2.1
**Average standardized test
composite scores of 8th-grade students,
by urbanicity: 1988**

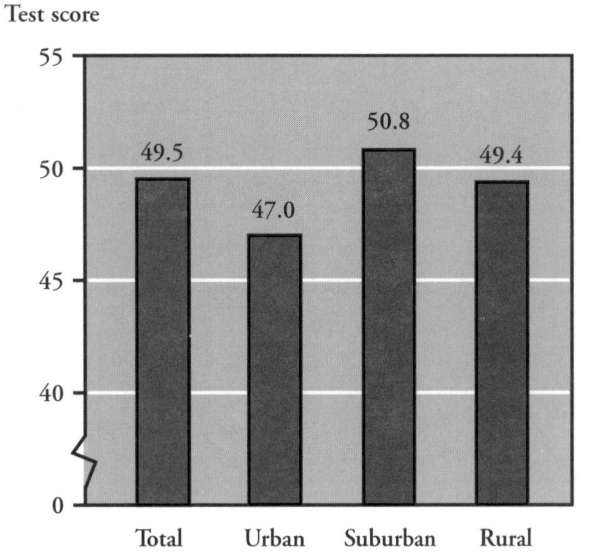

Test score

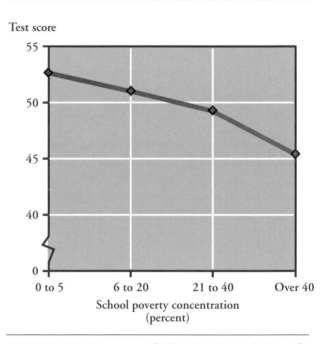

SOURCE: U.S. Department of Education, National Center for Education Statistics, National Education Longitudinal Study of 1988, Base Year Survey.

Figure 2.2
**Average standardized test
composite scores of 8th-grade students,
by school poverty concentration: 1988**

Test score

SOURCE: U.S. Department of Education, National Center for Education Statistics, National Education Longitudinal Study of 1988, Base Year Survey.

settings, but their scores were not statistically different from those in suburban settings (figure 2.3). Students in urban high poverty schools scored an average of 44, compared with an average of about 46 for students in suburban and rural high poverty settings. However, the lower scores of students in urban high poverty schools were not lower than predicted from the combined effect of the school's urban location and poverty concentration.

[2] As part of NELS:1988, the academic skills of a nationally representative sample of 8th-grade students were assessed. Tests of achievement were administered in mathematics and reading, and the number correct scores were standardized and rescaled to a mean of 50 and a standard deviation of 10. The standardized test composite is the equally weighted mean of the standardized reading and mathematics scores, restandardized to a mean of 50 and a standard deviation of 10. Because of missing data, the sample analyzed here has a weighted mean of 49.5. Percentiles were then identified for each subgroup based on the entire distribution.

Figure 2.3
Average standardized test composite scores of 8th-grade students,
by urbanicity and school poverty concentration: 1988

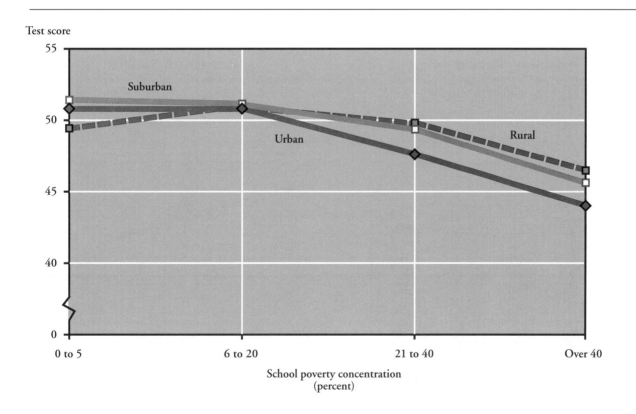

SOURCE: U.S. Department of Education, National Center for Education Statistics, National Education Longitudinal Study of 1988, Base Year Survey.

Academic Achievement of 10th Graders

Does the difference in achievement observed for urban 8th graders remain in 10th grade? This section presents evidence from the first follow-up of the same nationally representative survey, NELS:88—but 2 years later in 1990 when most of the 1988 8th graders were in 10th grade. However, not all of the same 8th graders were in this 10th-grade sample because some may have moved out of the country, dropped out of school, or repeated a grade. In addition, this 10th-grade sample has been "freshened" with 1990 10th graders who were not in the 8th-grade sample in 1988 to make it nationally representative of all public school 10th graders in 1990. Again, the indicator presented is an overall average test composite score calculated from mathematics and reading test scores.[3]

Are urban schools different? Urban 10th graders scored lower than their suburban counterparts on tests of achievement in mathematics and reading (figure 2.4). They had a composite test score of about 49, while suburban students had an average score of 51. Urban scores were no different than rural scores.

Are high poverty schools different? As with 8th graders, 10th-grade achievement was related to the concentration of poverty in the school (figure 2.5). Students in schools with the highest concentration of poverty had the lowest level of achievement (scoring 45 on average), whereas those in schools with the lowest poverty concentration scored an average of 53. Just like the 8th graders, the 10th graders in high poverty

Figure 2.4
Average standardized test composite scores of 10th-grade students, by urbanicity: 1990

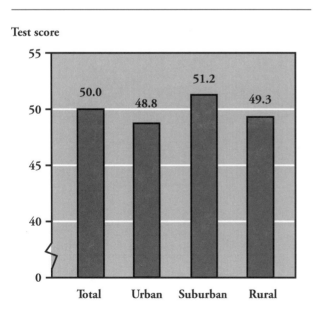

Test score

Figure 2.5
Average standardized test composite scores of 10th-grade students, by school poverty concentration: 1990

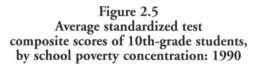
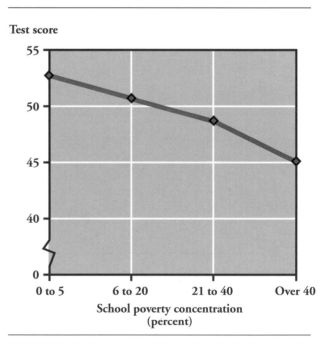

Test score

SOURCE: U.S. Department of Education, National Center for Education Statistics, National Education Longitudinal Study of 1988, First Follow-up Survey, 1990.

SOURCE: U.S. Department of Education, National Center for Education Statistics, National Education Longitudinal Study of 1988, First Follow-up Survey, 1990.

schools scored at a much lower percentile (the 30th) than students in low poverty schools (the 62nd).

Are urban schools different after accounting for the poverty concentration of the school? The difference between urban and suburban 10th graders on overall achievement observed in figure 2.4 did not hold after taking into account the differences in the concentration of poverty in urban compared with suburban schools. Thus, the lower performance of urban 10th graders is related to the higher concentration of poverty in urban schools.

Is 10th-grade student achievement in urban high poverty schools lower than predicted? Students in urban high poverty schools performed as predicted on achievement tests. In fact, they performed no differently than students

in high poverty schools in suburban or rural areas. Students in high poverty schools in every location scored an average of 45 on overall achievement tests. For urban and rural students, this was the lowest score among 10th graders in each location. Even though in figure 2.6 it also appears to be the lowest score for suburban students, the difference between students in suburban schools with the highest poverty concentration and those with the next highest level was not statistically significant.

[3]As part of the first follow-up survey of NELS:88, the academic skills of a nationally representative sample of 10th-grade students were assessed. Tests of achievement were administered in mathematics and reading, and the number correct scores were standardized and rescaled to a mean of 50 and a standard deviation of 10. The standardized test composite is the equally weighted mean of the standardized reading and mathematics scores, restandardized to a mean of 50 and a standard deviation of 10. Percentiles were then identified for each subgroup based on national distributions.

Figure 2.6
Average standardized test composite scores of 10th-grade students,
by urbanicity and school poverty concentration: 1990

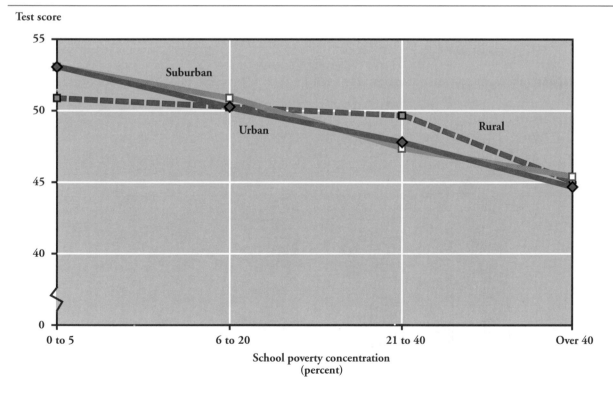

SOURCE: U.S. Department of Education, National Center for Education Statistics, National Education Longitudinal Study of 1988, First Follow-up Survey, 1990.

Did 10th-Grade Achievement Change Between 1980 and 1990?

The previous section compared the achievement of urban 10th graders with their suburban and rural counterparts. The discussion in this section turns to whether differences in achievement by school location have changed over the decade of the 1980s.

The source of data is a mathematics test given to a nationally representative sample of public high school sophomores in 1980 (from the HS&B Base Year Survey), which has been equated to the test given to the 1990 sample of sophomores from the NELS:88 First Follow-up Survey. (A composite score of mathematics and reading achievement, used in the preceding analysis, is unavailable for both groups of sophomores.) The 10th graders' average number of correct responses is compared according to the location of their school.[4] Since the definitions of poverty used in the two surveys were not comparable, comparisons could not be made by school poverty concentration.

Overall, sophomores in 1990 were able to correctly answer about two more items than sophomores in 1980 (figure 2.7). Students in all three locations improved their performance over the decade and exhibited similar levels of improvement. Urban 10th graders answered fewer items correctly than did their suburban or rural counterparts in 1980. By 1990, urban students again answered fewer items correctly than suburban students, but there was no significant difference between their performance and that of rural students. Urban students in **1990** performed at about the same level as suburban students had in **1980**.

---

[4]The data presented in this section are the estimated number of correct items on the mathematics assessments of two surveys: the 1980 HS&B Survey and NELS, 1990. The two assessments had enough items in common for them to be equated. Also, the number of correct items is used in this analysis, rather than standardized scores, to preserve the observed differences in the two groups. Standardizing each group's scores to have a mean of 50 and a standard deviation of 10 would obscure such observed differences.

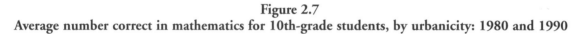

Figure 2.7
Average number correct in mathematics for 10th-grade students, by urbanicity: 1980 and 1990

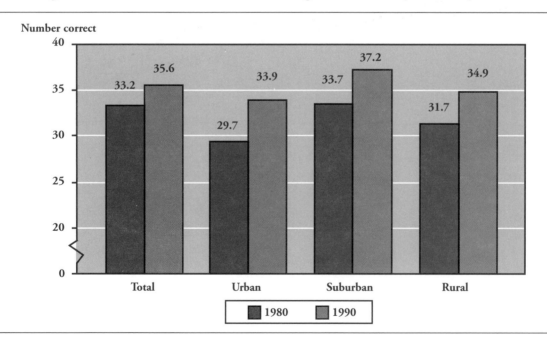

SOURCE: U.S. Department of Education, National Center for Education Statistics, High School and Beyond, Base Year Survey, 1980, and the National Education Longitudinal Study of 1988, First Follow-up Survey, 1990.

Educational Attainment

One of the most basic outcome measures of an education system is the educational attainment—that is, the amount of education or credentials attained—of the students who pass through the system. The level of education that students complete has a strong and direct impact on their employment and earnings potential.

It has been well documented that rates of employment are higher and more stable for those with higher educational attainment. While 70 percent of men ages 25–34 who did not complete high school were employed in 1991, 85 percent of men of this same age group who had completed high school were employed. Higher rates of employment were found among those who attended college: 89 percent of those with 1–3 years of college were employed, as were 92 percent of those with 4 or more years of college. In addition, the employment rates of college graduates remained stable during downturns in the economy over the last two decades, whereas they have declined for those with less education (U.S. Department of Education 1992).

Earnings are also strongly related to the level of education attained. Individuals who have completed high school and college earn more than those who have not. For example, white and black male high school graduates ages 25–34 earned about 27 percent more in 1990 than those who had not completed high school. In 1990, white and black males who had completed a college education earned 42 and 66 percent more, respectively, than those who had completed no more than a high school degree. The differential returns to education are even more dramatic for females (U.S. Department of Education 1992).

Educational attainment is related to the availability of opportunities, as well as the academic abilities, financial resources, and persistence of the individual. In this report, two measures of educational attainment are presented at two stages of completion that have a bearing on future opportunities. These measures are 1) the rate at which sophomores complete high school on time, from the HS&B survey; and 2) the rate at which young adults

complete any postsecondary degree, from the National Longitudinal Survey of Youth (NLSY). The measure of school poverty used in this section is the percentage of students in the school who are reported to be "disadvantaged" by school administrators, since this is the measure available in these two surveys.

The analysis described here will follow the same order as it did in the achievement section. First, measures of student attainment will be presented by urbanicity, followed by the level of concentration of disadvantaged students in the school, and by both characteristics combined. The statistical analysis presented in the previous section will be used to determine how the urbanicity and concentration of disadvantaged students in the school, separately and combined, are related to the educational attainment of students in those schools.

Findings

- Urban public school students were less likely to graduate from high school on time than suburban or rural students. This was related to the location of the school apart from the higher concentration of disadvantaged students in urban areas.

- Urban students were less likely to complete a postsecondary degree than suburban students. However, the differences appear to be related to the concentration of disadvantaged students in public schools in urban areas, rather than location.

- Students from urban schools with the highest proportion of disadvantaged students graduated from high school on time at rates that were lower than those in similar rural schools, but at rates that were not statistically different from similar suburban schools. They obtained higher education degrees at about the same rates as those from suburban and rural schools with the same high level of disadvantaged students.

High School Completion

Traditionally, one yardstick used to measure the outcomes of education has been students' completion of high school. This section looks at "on-time graduation" from high school, which is measured by the proportion of the high school sophomore class of 1980 who graduated with their class in 1982. The source of data for the measure is the HS&B Third Follow-up Survey.

A small, but significant, proportion of students complete high school beyond the traditional graduation age. In fact, some do not complete until their late 20s. However, these students are not considered to be on-time graduates in the measure of completion used here.

Are urban schools different? Almost 82 percent of the students in the sophomore class of 1980 attending public schools graduated on time with their classmates (figure 2.8). However, a smaller proportion of students in urban schools graduated on time compared with students in suburban or rural schools. Only 74 percent of students from urban schools graduated on time compared with 84 percent of students in suburban schools and 83 percent of students in rural schools.

Are schools with high concentrations of disadvantaged students different? Students from schools with fewer disadvantaged students were more likely to graduate on time than students from schools with large proportions of disadvantaged students. Only 73 percent of students in the most disadvantaged schools graduated on time compared with 80 percent or more of students in other schools (figure 2.9).

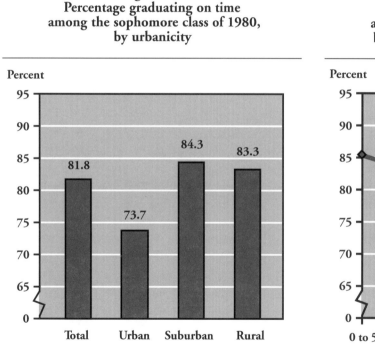

Figure 2.8
Percentage graduating on time among the sophomore class of 1980, by urbanicity

Percent

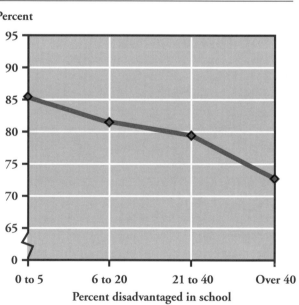
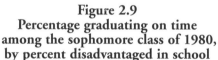

Figure 2.9
Percentage graduating on time among the sophomore class of 1980, by percent disadvantaged in school

Percent

Percent disadvantaged in school

SOURCE: U.S. Department of Education, National Center for Education Statistics, High School and Beyond Study, Third Follow-up, 1986.

SOURCE: U.S. Department of Education, National Center for Education Statistics, High School and Beyond Study, Third Follow-up, 1986.

Are urban schools different after accounting for concentrations of disadvantaged students in the school? An urban school location continues to be related to the lower on-time graduation rates of its students, even after accounting for the higher concentration of disadvantaged students in urban schools.

Were students in urban schools with the highest concentrations of disadvantaged students less likely to graduate than predicted? In figure 2.10, students in urban schools with the highest concentration of disadvantaged students appear to have the lowest rates of on-time graduation. However, their rates of graduation are significantly lower than only those of rural students, and are not statistically different from those of suburban students in similar schools. Sixty-six percent of urban students graduated on time compared with 74 percent of suburban and 80 percent of rural students in schools with similarly high concentrations of disadvantaged students. The combination of the schools' urban location and high proportions of disadvantaged students is not related to any additional risk of not graduating on time for these students. In fact, their graduation rates are no lower than what would be predicted from the separate effects of urbanicity and high concentrations of disadvantaged students added together.

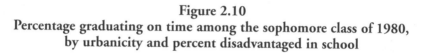

Figure 2.10
Percentage graduating on time among the sophomore class of 1980, by urbanicity and percent disadvantaged in school

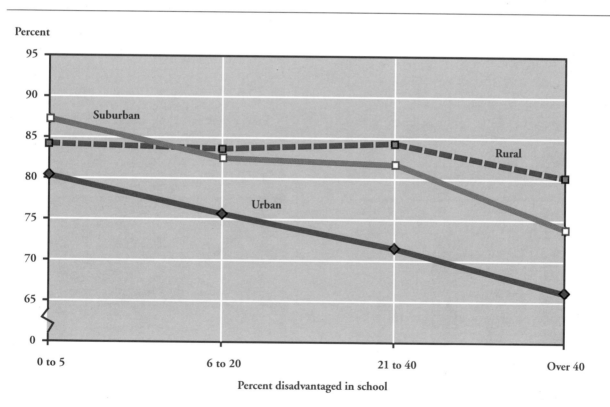

SOURCE: U.S. Department of Education, National Center for Education Statistics, High School and Beyond Study, Third Follow-up, 1986.

Postsecondary Degree Attainment

The next level of education a student may attain after high school is postsecondary education. Students' ability to enter a postsecondary institution and complete a degree depends upon their ability to finance their education and on their academic achievement and high school completion. Given urban students' lower levels of achievement and high school completion rates and disadvantaged students' inadequate financial resources, one would expect that those who had attended urban high schools with high proportions of disadvantaged students would have lower average postsecondary completion rates.

This section presents data from the National Longitudinal Survey of Youth (NLSY) on the percentage of students who had attended public high schools in urban, suburban, and rural areas and who had completed a bachelor's degree or more by 1990. (Those who completed an associates degree are not included in this measure.) This nationally representative sample of students was first interviewed in 1979 at ages 14–21 and reinterviewed in 1990 at ages 25–32, at which time information on their highest level of educational attainment

was obtained. These young adults were enrolled in high school in the late 1970s and early 1980s.

During the time that these students entered and completed postsecondary education, changes in the attainment of postsecondary education were evident nationwide. Although higher proportions of students were entering colleges and universities, some data suggest that smaller proportions were completing degrees. Financial and academic difficulties among this broader pool of college entrants may explain their lower completion rates (Knepper 1990). It is likely that the large age span of students in the following analysis masks these trends.

Are urban schools different? By 1990, 26 percent of the sampled youth ages 25–32 had completed a bachelor's degree or above. A smaller percentage of former urban and rural high school students than suburban students had completed a degree by 1990: 23 percent of former urban students and 22 percent of rural students had completed a degree, compared with 30 percent of former suburban students (figure 2.11).

Figure 2.11
Percentage of young adults completing a postsecondary degree by 1990, by high school urbanicity

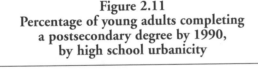

Percent

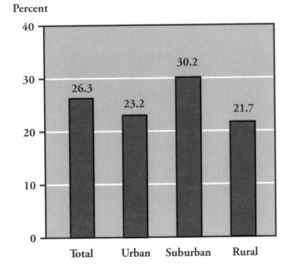

SOURCE: U.S. Department of Labor, National Longitudinal Survey of Youth, 1990.

Figure 2.12
Percentage of young adults completing a postsecondary degree by 1990, by percent disadvantaged in high school

Percent

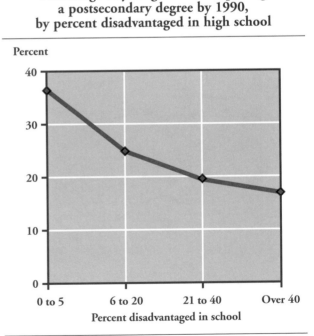

Percent disadvantaged in school

SOURCE: U.S. Department of Labor, National Longitudinal Survey of Youth, 1990.

Are schools with high concentrations of disadvantaged students different? The concentration of disadvantaged students in a high school was related to the likelihood that students from that school would complete a post-secondary degree. Thirty-six percent of high school students from schools with the lowest concentration of disadvantaged students had completed a degree, while less than half that percentage from schools with the highest concentration had done so (figure 2.12). No significant differences existed between the postsecondary completion rates of students in schools with the highest and next to highest concentrations of disadvantaged students.

Are urban schools different after accounting for differences in the concentration of disadvantaged students in the school? The differences in postsecondary completion rates seen in figure 2.11 by high school location disappeared when the differences in the concentration of disadvantaged students in schools in each location were considered. That is, the differences by urbanicity are related to differences in the proportion of students who are disadvantaged in urban, suburban, and rural schools.

Were students in urban schools with the highest concentration of disadvantaged students less likely to complete a postsecondary degree than predicted? About 15 percent of young adults who had attended urban schools with high concentrations of disadvantaged students had completed a postsecondary degree, a rate no different than for those who had attended suburban and rural schools with similarly disadvantaged populations (17 and 18 percent, respectively) (figure 2.13). There is no evidence to suggest that an urban setting combined with a high concentration of disadvantaged students was related to any additional penalty regarding postsecondary attainment.

The analysis by school location revealed that suburban high school students were more likely to complete a college degree than were urban and rural students (figure 2.11). However, when the average completion rates for each location were analyzed by the concentration of disadvantaged students in the school, it was apparent that only suburban students who came from schools with the lowest percentage of disadvantaged students had higher completion rates (figure 2.13). Students who had attended other suburban schools completed a degree at a similar rate as their urban and rural peers.

Figure 2.13
Percentage of young adults completing a postsecondary degree by 1990, by high school urbanicity and percent disadvantaged in high school

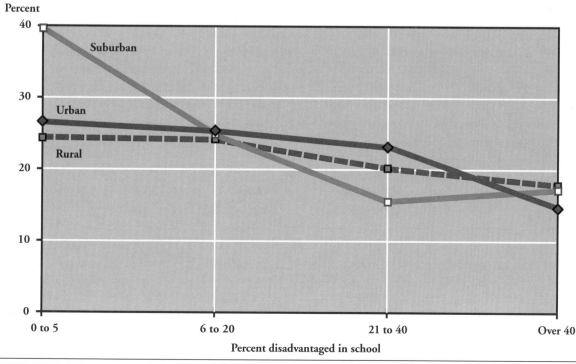

SOURCE: U.S. Department of Labor, National Longitudinal Survey of Youth, 1990.

Economic Outcomes

An individual's productivity, employment prospects, and risk of falling into poverty are often linked to the quality and extent of their schooling. To address this linkage, the analysis in this section will determine, first, whether students who emerge from urban public schools are more likely to be unproductive, unemployed, or living in poverty than those from suburban or rural schools, and second, whether students from urban schools with the highest concentration of disadvantaged students have less desirable economic outcomes than predicted.

It has been well-documented that people who have less education or who come from disadvantaged circumstances have more difficulty finding and sustaining employment, and that their earnings, on average, are lower than others. (See introduction to educational attainment section.) The last section demonstrated that students from urban public schools are least likely to graduate from high school on time or to obtain a higher education degree compared to students from public schools in other locations. Therefore, one would expect urban students, on average, to have poorer economic outcomes. In this analysis, students who attended urban and other high schools are followed to find out how they fared economically later in life.

All of the data reported in this section are from longitudinal surveys (which follow the same people through time). The economic outcomes of two groups of students who attended urban public high schools are compared with those who attended rural and suburban schools. The first outcome presented is the percentage of 1980 high school sophomores who were employed or enrolled in school full time in 1986—four years after the age at which most of them would have graduated from high school. Even though most people at this age do not settle into the types of jobs they will hold through most of their lives, this is an early indicator of economic productivity. It differs from standard measures of productivity in that the focus is on full-time activities, rather than on full-time and part-time activities. These data are from the HS&B Third Follow-up Survey.

The second group examined are young adults aged 25–32 in 1990—7 to 15 years after most would have graduated from high school. By this time, individuals are usually engaged in activities that are more likely to reflect lifetime employment patterns. Data for this group are drawn from the National Longitudinal Survey of Youth (NLSY). The three economic outcomes that are presented here are the percentage of young adults who are employed or attending school full time, the percentage who are unemployed, and the percentage who are living in poverty. The measure of school poverty used in this section is the percentage of students in the school who are reported to be "disadvantaged" by school administrators, since this is the measure available in these two surveys.

In this section, the analysis will follow the same order as it did in the previous sections. First, the indicators of economic outcomes will be presented by urbanicity, then by the concentration of disadvantaged students in the high school they attended, and then by both characteristics combined. As in previous sections, a statistical analysis is conducted to determine how the urbanicity and concentration of disadvantaged students in the school, both separately and combined, are related to the economic outcomes of students who have been educated in those schools.

Findings

- Young adults who had attended urban public schools were less likely than their suburban counterparts, but no different than their rural counterparts, to be productively engaged full time in work or school both 4 years after and 7 to 15 years after most had completed high school. An urban high school location was related to this outcome for students who had been out of school for

4 years, but not for those who had been out 7 to 15 years, even after accounting for the concentration of disadvantaged students in urban areas.

- Former students of urban public high schools were more likely to be unemployed and living in poverty later in life than those who had attended either rural or suburban high schools, even after accounting for the higher concentration of disadvantaged students in urban areas.

- Young adults who had attended an urban public high school with the highest percentage of disadvantaged students had higher poverty rates later in life, but no lower rates of productive activity, than those who had attended similar schools in other locations. Former urban students had unemployment rates that were higher than their suburban counterparts, but the same rates as those who had attended similar rural schools.

Early Productive Activities

The first economic outcome that will be examined is a measure of participation in productive activities 4 years after most students would have graduated from high school. This measure indicates whether students from urban schools are less likely than others to be involved in full-time productive activities (defined here as employment or enrollment in school full time, which differs from standard measures of productivity in that part-time work or school is not considered).[5] Early engagement in these activities is related to later economic returns, such as steady employment and higher earnings. Therefore, this indicator is both an outcome and a predictor of future economic well-being. The data used here are from the HS&B Third Follow-up Survey.

Are urban schools different? More than 60 percent of those surveyed were either enrolled in school or employed

full time in 1986 (figure 2.14). Those who had attended urban public high schools as sophomores in 1980 were less likely to have been either employed or in school in 1986 than those who had attended suburban schools (57 compared with 64 percent); however, they had about the same rates of participation as those who had attended rural schools (59 percent).

Are schools with high concentrations of disadvantaged students different? The concentration of disadvantaged students in the high school attended was also related to the likelihood of full-time participation in economic or educational activities 4 years after high school. Those who had attended high schools with the highest concentrations of disadvantaged students were much less likely to be enrolled or employed full time than other students. Forty-eight percent of students who had attended these

Figure 2.14
Percentage of young adults employed or attending school full time, 4 years after high school, by high school urbanicity: 1986

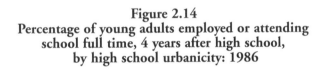

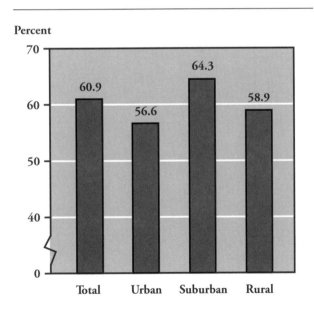

SOURCE: U.S. Department of Education, National Center for Education Statistics, High School and Beyond Study, Third Follow-up Survey, 1986.

Figure 2.15
Percentage of young adults employed or attending school full time, 4 years after high school, by percent disadvantaged in high school: 1986

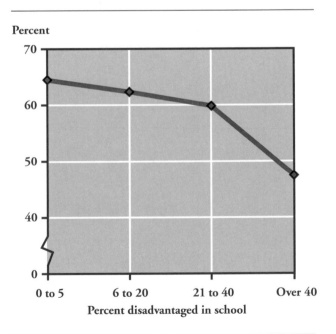

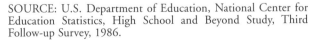

SOURCE: U.S. Department of Education, National Center for Education Statistics, High School and Beyond Study, Third Follow-up Survey, 1986.

schools were engaged in full-time economic or educational activities, compared with 60 to 64 percent of students in other schools (figure 2.15).

Are urban schools different after accounting for differences in the concentration of disadvantaged students in the school? The difference between urban and suburban students' rates of participation in full-time economic or educational activities remains when the higher concentration of disadvantaged students in urban schools is taken into account. Therefore, an urban school location is related to this outcome independent of the higher concentration of disadvantaged students found in urban schools.

Were students from urban high schools with the highest concentrations of disadvantaged students less likely than predicted to be employed or enrolled in school full time 4 years after high school? Less than half of students who had attended an urban high school with the highest concentration of disadvantaged students were employed or enrolled in school full time 4 years later (figure 2.16). However, this level of activity could be predicted from the combined effects of urbanicity and high poverty concentration. These students were about as active as those who had attended schools in suburban or rural areas with similarly disadvantaged populations.

---

[5]"Employment" is defined as working for pay full time or on active duty in the armed forces and not enrolled in college full time. An additional 10 percent of this group were employed part time, enrolled in school part time, or both, but these activities have been excluded from consideration. Expanding the analysis to include these activities produces similar results as for full-time employment or enrollment.

Figure 2.16
Percentage of young adults employed or attending school full time, 4 years after high school, by high school urbanicity and percent disadvantaged in high school: 1986

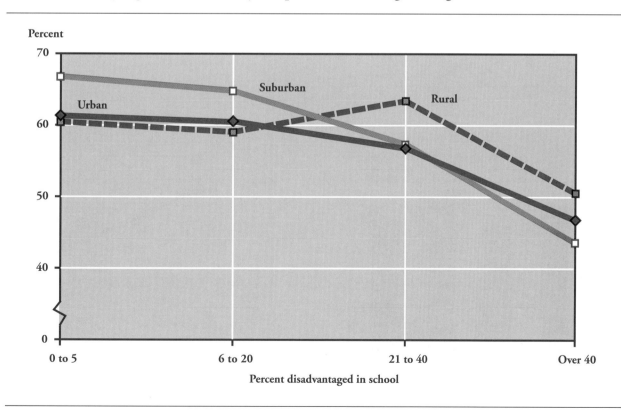

SOURCE: U.S. Department of Education, National Center for Education Statistics, High School and Beyond Study, Third Follow-up Survey, 1986.

Later Productive Activities

While the previous section examined productive activities 4 years after a student typically leaves high school, this section examines the productive activities of young adults after they have established patterns of activity that are more reflective of the ones they will have during their prime working years. The measure of participation in productive activities used here is the percentage of young adults ages 25–32 who were employed or attending school full time in 1990, 7 to 15 years after they typically would have finished high school. In 1990, these young adults were asked whether they were engaged in productive economic or educational activities full time. The NLSY is the source of data for this and the remaining economic indicators in this chapter. The urbanicity and proportion of disadvantaged students of the schools these young adults attended have been identified.

Are urban schools different? In 1990, 84 percent of young adults ages 25–32 were working at a job or enrolled in school full time. Young adults who had attended urban public schools were less likely to be employed or attending school (82 percent) than their counterparts who had attended suburban schools (86 percent); however, they were just as likely to be engaged in these activities as former rural students (82 percent) (figure 2.17).

Are schools with high concentrations of disadvantaged students different? Young adults were generally less likely to be engaged in productive activities if they had attended high schools with higher concentrations of disadvantaged students. Seventy-six percent of young adults who had attended high schools with the highest concentration of disadvantaged students were

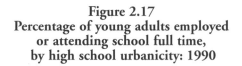

**Figure 2.17
Percentage of young adults employed
or attending school full time,
by high school urbanicity: 1990**

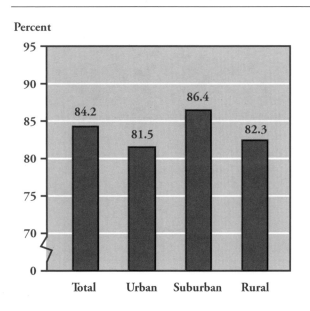

Percent

SOURCE: U.S. Department of Labor, National Longitudinal Survey of Youth, 1990.

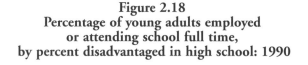

**Figure 2.18
Percentage of young adults employed
or attending school full time,
by percent disadvantaged in high school: 1990**

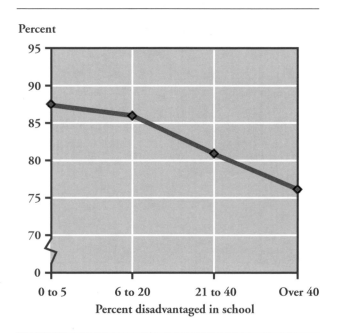

Percent

Percent disadvantaged in school

SOURCE: U.S. Department of Labor, National Longitudinal Survey of Youth, 1990.

working or enrolled in school full time, compared with 88 percent of their counterparts who had attended schools with less than 5 percent of the students disadvantaged (figure 2.18).

Are urban schools different after accounting for differences in the concentration of disadvantaged students in the school? The difference between the participation rates of former urban and suburban high school students disappeared after taking into account differences in the concentration of disadvantaged students in their high schools. The location of the school, then, was not related to later economic outcomes apart from differences by urbanicity in the proportion of disadvantaged students in the school.

Were young adults from urban schools with the highest concentration of disadvantaged students less likely than

predicted to be employed or enrolled in school 7 to 15 years after high school? In figure 2.19, young adults who had attended urban high schools with the highest concentration of disadvantaged students appear to be the least likely of any group to be working or attending school full time. However, their rates of participation are no different than predicted given the combined effects of urbanicity and a high proportion of disadvantaged students in the school. Moreover, the difference between their rates of participation in productive activities and those of young adults who attended suburban and rural schools with similarly disadvantaged populations are not statistically significant due to large sampling error. Seventy-three percent of these former urban students were engaged in these activities, compared with 81 percent of those who attended suburban schools and 76 percent of those who attended rural schools with similar levels of disadvantaged students (figure 2.19).

Figure 2.19
Percentage of young adults employed or attending school full time
by high school urbanicity and percent disadvantaged in high school: 1990

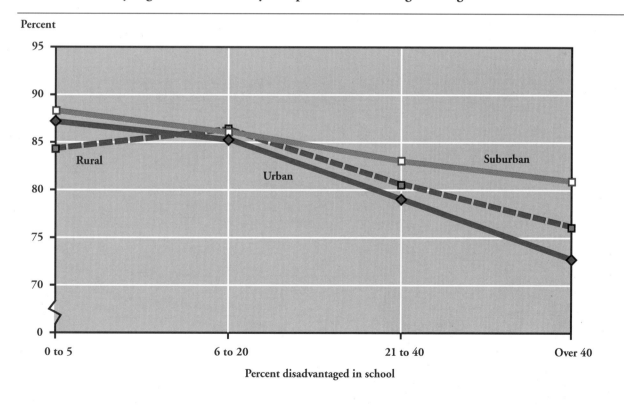

SOURCE: U.S. Department of Labor, National Longitudinal Survey of Youth, 1990.

Unemployment

The unemployment rate indicates the portion of the labor force that wish to be employed but are unable to find work.[6] The period during which the youth followed by the NLSY came of age and entered the labor market—the late 1970s through the 1980s—coincided with a period of higher overall unemployment, which disproportionately affected young, less educated, and minority populations (Freeman 1991). This section will examine the unemployment rates of young adults, ages 25–32, according to the urbanicity of the high school they attended in the late 1970s and early 1980s, rather than their place of residence at the time of the follow-up survey in 1990. Although the unemployment rates reported in 1990 were affected by the job markets in places where the young adults were residing in 1990, it was not possible to account for this effect in the following analysis.

Are urban schools different? In 1990, about 4 percent of young adults ages 25–32 were unemployed overall. But young adults who had attended public high schools in urban areas had an average unemployment rate of close to 6 percent, while those from suburban and rural schools had lower average unemployment rates of about 3 and 4 percent, respectively (figure 2.20).[7]

Are schools with high concentrations of disadvantaged students different? The unemployment rates of young adults generally increase with the proportion of disadvantaged students in the high school they attend. Young adults who had attended the schools with the highest concentrations of disadvantaged students were at least twice as likely to be unemployed as those from schools with lower levels of disadvantaged students (almost 8 percent unemployed compared with 2 to 4 percent from other schools) (figure 2.21).

Are urban schools different after accounting for differences in the concentration of disadvantaged students in the school? The urbanicity of the high school attended continues to be related to the unem-

Figure 2.20
Percentage of young adults unemployed, by high school urbanicity: 1990

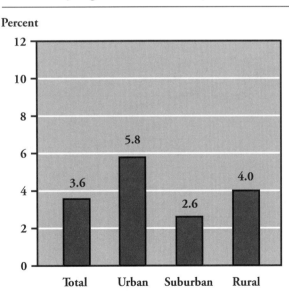

Percent

SOURCE: U.S. Department of Labor, National Longitudinal Survey of Youth, 1990.

Figure 2.21
Percentage of young adults unemployed, by percent disadvantaged in high school: 1990

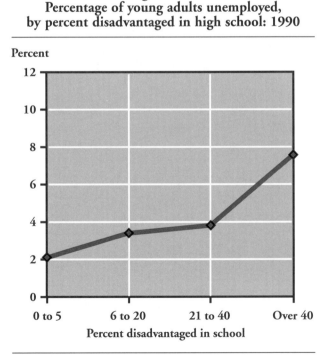

Percent

Percent disadvantaged in school

SOURCE: U.S. Department of Labor, National Longitudinal Survey of Youth, 1990.

ployment rates of young adults, even when differences by location in the proportion of disadvantaged students in the high school are considered. Young adults who had attended urban schools would still have higher unemployment rates, even if their schools had the same proportion of disadvantaged students as schools in other areas.

Were young adults from urban schools with the highest concentration of disadvantaged students more likely than predicted to be unemployed 7 to 15 years after high school? Young adults who had attended a high school located in an urban area with the highest levels of disadvantaged students had an average unemployment rate of 11 percent, which was more than twice the rate (5 percent) for those who went to similar schools in suburban areas (figure 2.22). The difference between the unemployment rates of those who had attended schools in urban and

rural areas with similarly high proportions of disadvantaged students appears large in the figure; however, it is not statistically significant. Although the urban unemployment rate of 11 percent is high, it is no higher than predicted from the combination of the unemployment rates observed separately for young adults from all urban schools and from all schools with high concentrations of disadvantaged students. There is no evidence to suggest that there was any additional unexplained unemployment for young adults who attended these schools that was related to the combination of the school's urban setting and highly disadvantaged population.

---

[6]"Unemployed" is defined as looking for work or on temporary layoff and not enrolled in school full time.

[7]The difference between urban and rural here is significant at the 90 percent confidence interval, rather than at the 95 percent confidence interval.

Figure 2.22
Percentage of young adults unemployed,
by high school urbanicity and percent disadvantaged in high school: 1990

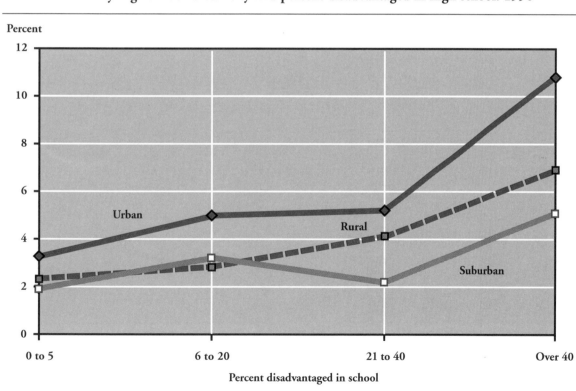

SOURCE: U.S. Department of Labor, National Longitudinal Survey of Youth, 1990.

Poverty Status

The average real earnings of young adults, in general, and of high school dropouts, in particular, declined between 1979 and 1988. This combined with higher levels of unemployment, as mentioned previously, drove many young adults in their prime into poverty by 1991 (Panel on High-Risk Youth 1993). Overall levels of poverty are affected by broad economic and demographic trends, but certain segments of the population are at higher risk for living in poverty than others.[8] Using data from the NLSY, this section addresses whether young adults 25–32 who attended public high school in urban areas in the late 1970s and early 1980s were more likely to be living in poverty in 1990, when they were in their prime years of life, than those who attended suburban or rural high schools.

Are urban schools different? In 1990, 8 percent of young adults 25–32 were living below the poverty line. Young adults who had attended urban public high schools were much more likely to be living in poverty (15 percent) than their counterparts who had attended suburban or rural high schools (6 and 9 percent, respectively) (figure 2.23).

Are schools with high concentrations of disadvantaged students in the school different? Young adults who had attended a high school with the highest concentrations of disadvantaged students were three times as likely to be living in poverty in 1990 (15 percent) as their counterparts who had attended schools with the lowest concentration of disadvantaged students (5 percent) (figure 2.24).

Figure 2.23
Percentage of young adults living in poverty, by high school urbanicity: 1990

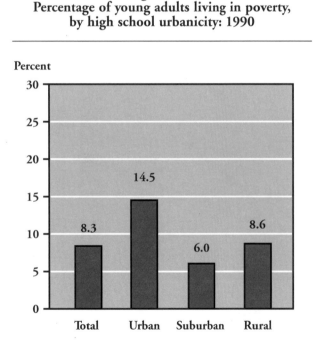

Percent

Figure 2.24
Percentage of young adults living in poverty, by percent disadvantaged in high school: 1990

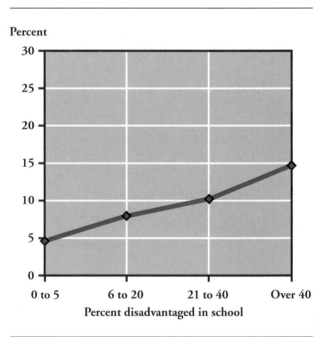

Percent

SOURCE: U.S. Department of Labor, National Longitudinal Survey of Youth, 1990.

SOURCE: U.S. Department of Labor, National Longitudinal Survey of Youth, 1990.

Are urban schools different after accounting for differences in the concentration of disadvantaged students in the school? Students who had attended urban high schools were more likely to be living in poverty later in life, even after the proportion of disadvantaged students in their schools was taken into account.

Were young adults from urban schools with the highest concentration of disadvantaged students more likely to be living in poverty 7 to 15 years after high school than predicted? One out of four young adults who had attended urban high schools with the highest proportions of disadvantaged students were living below the poverty line in 1990. This contrasts with one

out of seven young adults who had attended similar schools in suburban locations, and one out of 10 from rural locations (figure 2.25). One out of 27 students from suburban schools with the lowest level of disadvantaged students ended up living in poverty. The poverty rate in the prime of life for students from urban schools with high concentrations of disadvantaged students, though higher than other schools, is no higher than predicted from the additive effect of high concentrations of disadvantaged students and the urban location of the high schools.

---

[8]In addition to employment and earnings, family size and the age of the householder (in one- and two-person families) has an impact on the calculation of poverty status.

Figure 2.25
Percentage of young adults living in poverty,
by high school urbanicity and percent disadvantaged in high school: 1990

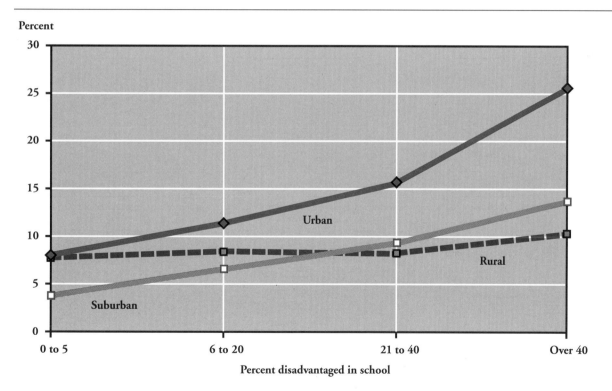

Percent

Percent disadvantaged in school

SOURCE: U.S. Department of Labor, National Longitudinal Survey of Youth, 1990.

Chapter 3

Student Background Characteristics and Afterschool Activities

This chapter examines the influences and activities that affect students' performance in school but that lie beyond the school's control. Although the chapter primarily focuses on family-related background characteristics, such as parental employment, it also addresses students' extracurricular activities and part-time work. Clearly, the choices students make about how they spend their time outside of school may affect their performance in school as well as their future employment.

The background characteristics of students that are discussed in this chapter were selected on the basis of previous research documenting their relationship to students' educational outcomes. Since Coleman's landmark study, *Equality of Educational Opportunity* (Coleman et al. 1966), numerous studies have found that family and socioeconomic characteristics are closely tied to a student's chances for academic success. For example, in a study of young adult literacy, parents' education was found to be significantly related to literacy behavior and type and amount of education young adults eventually achieve (Kirsch and Jungeblut 1986). Many believe that students in urban schools are less likely than students in other schools to have the family and economic resources that have been shown to predict academic success.

Further, it has been hypothesized that students who participate in school extracurricular activities are more likely to become engaged in school (Braddock 1991; Newmann 1992; Finn 1993). Research findings seem to show that students who participate in extracurricular activities have better grades, spend more time on homework, and have higher school aspirations.

While students' participation in extracurricular activities seems to positively affect their school performance, their working at a job during the school year may have mixed effects. On the positive side, working may increase the student's sense of responsibility, and early exposure to work experiences may promote future labor market success (Mangum 1988). On the negative side, however, student labor force participation has also been hypothesized to adversely affect student school engagement and outcomes (Newmann 1992).

Although this chapter examines each student background characteristic separately, the family characteristics that are discussed tend to be interrelated and linked to a student's likelihood of living in poverty. For example, a child from a one-parent family is more likely to be living in poverty, as is a child whose parent has lower educational attainment (Committee on Ways and Means, U.S. House of Representatives 1985). Similarly, because households with lower income levels are more mobile, the children in those households would be more likely to change schools. While this chapter discusses these and other selected family background characteristics, chapter 1 provides more descriptive information about the socioeconomic status of students according to the type of school they attend and its location.

The data in this chapter are drawn from the base year and first follow-up of a longitudinal survey that began with a cohort of 8th-grade students, the National Education Longitudinal Study of 1988 (NELS:88). In addition to information on students, NELS:88 includes information gathered directly from students' parents. Parents tend to be a more reliable source than the students themselves for information about parental and other family background characteristics.

Like the analysis in chapter 2, in this chapter students are grouped according to the urbanicity and the level of poverty concentration in the school they attended. The data for each measure are subjected to a series of statistical tests (using analysis of variance techniques) to determine:

1) If urban students, in general, have fewer family and economic resources and lower participation rates (in extracurricular activities or in the labor force) than suburban or rural students;

2) If students from schools with higher poverty concentrations have fewer background resources and different participation rates than students from schools with lower poverty concentrations;

3) If the background resources and participation rates of students from urban public schools would still differ from those of students from rural and suburban public schools if the level of poverty concentration poverty of their schools were held constant; and

4) If students in the urban schools with the highest poverty concentrations have fewer background resources and are less likely to participate in afterschool activities and less likely to be working part time than their suburban and rural counterparts and if so, were their family backgrounds and activities different than predicted.

Chart 3.1 lists the indicators that were used in this chapter and summarizes the findings for those indicators. The chart may be used as a reference, because the four basic questions addressed in this report are answered briefly for each characteristic discussed in this chapter.

This chapter is divided into two sections: student background characteristics and afterschool activities. The first section addresses whether a student lives with two parents, parental employment, whether a parent completed college, school mobility, parental expectations for the child to complete college, and parent and child conversations about school. The second section, on afterschool activities, focuses on sports-related activities offered by the schools attended by 8th graders, students' participation rates in these activities, and student employment.

Summary of This Chapter's Findings

Urban students and students who attend public schools with high poverty concentrations are, in general, more likely to have fewer economic and human resources—they are less likely to have two parents in the household and their parents have lower educational attainment. They are also likely to participate in extracurricular activities at lower rates. Even after accounting for school poverty concentration, the following patterns emerged for urban students:

- They were less likely to live in two-parent families;

- Those who lived in a two-parent family were less likely than suburban students to have a parent employed full time;

- They were more likely to have changed schools more than once; and

- They were less likely to participate in school-sponsored extracurricular sports activities.

For two of the indicators of student background and afterschool activities that were examined, students from an urban school with the highest poverty concentration experienced a higher level of risk than those in high poverty schools elsewhere.[9] These indicators for which urban high poverty students were at higher risk than high poverty students from other locations were:

- They were less likely to live in a two-parent family; and

- They were more likely to change schools more than once.

Of the remaining eight indicators, a similar level of risk was found among students in high poverty schools in suburban and rural locations.

For all of the indicators that were examined in this section, students attending urban high poverty public schools fared just as well as would be predicted from the combination of urban and high poverty school characteristics. That is, the students' background characteristics and afterschool activities could be predicted from the combined effects of an urban and a high poverty setting. There was no evidence that they were associated with an interaction, or compounding effect, of an urban setting and high poverty.

[9]The term *risk* is used because research findings indicate that these particular characteristics seem to be related to a greater likelihood of poor educational outcomes. For example, children living with only one parent and those whose parents are not employed do not perform as well in school as those living in two-parent households or those having at least one parent who is employed.

CHART 3.1—SUMMARY OF RESULTS: STUDENT BACKGROUND CHARACTERISTICS AND AFTERSCHOOL ACTIVITIES				
INDICATOR	Are Urban Schools Different?	Are High Poverty Schools Different?	Are Urban Schools Different after Accounting for Poverty Concentration?	Are Urban High Poverty Schools Different from Other High Poverty Schools? Are Urban High Poverty Schools Different than Predicted?
I. STUDENT BACKGROUND CHARACTERISTICS				
Living in Two-Parent Family	Yes, urban lower than suburban and rural	Yes, high poverty lower than all others	Yes, urban lower than others	Yes, lower than other high poverty No different than predicted
Single-Parent Family, Parent Works	Yes, urban lower than suburban, but same as rural	Yes, high poverty lower than all others	No, urban same as others	No, same as other high poverty No different than predicted
Two-Parent Family, at Least One Parent Works	Yes, urban lower than suburban, but same as rural	Yes, high poverty lower than all others	Yes, urban lower than suburban, same as rural	No, same as other high poverty No different than predicted
Parent Completed College	Yes, urban lower than suburban, same as rural	Yes, high poverty lower than all others	Yes, urban same as suburban, higher than rural	No, same as other high poverty No different than predicted

INDICATOR	Are Urban Schools Different?	Are High Poverty Schools Different?	Are Urban Schools Different after Accounting for Poverty Concentration?	Are Urban High Poverty Schools Different from Other High Poverty Schools? Are Urban High Poverty Schools Different than Predicted?
Student Changed Schools More Than Once	Yes, urban higher than suburban and rural	Yes, high poverty higher than most others	Yes, urban higher than others	Yes, higher than other high poverty

No different than predicted |
| Parent Expects Student to Complete College | Yes, urban lower than suburban, higher than rural | Yes, high poverty lower than most others | Yes, urban same as suburban, higher than rural | No, same as other high poverty

No different than predicted |
| Parent Talks with Student about School | Yes, urban lower than suburban and rural | Yes, high poverty lower than all others | No, urban same as others | No, same as other high poverty

No different than predicted |
| **II. AFTERSCHOOL ACTIVITIES** | | | | |
| School Sports Offerings | Yes, urban lower than suburban, higher than rural | Yes, high poverty lower than most others | Yes, urban higher than rural, same as suburban | Yes, higher than rural high poverty, same as suburban high poverty

No different than predicted |
| Student Sports Participation | Yes, urban lower than suburban and rural | Yes, high poverty lower than all others | Yes, urban lower than others | No, same as other high poverty

No different than predicted |
| Student Labor Force Participation | No, urban same as suburban and rural | Yes, high poverty lower than most others others | No, urban same as others | No, same as other high poverty

No different than predicted |

Student Background Characteristics

Family support and resources have been shown to significantly affect student's school progress. Thus, it is important to determine whether urban students have similar levels of family and socioeconomic resources as do students in suburban and rural schools.

Findings

- On all but one of the background indicators, student labor force participation, urban public school students fared less well than students who attended suburban public schools. However, on more than half of the indicators examined in this chapter, urban students fared as well as or better than rural students. Those indicators on which urban students fared less well than rural students were school mobility, talks with parents about school, sports participation, and family living arrangements.

- There appears to be a strong relationship between background characteristics that have been shown to put students at greater risk and the level of poverty concentration of the school that they attend. Among all the indicators reviewed, students attending high poverty schools generally fared less well than students attending schools with lower poverty concentrations.

- Even after accounting for the level of poverty in the schools, students who attended urban schools had a greater level of risk than those who attended suburban and rural schools in the areas of family structure and school mobility.[10] Among the remaining indicators, their level of risk was less than or equal to that of students attending other schools.

- Compared with students in high poverty schools in other locations, students who attended urban high poverty schools were less likely to live in a two-parent family and were more likely to have changed schools more than once.

---

[10]Chapter 1 contains a broad descriptive discussion of student characteristics by urbanicity.

Two-Parent Families

Whether a child lives with one parent or two has been found to be related to a child's success in school (Mulkey et al. 1992). All other things being equal, with only one parent in the household, that parent is likely to have less time to spend with the child than parents in two-parent households. Also, in one-parent households, household income is generally lower than it is in two-parent households, which may produce more economic stress in the household and, in turn, affect a student's school performance.

Are urban schools different? In 1988, about three-quarters of all 8th graders lived in households in which two parents were present (figure 3.1).[11] However, 8th-grade students in suburban or rural schools were more likely than urban students to be living with two parents. Approximately 80 percent of suburban and rural students lived with two parents, compared with only 68 percent of urban students.

Are high poverty schools different? Students in schools with higher concentrations of poverty were less likely to be living with two parents than students in schools with lower levels of poverty (figure 3.2). Eighty-five percent of 8th graders in schools with the lowest concentration of poverty lived with two parents, while 71 percent of students in schools with high poverty concentrations did so.

Are urban schools different after accounting for poverty concentration? While chapter 1 has shown that urbanicity and poverty concentration are highly related, students in urban schools were less likely than other students to be living in two-parent households

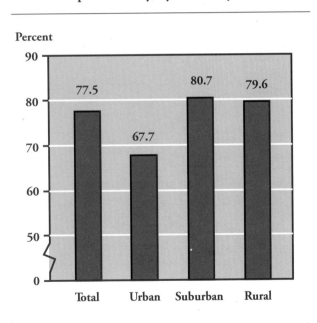

Figure 3.1
Percentage of 8th-grade students living in a two-parent family, by urbanicity: 1988

Percent

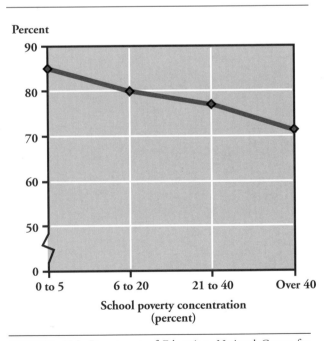

Figure 3.2
Percentage of 8th-grade students living in a two-parent family, by school poverty concentration: 1988

Percent

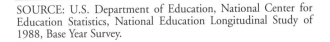

SOURCE: U.S. Department of Education, National Center for Education Statistics, National Education Longitudinal Study of 1988, Base Year Survey.

SOURCE: U.S. Department of Education, National Center for Education Statistics, National Education Longitudinal Study of 1988, Base Year Survey.

even after considering the effect of school poverty concentration (figure 3.3).

Is the percentage of students living in two-parent households lower than predicted in urban schools with high concentrations of poverty? Sixty-four percent of students in urban high poverty schools lived in two-parent families. This percentage is lower than that among students attending similar schools in suburban and rural locations. The percentage of students in urban high poverty schools who lived in two-parent families is no lower than would be predicted given the separate patterns for urban schools and high poverty schools overall. Moreover, it appears that the relationship between a school's level of poverty concentration

and family composition was weaker for rural students than for urban students (figure 3.3).

[11]Students were considered to be living in a two-parent family if they lived with their mother and father, their mother and a male guardian, or their father and a female guardian. Otherwise, if they lived with their mother or father only, they were considered to be living with one parent. Students living in any other type of family were excluded from this analysis. According to the report, *A Profile of Parents of Eighth Graders* (Horn and West 1992):

> 65 percent of students were living with both their mother and father;
> 12 percent were living with their mother and a male guardian;
> 3 percent were living with their father and a female guardian;
> 17 percent were living with their mother or female guardian (no other parent or guardian);
> 3 percent were living with their father or male guardian (no other parent or guardian); and
> 1 percent were living in other two-adult families.

Figure 3.3
Percentage of 8th-grade students living in a two-parent family, by urbanicity and school poverty concentration: 1988

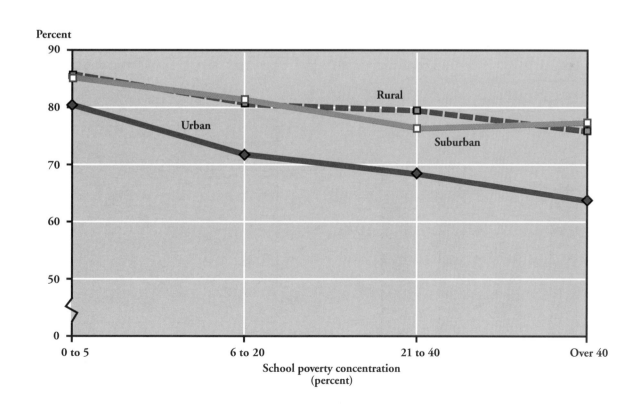

SOURCE: U.S. Department of Education, National Center for Education Statistics, National Education Longitudinal Study of 1988, Base Year Survey.

Parental Employment

There is evidence that parental employment influences family social and economic well-being in both negative and positive ways. This is true for several reasons. The number of earners in a family is related to the level of family income (U.S. Bureau of the Census 1993). In addition, if the male parent is not employed it can place great stress upon the family and may lead to a greater risk of family marital disruption (Bianchi and McArthur 1991). Thus parental employment can be seen as a positive attribute for a student in that the student is more likely to be living in a stable, more economically secure situation. Also, parents who are in the labor force may serve as positive role models for their children.

However, parental employment can have a negative impact when their working hours leave little time to spend with children, which may be especially true in families where there is a single parent.

Using information from NELS:88, this analysis breaks out employment status separately for parents of 8th graders when there is one parent in the household and when there are two.[12] For students living with one parent, the category of interest is whether that parent is working full time (contrasted to parents who are working part time, who are unemployed, or who are not in the labor force), because the primary interest in this

Figure 3.4
Percentage of 8th-grade students living in a one-parent family with parent working full time, by urbanicity: 1988

Percent

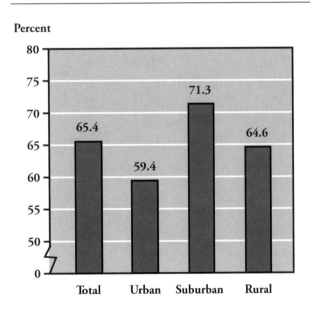

SOURCE: U.S. Department of Education, National Center for Education Statistics, National Education Longitudinal Study of 1988, Base Year Survey.

Figure 3.5
Percentage of 8th-grade students living in a one-parent family with parent working full time, by school poverty concentration: 1988

Percent

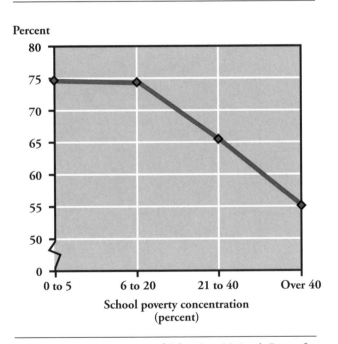

SOURCE: U.S. Department of Education, National Center for Education Statistics, National Education Longitudinal Study of 1988, Base Year Survey.

section is economic well-being. For students with two parents in the household, the indicator is whether at least one parent works full time.

Are urban schools different? In 1988, about 65 percent of *single* parents of 8th graders were working full time (figure 3.4). Children living in *two-parent* families were more likely to have at least one parent working than were children living with only one parent; about 94 percent of 8th graders in two-parent households had at least one parent working full time (figure 3.7). While urban 8th graders in *one-parent*

families were less likely to have that parent working full time than were the single parents of 8th graders in suburban locations (figure 3.4), they were no different on this measure than rural 8th graders. In 1988, 59 percent of urban students in single-parent families had their parent working full time, compared with about 71 percent of suburban and 65 percent of rural 8th-grade students in such families. Similarly, the proportion of students in *two-parent* families in urban and rural public schools with at least one parent working full time was less than that of their peers in suburban schools. Approximately 92 percent of these

Figure 3.6
Percentage of 8th-grade students living in a one-parent family with parent working full time, by urbanicity and school poverty concentration: 1988

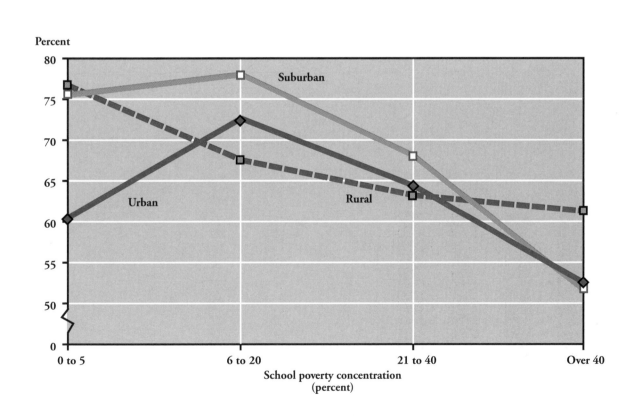

SOURCE: U.S. Department of Education, National Center for Education Statistics, National Education Longitudinal Study of 1988, Base Year Survey.

urban and rural students had at least one parent working, while 95 percent of suburban students did so (figure 3.7).

Are high poverty schools different? Students living in *single-parent* and *two-parent* families who attended schools serving large proportions of disadvantaged students were less likely than other students to have their parent working (figures 3.5 and 3.8). In the schools with the highest poverty concentrations, 55 percent of students in *one-parent* families had a working parent compared with over 74 percent of 8th graders in one-parent families from schools with the lowest poverty concentration. Similarly, of students in *two-parent* families in schools with the highest poverty concentrations, 88 percent had at least one parent working full time, compared with 97 percent of students in schools with the lowest poverty concentrations.

Are urban schools different after accounting for poverty concentration? Urban students who lived with *two* parents were less likely to have a parent employed full time even after accounting for differences in poverty concentration in each location (figure 3.9). After accounting for poverty concentration, differences in parental employment status between urban students who lived with one parent and their suburban and rural counterparts were not significant (figure 3.6).

Is the percentage of students with parents working full time lower than predicted in urban schools with high concentrations of poverty? Among students in urban high poverty schools, 53 percent of those living with *one* parent and 88 percent of those living with *two* parents had a parent working full time. These students were just as likely as comparable students attending high poverty

Figure 3.7
Percentage of 8th-grade students living in a two-parent family with at least one parent working full time, by urbanicity: 1988

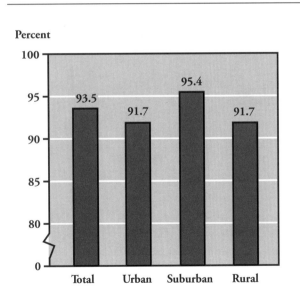

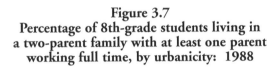

Figure 3.8
Percentage of 8th-grade students living in a two-parent family with at least one parent working full time, by school poverty concentration: 1988

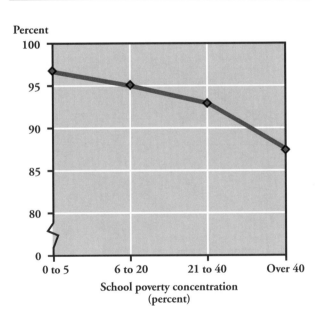

SOURCE: U.S. Department of Education, National Center for Education Statistics, National Education Longitudinal Study of 1988, Base Year Survey.

SOURCE: U.S. Department of Education, National Center for Education Statistics, National Education Longitudinal Study of 1988, Base Year Survey.

schools in suburban and rural locations to have a parent working full time. (The difference in figure 3.6 is not statistically significant.) The percentage of students, whether living in *one-* or *two-parent* families, with a parent working full time was no lower than predicted in urban schools with high concentrations of poverty.

[12]Information about "parental" labor force status was reported by the parent or guardian who responded to the parent questionnaire. That person reported his/her labor force status as well as that of a spouse/partner if one was present in the household. Refer to footnote 11 for more information about family composition.

Figure 3.9
Percentage of 8th-grade students living in a two-parent family with at least one parent working full time, by urbanicity and school poverty concentration: 1988

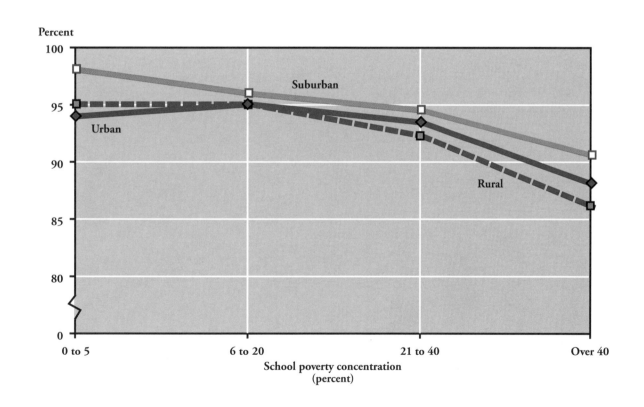

SOURCE: U.S. Department of Education, National Center for Education Statistics, National Education Longitudinal Study of 1988, Base Year Survey.

Parents' Educational Attainment

The association between parents' educational level and their children's potential academic success has been well documented. Children with more highly educated parents have higher educational achievement and attainment (Barro and Kolstad 1987; Kirsch and Jungeblut 1986; Kaufman and Bradby 1991; Horn and West 1992; McArthur 1993; Natriello et al. 1990). Further, parents with higher education also tend to have higher expectations for their children's educational outcomes (Horn and West 1992). If at least one parent has completed 4 or more years of college, household income tends to be higher, with parents having greater access to economic resources to support a child (U.S. Bureau of the Census 1992).

The NELS:88 parent survey asked the parent or guardian who responded to report his or her own highest level of education. If that person had a partner or spouse in the household, that person's educational level was also ascertained. In the analysis presented here, if there are two parent/guardians in the household, the highest level of education reported for either parent is used. For the sake of economy, the "parent or guardian" will be referred to as the "parent." (See footnote 11 for a description of family composition in the NELS:88 base year survey.)

Are urban schools different? In 1988, about 24 percent of all 8th graders had at least one parent in the household who had completed 4 years of college (figure 3.10). Children in urban schools were less likely to have a college-educated parent than were children in suburban schools. Twenty percent of urban children had at least one parent who had completed 4 years of

Figure 3.10
Percentage of 8th-grade students with a parent in the household who had completed 4 years of college, by urbanicity: 1988

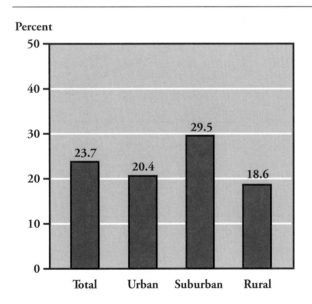

Figure 3.11
Percentage of 8th-grade students with a parent in the household who had completed 4 years of college, by school poverty concentration: 1988

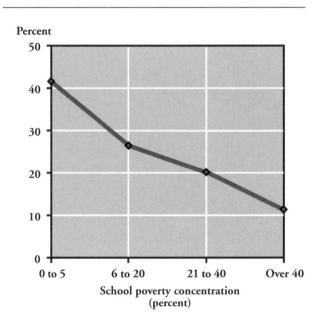

SOURCE: U.S. Department of Education, National Center for Education Statistics, National Education Longitudinal Study of 1988, Base Year Survey.

SOURCE: U.S. Department of Education, National Center for Education Statistics, National Education Longitudinal Study of 1988, Base Year Survey.

college or more, compared with almost 30 percent of suburban 8th graders. However, urban students were equally as likely to have a college-educated parent as were rural students.

Are high poverty schools different? Children from schools with the highest concentrations of poverty were much less likely to have at least one college-educated parent than students in schools with lower levels of school poverty (figure 3.11). Eleven percent of children in high poverty schools had a parent who had completed 4 years of college or more, compared with over 41 percent of children from low poverty schools.

Are urban schools different after accounting for poverty concentration? After the poverty concentra-

tion of the schools in each location was considered, urban and suburban students were equally likely to have at least one parent who had completed 4 years or more of college (figure 3.12). However, rural students were less likely than urban students to have at least one college-educated parent.

Is the percentage of students with a college-educated parent lower than predicted in urban schools with high concentrations of poverty? While 12 percent of students in urban high poverty schools had a college-educated parent, these students were equally as likely as students in similar schools in suburban and rural locations to have such parents. The percentage of students with a college-educated parent was no lower than predicted in urban schools with high concentrations of poverty.

Figure 3.12
Percentage of 8th-grade students with a parent in the household who had completed 4 years of college, by urbanicity and school poverty concentration: 1988

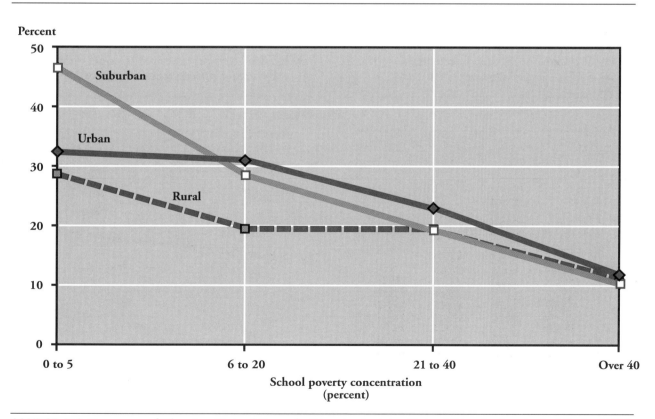

SOURCE: U.S. Department of Education, National Center for Education Statistics, National Education Longitudinal Study of 1988, Base Year Survey.

School Mobility

Previous research has linked student mobility (that is, changing schools) with students having increased academic and disciplinary problems in school (Bianchi 1993; Haveman, Wolfe, and Spaulding 1991; Straits 1987; Long 1975).[13] The negative impact of mobility upon schooling can be explained by a number of factors, for example, differences across schools or districts in academic requirements. Another explanation could be that students who frequently change schools may have difficulty becoming attached to a new school, which might decrease their motivation to learn. A student's likelihood of changing schools is also linked to the likelihood of being victimized at school (Bastian and Taylor 1991). This section focuses on school mobility by identifying 8th-grade students who changed schools two or more times since first grade for reasons *other than* a promotion to one grade or level or

a move from an elementary school building to a middle school building in the same district.

Are urban schools different? Eighth graders attending urban public schools in 1988 were more likely than other 8th-grade students to have changed schools two or more times since the first grade (figure 3.13). Almost 46 percent of urban students had changed school this often, compared with only 34 percent of suburban and 28 percent of rural students.

Are high poverty schools different? Students in schools with the highest concentrations of poverty had changed schools more often than students in schools with the lowest concentrations of poverty (figure 3.14). About 38 percent of students in schools with the highest level of school poverty concentration had changed schools

**Figure 3.13
Percentage of 8th-grade students who have changed schools more than once since first grade, by urbanicity: 1988**

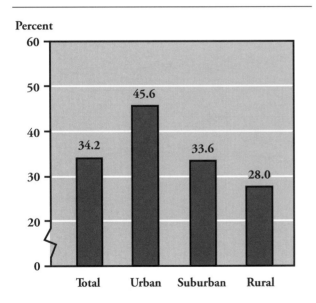

SOURCE: U.S. Department of Education, National Center for Education Statistics, National Education Longitudinal Study of 1988, Base Year Survey.

**Figure 3.14
Percentage of 8th-grade students who have changed schools more than once since first grade, by school poverty concentration: 1988**

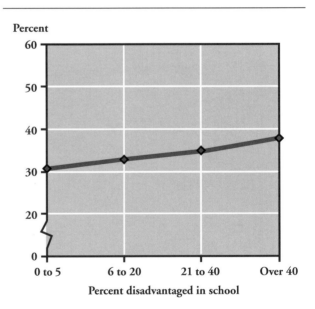

SOURCE: U.S. Department of Education, National Center for Education Statistics, National Education Longitudinal Study of 1988, Base Year Survey.

two or more times, compared with 31 percent of students in schools with the lowest concentration of poverty. There was no real difference between the mobility rates of students in schools with highest poverty and next to highest poverty concentrations.

Are urban schools different after accounting for poverty concentration? Even after the school poverty concentration in each location was considered, urban students were still more likely than suburban or rural students to have moved two or more times (figure 3.15).

Is student mobility higher than predicted in urban schools with high concentrations of poverty? Students in urban high poverty schools were more likely to have

changed schools two or more times than were students in similar suburban and rural schools. Forty-six percent of these students changed schools this often, compared with 37 percent of suburban and 29 percent of rural students in similar schools. The difference in student mobility between urban high poverty schools and other schools was no greater than would be predicted given the rates of student mobility for urban and high poverty schools taken separately. This suggests that the combination of high poverty concentration and an urban setting does not add to the already higher risk for these students to change schools.

---

[13]It should be noted that the negative impact of school mobility also could be due in part to underlying problems such as family instability.

Figure 3.15
Percentage of 8th-grade students who have changed schools more than once since first grade, by urbanicity and school poverty concentration: 1988

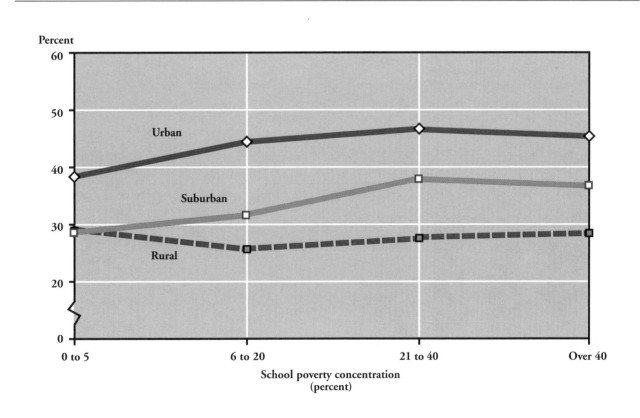

SOURCE: U.S. Department of Education, National Center for Education Statistics, National Education Longitudinal Study of 1988, Base Year Survey.

Parents' Expectations for Their Child's Education

A student's success in school is tied to parental expectations for their child's education. In many instances, parental expectations translate into prescriptions for their child's behavior, which include rules about homework and rules about maintaining a certain grade point average, as well as expectations about how well their child will do in school and how much education the child will eventually complete. Thus, at the same time that parental expectations may influence the student's immediate behavior, they may also affect the student's self-concept and motivation to learn (Horn and West 1992). For this analysis, the measure of parental expectations used is whether parents expect their 8th grader to complete 4 or more years of college, since college completion directly affects labor market success. As with previous sections on parental labor force partici-

pation and their education, both parents and guardians are included here and referred to simply as "parents." (See footnote 11 for a discussion of family composition in NELS:88.)

Are urban schools different? In 1988, the parents of most 8th graders held high expectations for their children's education (figure 3.16). The parents of over half the children expected them to graduate from college with a 4-year degree.[14] Parental expectations on average were higher for students in urban schools than for rural students, but were lower than those for suburban students. Almost 56 percent of urban students had parents who expected them to eventually receive a 4-year degree, compared with 49 percent of rural students and 60 percent of suburban students.

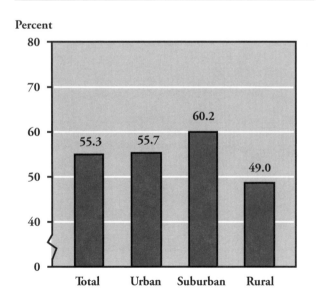

Figure 3.16
Percentage of 8th-grade students whose parents expect them to complete 4 years of college, by urbanicity: 1988

Percent

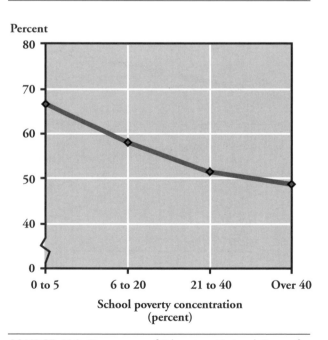

Figure 3.17
Percentage of 8th-grade students whose parents expect them to complete 4 years of college, by school poverty concentration: 1988

Percent

School poverty concentration (percent)

SOURCE: U.S. Department of Education, National Center for Education Statistics, National Education Longitudinal Study of 1988, Base Year Survey.

SOURCE: U.S. Department of Education, National Center for Education Statistics, National Education Longitudinal Study of 1988, Base Year Survey.

Are high poverty schools different? Parents of children in schools with relatively large concentrations of poor children were far less likely to expect their children to finish college than parents of children in other schools (figure 3.17). The parents of almost two-thirds of the 8th graders in low poverty schools expected them to finish a 4-year college program, compared with 49 percent of the parents of 8th graders in high poverty schools.

Are urban schools different after accounting for poverty concentration? Only the difference between urban and rural schools remained significant after accounting for poverty concentration. However, there were no significant differences between urban and suburban schools after accounting for poverty concentration. The educational expectations of the parents of urban and suburban students declined similarly

with increasing school poverty (figure 3.18). But for rural students, the parents' expectations varied little across the categories of concentrations of poverty: about 50 percent of all rural students had parents who thought their child would complete a 4-year college program, regardless of poverty concentration level.

Are parental expectations lower than predicted in urban schools with high concentrations of poverty? The parental expectations of students in urban high poverty concentration schools were no lower than would be predicted. In fact, regardless of urbanicity, the parents of about half of students in high poverty schools expected them to complete 4 years of college.

---

[14]Given the fact that in 1990 less than a third of all 25- to 32-year-olds held a bachelor's degree or higher, these expectations may be unrealistically high. See figure 2.11 in chapter 2 of this report.

Figure 3.18
Percentage of 8th-grade students whose parents expect them to complete 4 years of college, by urbanicity and school poverty concentration: 1988

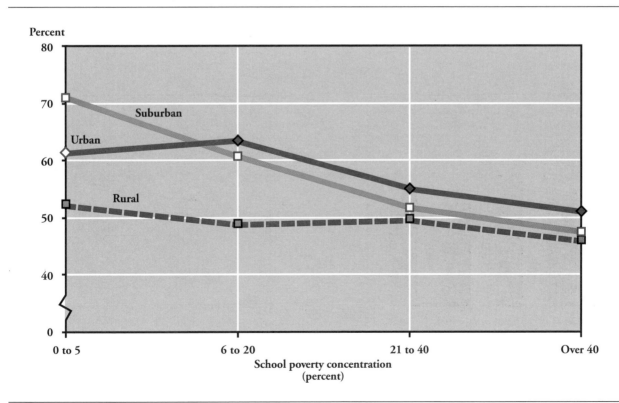

SOURCE: U.S. Department of Education, National Center for Education Statistics, National Education Longitudinal Study of 1988, Base Year Survey.

Parent and Child Conversations About School

Parent involvement in their child's education may take many forms. These include participation in parent/teacher organizations, volunteering at the school, contacting the school about the child's progress, monitoring homework, talking with their child about what they do in school, and talking about future education plans.

This section addresses one such aspect of parent involvement, the frequency with which the parents talk with their 8th-grade students about school. The assumption made is that talking with the child about school on a regular basis shows the student that the parent cares about school issues and keeps the parent informed about school activities.

Are urban schools different? In 1988, the parents of more than three out of four 8th graders talked with their child about school (figure 3.19), but the parents of 22 percent of public school students rarely did so.[15] Parents of urban students were less likely to regularly talk to their child than were parents of rural or suburban students. The differences by urbanicity, while small, were significant: the parents of about one-fourth of urban students rarely talked to their child about school, compared with the parents of about 23 percent of rural students and one-fifth of suburban students.

Are high poverty schools different? Parents of students in schools with high concentrations of poverty were less likely than parents of students in other schools to have

Figure 3.19
Percentage of 8th-grade students whose parents rarely talk to them about school, by urbanicity: 1988

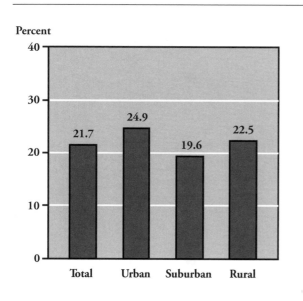

Percent

SOURCE: U.S. Department of Education, National Center for Education Statistics, National Education Longitudinal Study of 1988, Base Year Survey.

Figure 3.20
Percentage of 8th-grade students whose parents rarely talk to them about school, by school poverty concentration: 1988

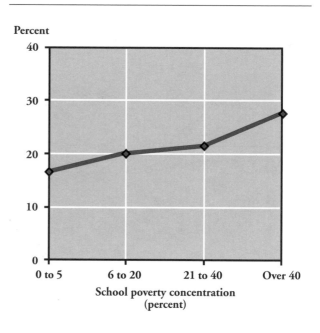

Percent

School poverty concentration (percent)

SOURCE: U.S. Department of Education, National Center for Education Statistics, National Education Longitudinal Study of 1988, Base Year Survey.

regular conversations with their child about school (figure 3.20). The parents of almost 28 percent of students in schools with high concentrations of poverty rarely talked to their child about school, compared with the parents of 17 percent of students in low poverty schools.

Are urban schools different after accounting for poverty concentration? After taking into account differences in the poverty concentration of schools in each location, differences between urban, suburban, and rural schools in the frequency of parent/child conversations about school were no longer statistically significant. The differences between parents of students in urban, suburban, and rural schools shown in figure 3.19 were probably due to the fact that urban schools were more likely to have high concentrations of poverty, and that

parents of students in such schools talked less frequently to their child about school (figure 3.20).

Is the percentage of students whose parents rarely talk with them about school higher than predicted in urban schools with high concentrations of poverty? In urban high poverty schools, the percentage of students whose parents rarely talk with them about school (28 percent) is no higher than it is for suburban or rural high poverty schools, and is no higher than predicted (figure 3.21).

---

[15]These data are based on a questionnaire item asking parents (or guardians) how often they talk with their children about school. There may be some amount of upward bias in these items due to the social desirability of the positive responses.

Figure 3.21
Percentage of 8th-grade students whose parents rarely talk to them about school, by urbanicity and school poverty concentration: 1988

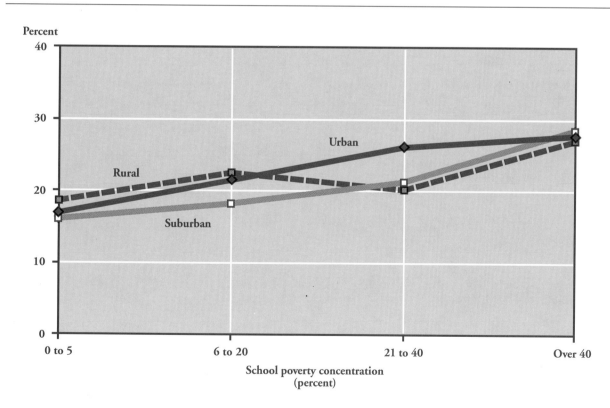

SOURCE: U.S. Department of Education, National Center for Education Statistics, National Education Longitudinal Study of 1988, Base Year Survey.

Afterschool Activities

In this section the relationship between urbanicity, school poverty concentration, and afterschool activities is discussed. For the purposes of this report, it is assumed that participation in school-sponsored, afterschool sports activities benefits students overall. However, as mentioned earlier, there is lively debate about whether working while in school—and, if so, how many hours of work per week—is in the student's best interests.

Findings

- While urban public schools were in between suburban and rural schools in the number of sports-related activities offered, urban students' participation in those activities was lower than that of either suburban or rural students, even after accounting for poverty concentration.

- Students in urban high poverty schools participated in sports-related activities at similar rates as did students in high poverty schools in suburban or rural locations.

- In rural schools, while there were generally fewer types of activities offered than in similar urban or suburban schools, a higher proportion of students participated. This higher participation rate may be due to rural schools generally being smaller and, hence, students being more likely to be drawn into school activities than they might be in larger schools with less individualized attention. Another explanation may be that there is less competition for a limited number of slots in rural schools, so the ratio of students to opportunities is higher.

- As the concentration of poverty in the school increases, both the number of sports-related activities offered and the proportion of students who participate decline.

- There was no difference between urban, suburban, and rural students in the proportion working 11 or more hours per week, even when accounting for poverty and even in schools with the highest poverty concentrations.

Student Participation in Extracurricular Sports

Participation in school extracurricular activities may increase students' interest in school. Students who participate in school-sponsored sports activities (and academic clubs) seem to have better grades, spend more time on homework, and have higher school aspirations (Newmann 1992). Moreover, afterschool activities may enable students to use their time more constructively, thus decreasing their likelihood of getting into trouble in school or elsewhere.

In the next section, the discussion focuses on school sports as an example of the many activities available, because research indicates that sports activities influence students' engagement in schools as much as other afterschool activities (Newmann 1992). The data that were used in the following analysis are drawn from the first follow-up of the NELS:88 collected in 1990 on 10th graders and their schools. The first part of the discussion examines differences in the number of sports activities offered by schools according to urbanicity and level of poverty concentration. This is necessary to understand whether opportunities to participate in sports differ by school type, which might influence whether students in different types of schools vary in the degree to which they participate in sports. The discussion then turns to students' rates of participation in school-sponsored sports.

School Sports Offerings

Are urban schools different? In 1990, 10th graders were offered an average of 7.3 sports-related activities in schools nationwide (figure 3.22).[16] Urban schools offered 7.4 sports-related activities, while students in suburban public schools were offered similar numbers of activities (7.7). On average, students in rural schools had fewer such activities (6.7) available to them. This may be due, in part, to the fact that the student membership of rural schools tends to be smaller than those of schools in other locations.[17] Another factor may be that rural schools tend to have a more geographically dispersed student membership, which might make supporting a larger number of sports-related offerings infeasible. Though the differences in numbers of activities offered are small, they are statistically significant.

Are high poverty schools different? Students in schools with high concentrations of poverty had fewer sports activities available to them than students in low poverty schools (figure 3.23). However, these differences were not large. In the schools with the highest concentrations of poverty about seven sports activities were offered, compared with about eight activities offered in schools with low poverty concentrations.

Are urban schools different after accounting for poverty concentration? After the school's level of poverty concentration was considered, the numbers of sports-related activities offered by urban and suburban schools were no longer different; however, the difference in the numbers of sports-related activities offered

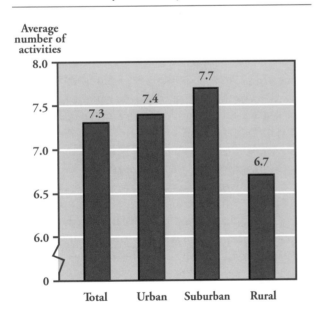

Figure 3.22
Average number of sports-related activities offered by the schools attended by 10th-grade students, by urbanicity: 1990

SOURCE: U.S. Department of Education, National Center for Education Statistics, National Education Longitudinal Study of 1988, First Follow-up Survey.

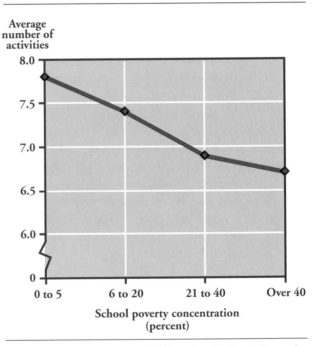

Figure 3.23
Average number of sports-related activities offered by the schools attended by 10th-grade students, by school poverty concentration: 1990

SOURCE: U.S. Department of Education, National Center for Education Statistics, National Education Longitudinal Study of 1988, First Follow-up Survey.

by urban and rural schools remained. Fewer activities were offered to 10th-grade students in rural schools than in urban schools at every level of poverty concentration except the lowest (figure 3.24).

Is the number of sports-related activities lower than predicted in urban schools with high concentrations of poverty? Students in urban high poverty schools had access to a similar number of activities as those in suburban high poverty schools (about seven), and slightly more than rural high poverty schools (about six). The number of activities in urban high poverty schools could be predicted given the patterns for urban schools and high poverty schools considered separately. That is, being in a poor urban school did not present any disadvantage in the number of sports-related activities offered beyond that observed for high poverty schools in general.

---

[16]Sports-related activities included baseball/softball, basketball, football, soccer, swim team, other team sports, other individual sports, cheerleading, and drill team.

[17]See chapter 1 above.

Figure 3.24
Average number of sports-related activities offered by the schools attended by 10th-grade students, by urbanicity and school poverty concentration: 1990

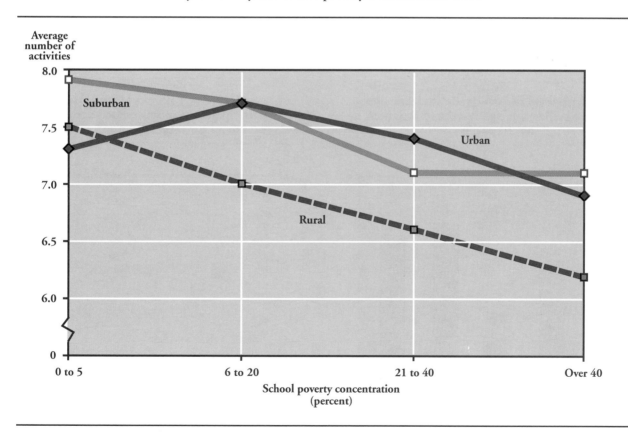

SOURCE: U.S. Department of Education, National Center for Education Statistics, National Education Longitudinal Study of 1988, First Follow-up Survey.

Sports Participation

Are urban schools different? In 1990, a little more than half of all 10th-grade students participated to some extent in sports-related school activities (figure 3.25).[18] However, urban students were less likely than either suburban or rural students to have participated—45 percent compared with 54 percent and 53 percent, respectively.

Are high poverty schools different? Students in high poverty schools were less likely to participate in school sports-related activities than other students (figure 3.26). Approximately 56 percent of students in schools with low poverty concentrations were involved in sports-related activities, compared with 44 percent of students in high poverty schools.

Are urban schools different after accounting for poverty concentration? When the school's level of poverty concentration was taken into account, urban students' participation rates in sports-related activities generally remained lower than those of other students (figure 3.27). Among students enrolled in schools with lower poverty concentrations (20 percent or less), urban students tended to be less likely to participate in sports-related activities than students in similar suburban and rural schools.

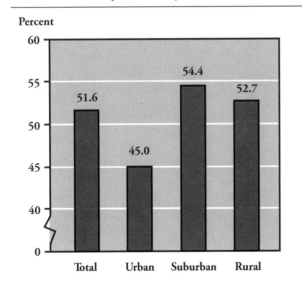

Figure 3.25
Percentage of 10th-grade students who participated in sports-related activities, by urbanicity: 1990

Percent

SOURCE: U.S. Department of Education, National Center for Education Statistics, National Education Longitudinal Study of 1988, First Follow-up Survey.

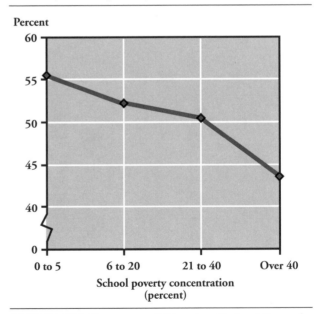

Figure 3.26
Percentage of 10th-grade students who participated in sports-related activities, by school poverty concentration: 1990

Percent

SOURCE: U.S. Department of Education, National Center for Education Statistics, National Education Longitudinal Study of 1988, First Follow-up Survey.

Is the percentage of students participating in sports-related activities lower than predicted in urban schools with high concentrations of poverty? At the highest level of poverty concentration, the participation rates of urban, suburban, and rural students did not differ significantly. The combination of being in an urban school with a high poverty concentration was not related to any additional disadvantage for these students. That is, students in these schools participated in sports-related activities at rates that would be predicted for students in schools that were both urban and high poverty.

---

[18]Participation was defined as being involved in one or more intramural sports, junior varsity, freshman or varsity team sports, or cheerleading or drill teams for such sports.

Figure 3.27
Percentage of 10th-grade students who participated in sports-related activities, by urbanicity and school poverty concentration: 1990

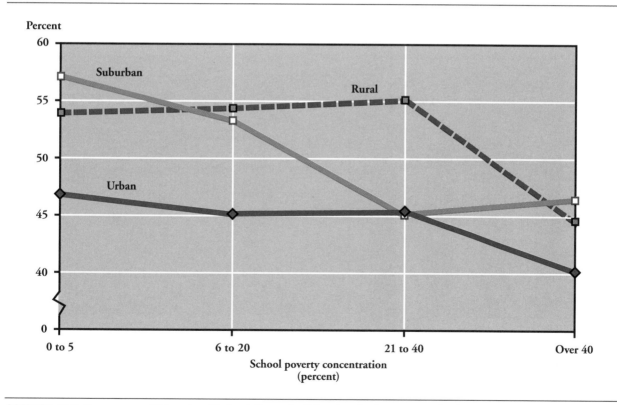

SOURCE: U.S. Department of Education, National Center for Education Statistics, National Education Longitudinal Study of 1988, First Follow-up Survey.

Employment of 10th-Grade Students

Employment while attending high school appears to have both short-term effects upon students' degree of engagement in school and long-term effects upon students' future labor market activities. While previously many researchers had argued that overall students benefited from their early labor market experiences (Mangum 1988; Lewin-Epstein 1981), the picture is not nearly so clear based on recent research (Greenberger and Steinberg 1986).

Many researchers now argue that part-time employment has a deleterious effect on educational outcomes and on future labor market experience. Students who work during the school year have less time for homework and may be too tired to accomplish their school

work successfully. In addition, as students become more involved in the labor force, they may become less interested in school. In terms of future labor market experiences, the downside to part-time employment was unforeseen during the 1970s. The reality is that most part-time jobs currently available to students are high stress, dead-end jobs (store clerk, food service worker), which actually promote delinquent behaviors and encourage students to develop negative attitudes toward work itself (Greenberger and Steinberg 1986).

Some research (Newmann 1992) has found that students who work 20 or more hours per week are more likely to experience negative effects from working. In this section, the measure examined is whether or not

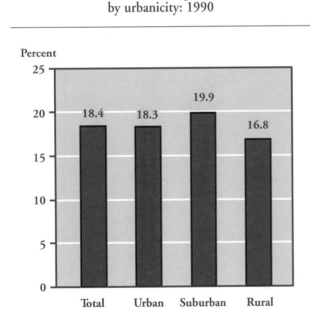

Figure 3.28
Percentage of 10th-grade students who worked
11 or more hours per week,
by urbanicity: 1990

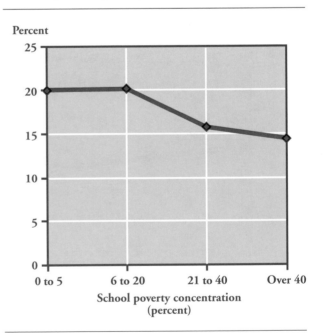

Figure 3.29
Percentage of 10th-grade students who worked
11 or more hours per week,
by school poverty concentration: 1990

SOURCE: U.S. Department of Education, National Center for Education Statistics, National Education Longitudinal Study of 1988, First Follow-up Survey.

SOURCE: U.S. Department of Education, National Center for Education Statistics, National Education Longitudinal Study of 1988, First Follow-up Survey.

10th-grade students work 11 or more hours per week during the school year, because few students in the 10th grade work 20 hours or more per week.

Are urban schools different? In 1990, about 18 percent of 10th graders were employed 11 or more hours per week (figure 3.28). However, urban 10th graders were just as likely as other students to be working this many hours. While it appears that rural students were less likely than urban students to work 11 or more hours, this difference is not statistically significant.

Are high poverty schools different? While the proportions of urban, suburban, and rural students who worked 11 or more hours varied little, the proportions of such students did vary according to the level of poverty concentration in the school (figure 3.29). A lower proportion of students in schools with the highest concentration of poverty worked 11 or more hours than students in schools with lower poverty concentrations (20 percent or less). For example, about 14 percent of students in schools with the highest poverty concentration worked 11 or more hours, compared with about 20 percent of 10th graders attending schools with less than 20 percent poverty concentration. For students in schools with the highest and next to highest poverty concentrations, however, there was no statistically significant difference in their likelihood of working.

Figure 3.30
Percentage of 10th-grade students who worked 11 or more hours per week, by urbanicity and school poverty concentration: 1990

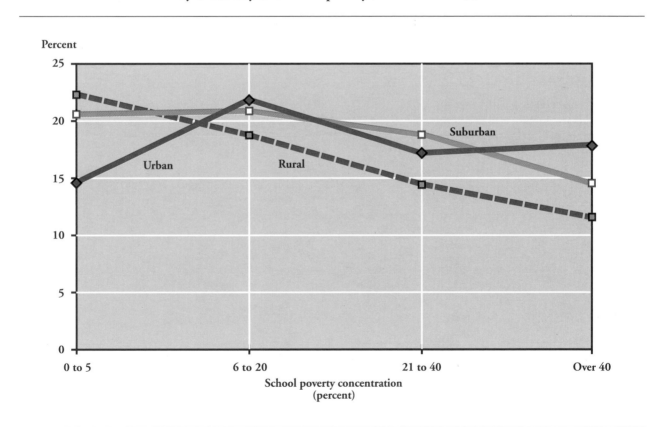

SOURCE: U.S. Department of Education, National Center for Education Statistics, National Education Longitudinal Study of 1988, First Follow-up Survey.

Are urban schools different after accounting for poverty concentration? There were no significant differences by urbanicity after taking into account poverty concentration.

Is the percentage of students who work part time higher than predicted in urban schools with high concentrations of poverty? Students in urban high poverty schools were as likely to be employed as those in other high poverty schools, and their employment levels could be predicted from the combination of location and level of poverty concentration (figure 3.30).

Chapter 4

School Experiences

The national interest in developing programs to improve the schooling and educational outcomes of children attending urban public schools and particularly high poverty urban schools has never been greater. Many authors have debated how resources contribute to differences in the quality of the educational experiences found in urban schools generally and, particularly, in those that serve poor students.[19] This chapter contributes to that debate by presenting empirical evidence from nationally representative surveys to show whether and how the school experiences of these children differ from those of other students.

This chapter addresses three key areas that affect a child's public school experience: school resources and staff, school programs and coursetaking, and student behavior. Meaningful differences in these areas between schools in different locations lend support to the contention that some groups of students have less desirable educational experiences and more limited opportunities than other groups. These differences may be related, in turn, to the poorer outcomes for some groups of students observed in chapter 2. Further, they can help focus the national policy and research agenda on those areas that need to be improved for students attending high poverty public schools in urban locations.

The same analysis model that was used in previous chapters is used in this chapter to distinguish differences by school urbanicity and poverty concentration, separately and in combination with one another. Schools and students were grouped according to the urbanicity and level of poverty concentration in the school. Specifically, the analysis determines:

1) whether students' school experiences differ by location;

2) whether their school experiences differ by school poverty concentration;

3) whether differences by school location remain after accounting for the variation in school poverty concentration; and

4) whether the school experiences of students in urban high poverty schools differs from that of students in high poverty schools in other locations, and whether urban high poverty schools are different than predicted on the measures examined.

The phrase *greater than predicted* means that the differences between urban high poverty and other schools were larger than would be predicted from the additive effects of an urban and high poverty setting, indicating an interaction, or compounding effect, of the two. This chapter presents data separately for elementary and secondary schools when there are meaningful differences by level.

Current measures of school quality that are available in national surveys reflect neither the depth nor breadth of a student's school experiences (Bobbitt et al. 1992). Thus, the indicators presented in this chapter are limited by the available data and do not provide a thorough review of student experiences. Rather, they are a selective set of indicators for public schools and students. These indicators were chosen through a process that included a review of available data and research to identify important aspects of the school environment and an analysis that revealed those indicators that varied meaningfully by location and level of poverty in the school (see appendix C for a list of data reviewed).

Chart 4.1 displays the indicators for the three sections in this chapter—school resources and staff, school programs and coursetaking, and student behavior—as well

---

[19]For example, Hedges, Laine, and Greenwald April 1994; Hanushek 1994; Hedges, Laine, and Greenwald May 1994.

as the results of the analyses (discussed in the next section). First, the school resources and staff section addresses the issue of the distribution of financial resources through teachers' rating of the adequacy of school resources and teacher salaries. The experience and availability of teachers are measured by years of teaching experience and the difficulties that administrators encounter in hiring teachers. Next, the demographics of the teaching force are characterized by the percentage of teachers who are minority and male. Finally, this section presents data on teachers' influence over the curricula they teach and teacher absenteeism as indicators of the control that teachers have over their work and teacher morale.

The second section presents indicators of student participation in public school programs and student coursetaking in four areas: preschool attendance, availability of gifted and talented programs, participation in vocational education, and mathematics coursetaking (geometry).

Finally, the third section presents indicators of student behaviors, both in and out of school, that affect their academic performance. Behaviors of individual students can affect their own as well as other students' academic performance. The first group presented are those that affect one's own performance: the amount of time spent doing homework, the amount of television watched on weekdays, and absenteeism from school. The second group reflect the influence of the classroom and school environment: the amount of time teachers spend maintaining discipline in the classroom, and students' perception of their own safety and the threat of weapons in their schools. Finally, this section presents two additional risk-taking behaviors outside of school that affect academic performance and completion: students' use of alcohol, and pregnancy.

Chart 4.1 reports the answers to the questions that were asked of the data for each indicator of school experience. Although the table presents the results of the complete analysis, this discussion will focus on the questions in the third and fourth columns: Are urban public schools different after accounting for the higher poverty concentration in urban schools? Are urban high poverty schools different from suburban and rural high poverty schools? Are the school experiences of students in urban high poverty schools different than predicted?

Summary of This Chapter's Findings

- Students in urban public schools overall had less desirable experiences than those in other locations on 8 of the 20 measures analyzed, even after accounting for the higher poverty concentration in urban schools.

- Students in public schools with high poverty concentrations had less desirable school experiences than those in low poverty schools on every measure except the availability of minority staff and student use of alcohol.

- Students in high poverty urban public schools had less desirable school experiences than those in high poverty rural schools on nearly half of the measures, and had less desirable experiences than those in high poverty suburban schools on two of the indicators.

- Students in high poverty urban schools had unusually high rates of television watching compared with other groups of students, exceeding the rates that would be predicted from the differences by location and poverty concentration combined.

- Among the school resources and staff indicators, fewer necessary resources for teachers, hiring difficulties, lack of teacher influence over curriculum, and higher teacher absenteeism were problems affecting urban schools more than suburban and rural schools, and urban high poverty schools more than rural high poverty schools. However, urban high poverty schools had a more diverse staff than other schools, and more minority teachers than would be predicted from the combination of their location and poverty concentration compared with rural schools.

- School program and coursetaking indicators suggest that students in urban schools, overall, were at a disadvantage compared with those in suburban schools in their access to gifted and talented programs, but this disadvantage did not hold for urban high poverty schools compared with similar suburban schools.

- With regard to the other school program and coursetaking indicators—preschool attendance, participation in vocational education, and mathematics coursetaking—students in urban public schools, after accounting for poverty, and in urban high poverty schools were no different than others.

Moreover, both students in urban and urban high poverty schools had higher preschool attendance rates than their rural counterparts.

- In the area of student behavior, absenteeism, class discipline, feeling safe at school, weapons possession, and pregnancy were more likely to be problems among urban students overall than among other students.

- In general, students in urban high poverty schools had more disciplinary problems and were much more likely to watch a lot of television. Otherwise, they behaved similarly to their suburban and rural counterparts with two exceptions: they were more likely to be absent than rural students, and weapons possession was more likely to be a problem in their schools than in rural schools.

CHART 4.1—SUMMARY OF RESULTS: SCHOOL EXPERIENCES				
INDICATOR	Are Urban Schools Different?	Are High Poverty Schools Different?	Are Urban Schools Different after Accounting for Poverty Concentration?	Are Urban High Poverty Schools Different from Other High Poverty Schools? Are Urban High Poverty Schools Different than Predicted?
I. SCHOOL RESOURCES AND STAFF				
Necessary Resources Available	Yes, urban lower than suburban and rural	Yes, high poverty lower than all others	Yes, urban lower than others	Yes, lower than rural high poverty, same as suburban high poverty No different than predicted
Teacher Salary	Yes, urban **higher** than rural, lower than suburban	Yes, high poverty lower than most others	Yes, urban **higher** than rural, same as suburban	Yes, **higher** than rural high poverty, same as suburban high poverty No different than predicted

INDICATOR	Are Urban Schools Different?	Are High Poverty Schools Different?	Are Urban Schools Different after Accounting for Poverty Concentration?	Are Urban High Poverty Schools Different from Other High Poverty Schools? / Are Urban High Poverty Schools Different than Predicted?
Teaching Experience	Yes, urban lower than suburban, **higher** than rural	Yes, high poverty lower than all others	Yes, urban **higher** than rural, same as suburban	No, same as other high poverty / No different than predicted
Difficulties Hiring Teachers	Yes, urban more than suburban and rural	Yes, high poverty more than all others	Yes, urban more than others	Yes, more than rural high poverty, same as suburban high poverty / No different than predicted
Percent Minority Teachers	Yes, urban **higher** than suburban and rural	Yes, high poverty **higher** than all others	Yes, urban **higher** than others	Yes, **higher** than other high poverty / Yes, **higher** than predicted
Percent Male Secondary Teachers	No, urban same as suburban and rural	Yes, high poverty lower than most others	No, urban same as others	Yes, **higher** than rural high poverty, same as suburban high poverty / Yes, **higher** than predicted
Teachers' Influence over Curriculum	Yes, urban lower than suburban or rural	Yes, high poverty lower than all others	Yes, urban lower than others	Yes, lower that rural high poverty, same as suburban high poverty / No different than predicted
Teacher Absenteeism	Yes, urban higher than suburban, and rural	Yes, high poverty higher than all others	Yes, urban higher than others	Yes, higher than rural high poverty, same as suburban high poverty / No different than predicted

INDICATOR	Are Urban Schools Different?	Are High Poverty Schools Different?	Are Urban Schools Different after Accounting for Poverty Concentration?	Are Urban High Poverty Schools Different from Other High Poverty Schools? / Are Urban High Poverty Schools Different than Predicted?
II. SCHOOL PROGRAMS AND COURSETAKING				
Preschool Attendance Rates	Yes, urban lower than suburban, **higher** than rural	Yes, high poverty lower than all others	Yes, urban **higher** than rural, same as suburban	Yes, **higher** than rural high poverty, same suburban high poverty No different than predicted
Gifted and Talented Programs	Yes, urban lower than suburban, same as rural	Yes, high poverty lower than all others	Yes, urban lower than suburban, same as rural	Yes, lower that rural high poverty, same as suburban high poverty Yes, lower than predicted
Vocational Education Credits	No, urban same as suburban and rural	Yes, higher as poverty increases*	No, urban same as others	* No different than predicted
Percentage of Seniors Who Took Geometry	Yes, urban lower than suburban, same as rural	Yes, lower as poverty increases*	No, urban same as others	* No different than predicted
III. STUDENT BEHAVIOR				
Television Watching on Weekdays	Yes, urban higher than suburban, same as rural	Yes, high poverty higher than all others	No, urban same as others	Yes, higher than other high poverty Yes, higher than predicted
Hours of Homework Completed	No, urban same as suburban and rural	Yes, high poverty lower than all others	No, urban same as others	No, same as other high poverty No different than predicted

*This indicator was tested using poverty concentration as a continuous rather than categorical variable. Since the sample sizes for schools by urbanicity and poverty concentration combined were too small to produce reliable estimates, no comparisons were made between urban high poverty and other high poverty schools.

INDICATOR	Are Urban Schools Different?	Are High Poverty Schools Different?	Are Urban Schools Different after Accounting for Poverty Concentration?	Are Urban High Poverty Schools Different from Other High Poverty Schools? Are Urban High Poverty Schools Different than Predicted?
Student Absenteeism	Yes, higher than suburban	Yes, high poverty higher than all others	Yes, urban higher than others	Yes, higher than rural high poverty, same as suburban high poverty No different than predicted
Time Maintaining Discipline	Yes, urban higher than suburban and rural	Yes, high poverty higher than most others	Yes, urban higher than others	Yes, higher than other high poverty No different than predicted
Feeling Unsafe in School	Yes, urban higher than suburban and rural	Yes, high poverty higher than most others	Yes, urban higher than rural, same as suburban	No, same as other high poverty No different than predicted
Student Weapons Possession	Yes, urban higher than suburban and rural	Yes, high poverty higher than all others	Yes, urban higher than others	Yes, higher than rural high poverty, same as suburban high poverty No different than predicted
Student Use of Alcohol	Yes, urban **lower** than suburban and rural	Yes, high poverty **lower** than all others	Yes, urban **lower** than rural, same as suburban	No, same as other high poverty No different than predicted
Student Pregnancy	Yes, urban higher than suburban, and rural	Yes, high poverty higher than all others	Yes, urban higher than others	No, same as other high poverty No different than predicted

School Resources and Staff

Adequate resources and a committed, well-qualified, and professional staff of teachers are key elements of a vital learning environment which leads to high academic achievement (Special Study Panel on Education Indicators 1991). Yet urban high poverty public schools are often assumed to have fewer well-qualified teachers and fewer resources—issues that strike at the heart of what it means to provide high-quality education for all youngsters.

This section examines three aspects of school resources and staffing: availability of resources and teacher salaries, teacher experience and supply, and teacher characteristics and behavior. Each indicator has been selected for its relevance to policy debates about the quality of the school environment, but the indicators presented are by no means exhaustive.[20]

Findings

- Public urban schools did less well in providing necessary resources to teachers, and urban high poverty public schools did less well in this area than rural high poverty schools. However, urban teacher salaries were, in fact, higher than those for rural teachers. Teachers in high poverty urban schools also had higher salaries than their rural counterparts, and had about the same salaries as those in suburban high poverty schools.

- Teachers in urban public schools, after accounting for poverty, and urban high poverty schools were just as experienced as their suburban and rural counterparts. In fact, urban teachers, over-all, were more experienced than rural teachers. However, administrators of urban schools, in general, and urban high poverty schools in particular, were more apt to complain about difficulties in hiring qualified teachers than most other administrators.

- Teachers in urban and urban high poverty public schools were more likely to be minorities, but just as likely to be male as those in comparable schools in other locations. In fact, teachers in urban high poverty schools were more likely to be male than those in rural high poverty schools.

- Urban teachers and those in urban high poverty schools reported less influence over their curriculum than most teachers in other locations. Teachers' perceptions of the level of teacher absenteeism were higher among urban teachers than among teachers in other locations, even after taking poverty into account; however, teachers in urban high poverty schools did not consider teacher absenteeism more serious than those in suburban high poverty schools.

- Higher concentrations of poverty in schools had a consistent and pervasive relationship to poorer quality resources and staff. Only one resource and staffing indicator was favorable in high poverty schools: there were higher percentages of minority staff.

---

[20]See appendix C for a discussion of the criteria used in selecting indicators.

Availability of Resources

The issue of how school financial resources are distributed is controversial, with some arguing that the amount of expenditures has little effect on student outcomes (Hanushek 1989). Others have reported that school finances do make a difference (Rotberg 1993; Berliner 1993). According to a recent report from the Council of the Great City Schools, the average per pupil expenditure for large city public school students was less than the national average and was also less than the expenditure in suburban and rural public school districts (Council of the Great City Schools 1992).

National data on school finance were not available by the classifications of school location and poverty concentration required for this analysis. In addition, public school finances are determined primarily at the district level and are reported by district in national surveys.[21] Both the urbanicity and poverty

concentration of schools can vary within a school district, as do expenditures and resource availability.

The school-level indicator presented in this section is derived from teacher opinion data on the availability of necessary materials (e.g., textbooks, supplies, copy machines) for the staff. Teacher responses can provide an indication of resource availability at the school level since teachers may be in the best position to judge whether the resources available in the school are adequate to meet the demands of instruction.

Are urban schools different? Seventy-six percent of public school teachers nationwide agreed that necessary materials were available in their schools in 1987–88. However, urban teachers were less likely to report that needed materials were available than teachers in either suburban or rural schools (figure 4.1). Seventy percent

Figure 4.1
Percentage of teachers who agreed that necessary materials are available in their schools, by urbanicity: 1987–88

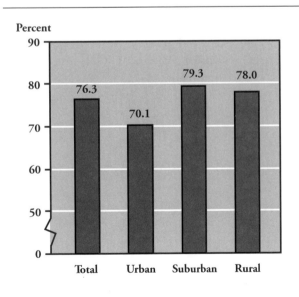

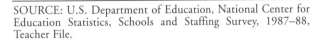

SOURCE: U.S. Department of Education, National Center for Education Statistics, Schools and Staffing Survey, 1987–88, Teacher File.

Figure 4.2
Percentage of teachers who agreed that necessary materials are available in their schools, by school poverty concentration: 1987–88

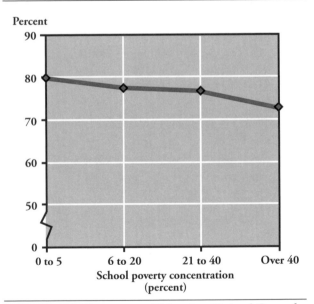

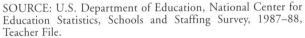

SOURCE: U.S. Department of Education, National Center for Education Statistics, Schools and Staffing Survey, 1987–88, Teacher File.

of urban teachers reported that materials were adequate compared with 79 percent of suburban and 78 percent of rural teachers.

Are schools with high poverty concentrations different? There were also differences by concentration of poverty in the schools. Teachers in schools with the highest concentration of poverty reported less frequently than teachers in any other school type that the resources available to the staff were adequate (72 percent compared with 80 percent of teachers in the low poverty schools) (figure 4.2).

Are urban schools different after accounting for the poverty concentration of the school? After accounting for differences in poverty concentration across school locales, teachers in urban schools were still less likely to report that necessary materials were available (figure 4.3). That is, the fact that urban schools are more like-

ly to have high concentrations of poverty is not the only explanation for why urban teachers were less likely to feel that resources were adequate.

Were teachers from urban high poverty schools less likely to have necessary materials than predicted? Teachers in urban high poverty schools were less likely to feel they had necessary materials than teachers in every other school type with the exception of teachers in suburban high poverty schools. Sixty-seven percent of teachers in urban high poverty schools felt that resources were adequate. However, an urban location and a high poverty concentration do not combine to create any additional disadvantage above and beyond that observed separately for urban teachers and teachers in high poverty schools.

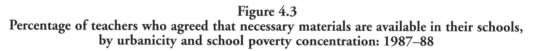

[21]An interesting discussion on the differences in spending between districts can be found in William T. Hartman (Spring 1988, 436–459).

Figure 4.3
Percentage of teachers who agreed that necessary materials are available in their schools, by urbanicity and school poverty concentration: 1987–88

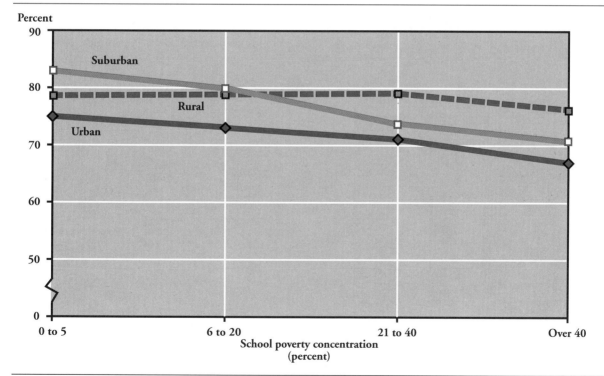

SOURCE: U.S. Department of Education, National Center for Education Statistics, Schools and Staffing Survey, 1987–88, Teacher File.

Teacher Salaries

One of the largest components of education expenditures is teacher salaries. In the public schools, teacher salaries are often set as part of district policy and are dependent on the teacher's education level and experience. In 1990–91, 94 percent of all public school districts used teacher salary schedules (Choy et al. 1993). Given this fact, variations in teacher salaries are likely to reflect differences in teacher experience as well as regional economic differences. Comparing teacher salaries revealed meaningful differences by location and poverty concentration.

Are urban schools different? Nationally, the average academic base salary for public school teachers was $25,507 in 1987–88.[22] Average salaries varied for teachers by the location of their schools, with rural salaries being notably lower than urban and suburban salaries. Teachers in urban schools averaged $27,372,

which was lower than $28,528 for teachers in suburban schools and higher than $23,293 for teachers in rural schools (figure 4.4).

Are high poverty schools different? Average salaries also differed by school poverty concentration. The average base salary of $28,841 for teachers in low poverty schools exceeded the national average of $25,507, while the average salary of teachers in schools with the two highest levels of poverty concentration was lower than the national figure of about $24,000 (figure 4.5). Salaries of teachers in schools with poverty concentrations of more than 40 percent and 21 to 40 percent were not statistically different from each other.

Are urban schools different after accounting for poverty concentration? When varying school poverty concentration was taken into account, the small disparity

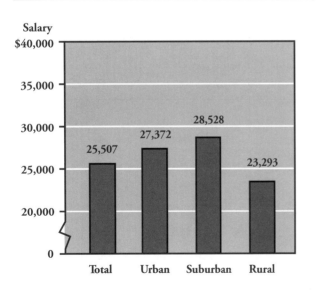

**Figure 4.4
Average academic base teacher salary,
by urbanicity: 1987–88**

SOURCE: U.S. Department of Education, National Center for Education Statistics, Schools and Staffing Survey, 1987–88, Teacher File.

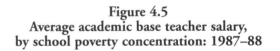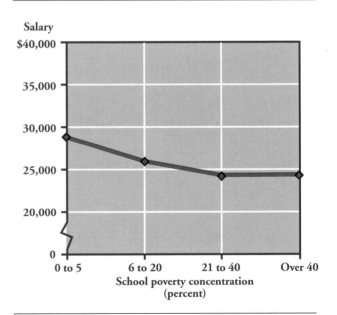

**Figure 4.5
Average academic base teacher salary,
by school poverty concentration: 1987–88**

SOURCE: U.S. Department of Education, National Center for Education Statistics, Schools and Staffing Survey, 1987–88, Teacher File.

in the average urban and suburban teacher salaries cited above disappeared and could no longer be considered different. Only the rural average teacher salary was different from the average urban salary. Figure 4.6 clearly shows the low level of the rural salaries when compared with the salaries in the other two locations. By contrast, suburban and urban salaries appear to be very similar at all levels of poverty concentration, with the exception of the low poverty category.

One factor that may explain these differences is the variation in the average years of experience for teachers by urbanicity and school poverty concentration. The average years of teaching experience seems to mirror average teacher salaries, with rural teachers and teachers in schools with higher poverty concentrations having less experience. (See appendix table 4.2.) Since public school teacher salaries are typically based on a salary schedule tied to teaching experience, as mentioned above, variation in salaries by years of teaching experi-

ence would be expected. (See the next section for further analysis of teacher experience.) Other factors affecting the urban-rural differential may include cost of living differences between rural and urban locations.

Were teachers in urban high poverty schools likely to have lower salaries than predicted? The salaries of teachers in urban high poverty schools were higher than those for rural teachers in similar schools ($26,772 compared with $21,470), and were no different from salaries for teachers in similar suburban schools. The salaries for teachers in urban high poverty schools were no lower than would be predicted from their location and poverty concentration (figure 4.6).

---

[22]Academic base salary refers to the teacher salary received for teaching in the school year 1987–88. Not included are earnings from the summer of 1987 or additional compensation for extracurricular or additional activities such as coaching, student activity sponsorship, or evening classes. Also, earnings from non-school employment are not included.

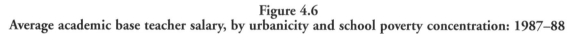

Figure 4.6
Average academic base teacher salary, by urbanicity and school poverty concentration: 1987–88

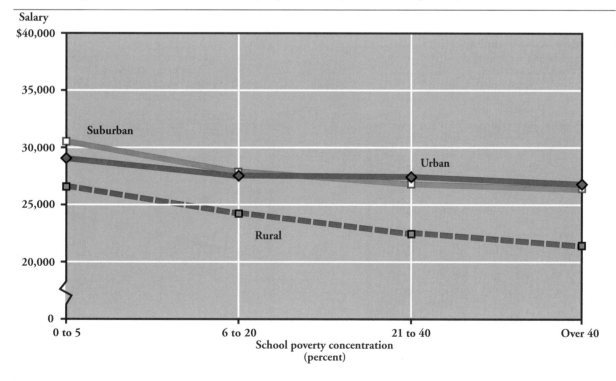

SOURCE: U.S. Department of Education, National Center for Education Statistics, Schools and Staffing Survey, 1987–88, Teacher File.

Teacher Experience

Some education policy research has linked teacher ability and qualifications with student achievement. For example, according to Hanushek (1989), "there are striking differences in average gain in student achievement across teachers." Citing a study in Texas, David Berliner (1993) stated, "The percentage of teachers with master's degrees accounted for 5% of the variation in student scores across districts in grades 1–7."

Although teacher quality is easy to understand, it is difficult to measure. Many indirect measures exist—ranging from objective data, such as the rates of teacher certification, level of education, coursework in the fields they teach, and number of years of teaching experience—to more subjective indicators such as administrators' and students' ratings of teacher performance. When discussing the limited explanatory power of current measures of teacher quality, Hanushek (1989) noted that one indicator of teacher quality, teacher experience, yielded the most statistically significant findings in a summary of studies attempting to

find links between achievement and education "inputs." Further, recent reports indicate that teacher quality varies by poverty concentration in the school. Jonathan Kozol (1991), quoting a principal from a high poverty New York public school, presents anecdotal evidence that teachers in these schools may be less qualified than those in higher income schools:

> "These are the kids most in need," says Edward Flanery, the principal of one of the low-income schools, "and they get the worst teachers." For children of diverse needs in his overcrowded rooms [Flanery] says you need an outstanding teacher. "And what do you get? You get the worst."

Although no single indicator seems adequate to fully address the complex issues surrounding teacher quality, for the purposes of this analysis, data on the percentage of teachers with 3 years or less of teaching experience from the 1987–88 Schools and Staffing Survey (SASS) were compared by school location and poverty concentration. Other indicators examined—such as the

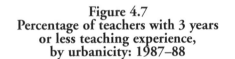

Figure 4.7
Percentage of teachers with 3 years
or less teaching experience,
by urbanicity: 1987–88

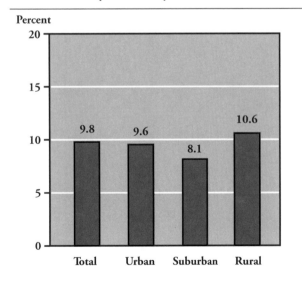

SOURCE: U.S. Department of Education, National Center for Education Statistics, Schools and Staffing Survey, 1987–88, Teacher File.

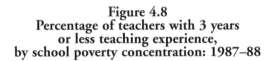

Figure 4.8
Percentage of teachers with 3 years
or less teaching experience,
by school poverty concentration: 1987–88

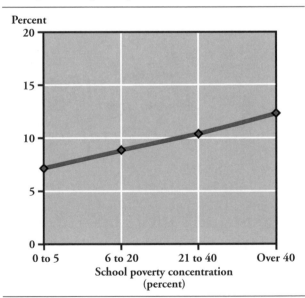

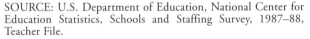

SOURCE: U.S. Department of Education, National Center for Education Statistics, Schools and Staffing Survey, 1987–88, Teacher File.

percentage of teachers who were certified, the number of courses they took in their main assignment field, and teacher degree attainment—did not reveal much variation by urbanicity or school poverty concentration. (See appendix C.)

Are urban schools different? On average, 10 percent of public school teachers nationwide had 3 years or less teaching experience in the 1987–88 school year. Ten percent of urban teachers had 3 years or less experience, which was greater than the 8 percent for suburban teachers but less than the 11 percent for rural teachers (figure 4.7).

Are high poverty schools different? The number of years of teaching experience varied by school poverty concentration (figure 4.8). High poverty schools had the highest percentage of teachers with 3 years or less teaching experience (12 percent), which was 70 percent higher than that of low poverty schools (7 percent).

Are urban schools different after accounting for poverty concentration? Once the association between the schools' poverty concentration and teacher experience was taken into account, there was no difference between urban and suburban schools in teacher experience. The rural-urban difference, remained, however. As shown in figure 4.9, the urban and suburban percentages are very close at all levels of school poverty, while rural schools have a greater proportion of less experienced teachers in general.

Were teachers in urban high poverty schools more likely to have 3 years or less teaching experience than would be predicted? Urban teachers in high poverty schools were as likely as predicted to have 3 years or less teaching experience. In fact, the percentage of these teachers having less than 4 years of teaching experience (12 percent) was no different than in high poverty schools in other locations. The relatively high percentage of less experienced teachers in urban high poverty schools reflects the high poverty concentration of their schools, not the urban location (figure 4.9).

Figure 4.9
Percentage of teachers with 3 years or less teaching experience,
by urbanicity and school poverty concentration: 1987–88

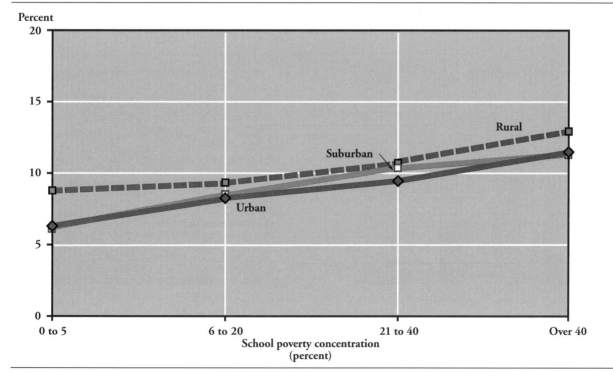

SOURCE: U.S. Department of Education, National Center for Education Statistics, Schools and Staffing Survey, 1987–88, Teacher File.

Difficulty Hiring Teachers

Although predicted teacher shortages did not materialize in the late 1980s (Bobbitt 1991), reports persist that shortages of well-qualified teachers exist for schools in the inner cities serving large numbers of disadvantaged children (Oakes 1990). This section looks at evidence that the supply of teachers may vary by urbanicity and school type. The indicator below, drawn from the 1987–88 SASS, compares administrator reports of having general difficulties hiring teachers for their schools.[23]

Are urban schools different? Nationally, 16 percent of public school administrators reported that they experienced general difficulties hiring teachers when surveyed in 1987–88. For urban schools, this percentage was much higher (23 percent) than it was for suburban and rural schools, which were both at 13 percent (figure 4.10).

Are high poverty schools different? Administrators from high poverty schools were more likely than their peers in other schools to have difficulty hiring teachers. Twenty-four percent of the administrators from the highest poverty schools reported having difficulties—twice the proportion of the administrators from the lower poverty schools (those with 0–5 percent and 6–20 percent poverty concentration) and somewhat less than twice the proportion when compared with administrators from schools with 21–40 percent poverty concentration (figure 4.11).

Are urban schools different after accounting for poverty concentration? The differences between the high poverty schools and all other school types were quite large, and when the poverty concentration of schools in each location was taken into account, the

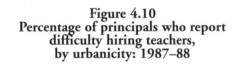

Figure 4.10
Percentage of principals who report difficulty hiring teachers, by urbanicity: 1987–88

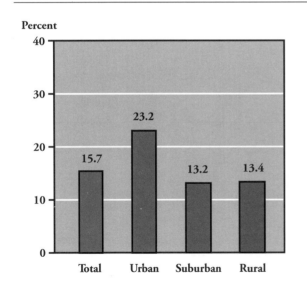

SOURCE: U.S. Department of Education, National Center for Education Statistics, Schools and Staffing Survey, 1987–88, Administrator File.

Figure 4.11
Percentage of principals who report difficulty hiring teachers, by school poverty concentration: 1987–88

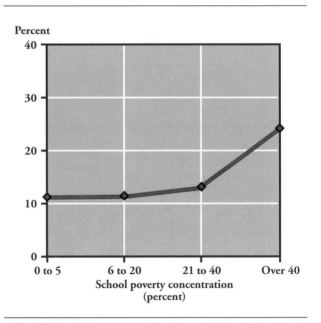

SOURCE: U.S. Department of Education, National Center for Education Statistics, Schools and Staffing Survey, 1987–88, Administrator File.

differences by location remained. Urban administrators were still more likely to have difficulties hiring teachers than their peers in other locations.

Were administrators in urban high poverty schools more likely to have hiring difficulties than predicted? Administrators from urban high poverty schools were more likely than their rural counterparts to experience difficulties in hiring teachers. Although it appears that they were more likely to experience difficulties than suburban administrators (31 percent of administrators in urban high poverty schools compared with 26 percent of administrators in suburban high poverty schools), this difference was not statistically significant.

In general, administrators in urban high poverty schools did not appear to have hiring difficulties beyond what would be predicted given their school location and poverty concentration (figure 4.12). This suggests that the combination of high poverty concentration in an urban setting does not add to the already greater hiring difficulties in these schools.

---

[23]In the context of the 1987–88 SASS survey, "general difficulties" refers to hiring teachers in all subject matters. The administrators were also asked to report on their difficulties in hiring teachers in different fields. However, since the fields were not defined for the 1987–88 survey, this study relies on the reports of general difficulties.

Figure 4.12
Percentage of principals who report difficulty hiring teachers,
by urbanicity and school poverty concentration: 1987–88

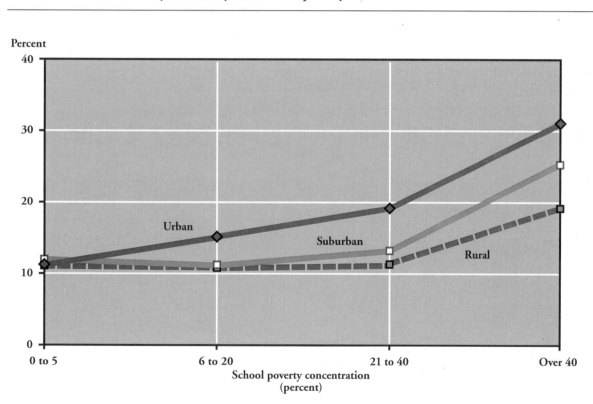

SOURCE: U.S. Department of Education, National Center for Education Statistics, Schools and Staffing Survey, 1987–88, Administrator File.

Percent Minority Teachers

In chapter 1, it was shown that minority student enrollment is largest in high poverty urban schools. Urban schools, overall, are also more likely to serve greater percentages of minority students than rural and suburban schools. Even though researchers have debated this issue, policymakers are interested in the possible link between having strong minority representation among teachers and the high achievement and aspirations of minority students (King 1993). Recent reports suggest that the number of minority teachers in the public schools has not risen to meet the level of minority student enrollment. According to the Vice President of the National Education Association, teacher recruitment has not met the demands of creating a more diversified teaching force:

> It's very disheartening to see that we have not made significant progress in these areas of teacher recruitment. . . . Students learn lessons about life both through formal instruction and what they see around them. We need more male elementary school teachers and more people of color at all grade levels (Jordan 1992).

A recent report by the Council of the Great City Schools (1992) also noted,

> [T]he demography of urban teachers does not match that of urban students . . . viewed from a different angle, these demographic patterns meant that there was one African-American teacher for every 25.4 African-American students in the Great City Schools, one white teacher for every 7.4 white students, one Hispanic teacher for every 62.9 Hispanic students, one Asian-American teacher for every 46.2 Asian-American students (see also King 1993).

Given student demographics, are schools in urban locations and those with high poverty concentrations more likely to employ greater numbers of teachers from minority backgrounds? The 1987–88 SASS asked schools to list the racial-ethnic backgrounds of all teachers using the categories of black non-Hispanic, white non-Hispanic, Native American, Asian or Pacific Islander, and Hispanic origin regardless of race. An indicator of the percentage of teachers who were members of a racial-ethnic minority was created by

Figure 4.13
Percentage of teachers who are minority, by urbanicity: 1987–88

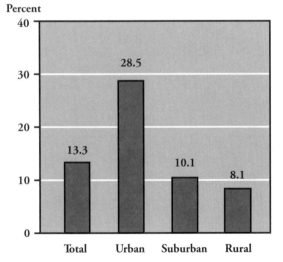

SOURCE: U.S. Department of Education, National Center for Education Statistics, Schools and Staffing Survey, 1987–88, Teacher File.

Figure 4.14
Percentage of teachers who are minority, by school poverty concentration: 1987–88

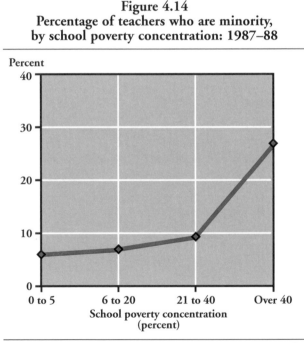

SOURCE: U.S. Department of Education, National Center for Education Statistics, Schools and Staffing Survey, 1987–88, Teacher File.

combining all of the categories with the exception of white, non-Hispanic.

Are urban schools different? Nationally, 13 percent of the total public school teaching force in 1987–88 identified with a race-ethnicity other than white. The percentage of minority teachers in urban schools was almost three times higher (29 percent) than that of suburban schools (10 percent), and more than three times higher than that of rural schools (8 percent) (figure 4.13). In comparison, the percentage of minority students enrolled in urban schools was almost twice as high as the percentage of minority teachers (49 percent), and was twice as high as that in suburban and rural schools (20 percent and 16 percent, respectively).

Are high poverty schools different? Similarly, teachers in high poverty schools were three to four times more likely to belong to a racial-ethnic minority group than schools with lower poverty concentrations. Twenty-seven percent of the staff in schools with the highest poverty concentration were minorities, compared with 6 percent for schools with 0–5 percent of students living in poverty (figure 4.14).

Are urban schools different after accounting for poverty concentration? Despite the connection between school poverty concentration and the percentage of the teaching force that was from a minority background, differences between urban schools and those in other locations could not be attributed solely to differences in poverty concentration—in other words, the location of the school still mattered. Urban schools were more likely to have minority staff at all levels of school poverty (figure 4.15).

Were urban high poverty schools more likely to employ minority staff than predicted? Urban high poverty schools employed a higher proportion (39 percent) of minority staff than schools with similar poverty concentrations in suburban and rural locations (29 percent and 19 percent, respectively) (figure 4.15). This percentage is higher than predicted relative to rural high poverty schools. However, even this high percentage is lower than the percentage of minority students who are in high poverty urban schools. According to the 1987–88 SASS, 68 percent of students in urban schools with the highest concentration of poverty were from minority groups.

Figure 4.15
Percentage of teachers who are minority, by urbanicity and school poverty concentration: 1987–88

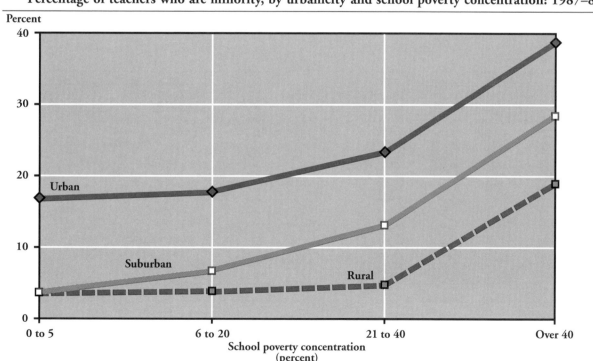

SOURCE: U.S. Department of Education, National Center for Education Statistics, Schools and Staffing Survey, 1987–88, Teacher File.

Teacher Gender

The public school teaching force is predominantly female. This is especially true at the elementary school level, where females make up 79 to 90 percent of all teachers, depending upon the combination of school location and poverty concentration. As with the issue of teacher minority background, researchers have not proven that students will achieve more if they are exposed to a mix of teachers that closely reflects student demographics. However, some researchers examining education issues in urban schools have highlighted the need for recruiting male teachers who could serve as role models for male students, particularly those who live in single-parent families (Jordan 1992). For example, in a report by the Council of the Great City Schools, the authors noted that during the 1990–91 school year there was one male teacher for every 34 male students in urban schools, while there was one

female teacher for every 12.3 female students (Council of the Great City Schools 1992). Since there was greater variation in the gender of secondary school teachers (secondary schools are more likely to employ male teachers than elementary schools), only secondary teachers are examined by gender in this section.

Are urban schools different? Nationally, 48 percent of public secondary school teachers in 1987–88 were male, and these proportions did not differ by school location. Forty-eight percent of teachers in urban secondary schools were male compared with 49 percent in suburban schools and 47 percent in rural schools (figure 4.16).

Are high poverty schools different? When schools were compared based on poverty concentration, differences

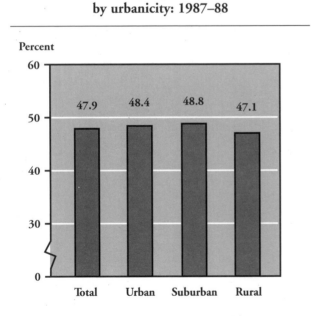

Figure 4.16
Percentage of secondary school teachers who are male, by urbanicity: 1987–88

SOURCE: U.S. Department of Education, National Center for Education Statistics, Schools and Staffing Survey, 1987–88, Teacher File.

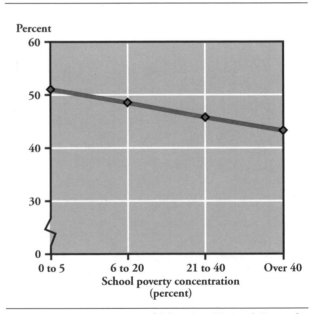

Figure 4.17
Percentage of secondary school teachers who are male, by school poverty concentration: 1987–88

SOURCE: U.S. Department of Education, National Center for Education Statistics, Schools and Staffing Survey, 1987–88, Teacher File.

in the gender of the teaching force emerged. High poverty schools had a lower percentage of male teachers than low poverty schools (43 percent and 51 percent, respectively). However, there was no significant difference in the proportion of male teachers between the schools with the highest and next to highest poverty concentration (figure 4.17).

Are urban schools different after accounting for poverty concentration? Taking into account the school poverty concentration, the results by school location remained the same. There were still no differences in the proportion of teachers that were male in urban, suburban, and rural schools.

Were urban high poverty schools more likely to employ male teachers than predicted? Urban high poverty schools were actually more likely than predicted to employ male teachers when compared with most rural schools; however, they were no different than predicted compared with suburban schools. Male teachers made up about half of all teachers in high poverty urban schools, which is about the same proportion as the national average. In fact, as can be seen in figure 4.18, high poverty schools in urban locations were more likely than those in rural locations to employ male teachers. Though it appears from figure 4.18 that high poverty urban schools were also more likely to have male teachers than suburban high poverty schools, this difference was not statistically significant.

Figure 4.18
Percentage of secondary school teachers who are male,
by urbanicity and school poverty concentration: 1987–88

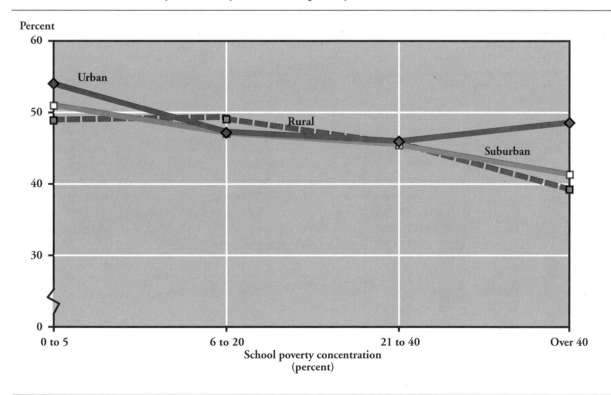

SOURCE: U.S. Department of Education, National Center for Education Statistics, Schools and Staffing Survey, 1987–88, Teacher File.

Teacher Influence Over Curriculum

In recent years, reforms have stressed the importance of increasing the autonomy of school staff to make decisions on various aspects of school policy. These reforms not only advocate giving authority to those closest to the student but also seek the overall improvement of teaching as a profession. According to the Special Study Panel on Education Indicators (1991):

> Recent research on effective schools . . . draws attention to very basic needs of teachers if they are to sustain their best efforts. Today's reform effort understands that better schools depend on teachers vested with greater authority to control classroom resources and determine curriculum and other core matters of their professional lives.

Social science researchers have established that workers who feel that they have control over their work have more positive attitudes toward their jobs and will therefore perform better (Special Study Panel on Education Indicators 1991; Choy et al. 1993a; Jones 1992). Although there is a growing body of research on teacher control and decision making in the classroom, there is little research that

directly links teacher decision making to student achievement (Rowen 1990).

In 1987–88, teachers were asked to rate teachers' level of influence on several school policies as part of the SASS. Noticeable differences, both by school location and poverty concentration, were found in how teachers rated the influence of teachers over curriculum, and these findings are presented below. Interestingly, when asked about teachers' influence over other policy areas such as determining discipline, determining the content of in-service training programs, and ability grouping of students by classes, teacher responses did not vary by school poverty concentration or location. In addition, teachers' job satisfaction did not appear to vary by these school characteristics.

Are urban schools different? Nationally, 35 percent of public school teachers felt that teachers had a great deal of influence over establishing curriculum in their school.

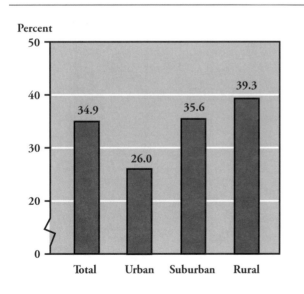

Figure 4.19
Percentage of teachers who think that teachers have a great deal of influence on establishing curriculum, by urbanicity: 1987–88

SOURCE: U.S. Department of Education, National Center for Education Statistics, Schools and Staffing Survey, 1987–88, Teacher File.

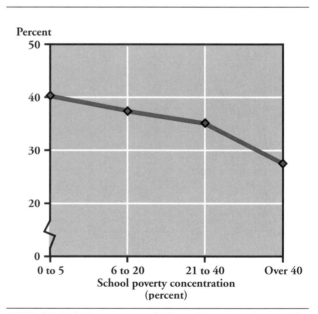

Figure 4.20
Percentage of teachers who think that teachers have a great deal of influence on establishing curriculum, by school poverty concentration: 1987–88

SOURCE: U.S. Department of Education, National Center for Education Statistics, Schools and Staffing Survey, 1987–88, Teacher File.

When comparisons were made based on school location, however, urban teachers were less likely than suburban or rural teachers to feel that teachers had a great deal of influence in this area. Twenty-six percent of urban teachers thought that teachers had a great deal of influence over curriculum, as opposed to 36 percent of suburban and 39 percent of rural teachers (figure 4.19).

Are high poverty schools different? Teachers' perceived influence over curriculum tended to diminish as the concentration of poverty in their schools increased. While 41 percent of teachers in low poverty schools reported that teachers had a great deal of influence over curriculum, 28 percent of teachers in high poverty schools did so (figure 4.20).

Are urban schools different after accounting for poverty concentration? School location still mattered after taking into account differences in school poverty concentration. Teachers from schools in urban locations were still less

likely than teachers from suburban or rural schools to think that teachers have a great deal of influence over establishing curriculum when the concentration of poverty in their schools was held constant.

Were teachers in urban high poverty schools less likely to have a great deal of influence over establishing curriculum than predicted? Teachers in urban high poverty schools were less likely to report that teachers have a great deal of influence over curriculum than teachers in rural high poverty schools, but they reported a similar level of influence compared with teachers in suburban high poverty schools (figure 4.21). Twenty-two percent of teachers in high poverty urban schools thought that teachers had a great deal of influence over curriculum. However, it did not appear that teachers in urban high poverty schools considered teachers to be less influential than would be predicted based on the patterns for urban and high poverty schools separately.

Figure 4.21
Percentage of teachers who think that teachers have a great deal of influence on establishing curriculum, by urbanicity and school poverty concentration: 1987–88

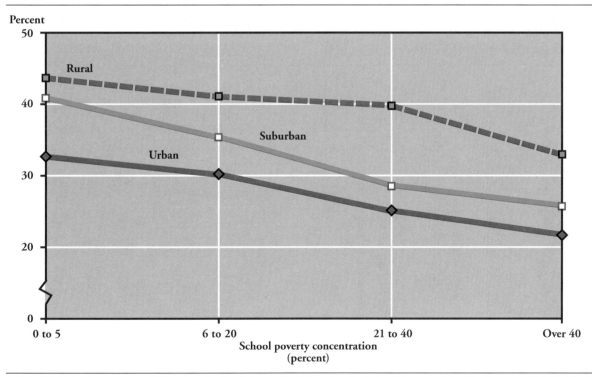

SOURCE: U.S. Department of Education, National Center for Education Statistics, Schools and Staffing Survey, 1987–88, Teacher File.

Teacher Absenteeism

Clearly, the consistent presence of the teacher in the classroom is of paramount importance in providing instruction to students. Beyond this, some research has suggested that high staff absenteeism indicates poor worker morale. Is there evidence to suggest that teacher absenteeism is a greater problem in urban schools, high poverty schools, or both? Teacher ratings of the seriousness of the problem of teacher absenteeism in their school, drawn from the 1987–88 SASS, are reported below.[24]

Are urban schools different? Nationally, 23 percent of teachers viewed teacher absenteeism as a moderate to serious problem in their schools. When responses were compared by the location of the school, urban teachers were more likely than teachers in both suburban and rural schools to consider teacher absenteeism as a problem. This can be clearly seen in figure 4.22, which

shows that approximately 31 percent of urban teachers reported their co-workers' attendance as a moderate or serious problem, as compared with 23 percent of suburban and 20 percent of rural teachers.

Are high poverty schools different? A clear relationship was also found between school poverty concentration and teachers' perception of teacher absenteeism. Thirty-one percent of teachers in the high poverty schools reported that they considered teacher absenteeism a problem, while 21 percent of teachers in the low poverty schools reported similarly. In fact, when the teachers from the high poverty schools were compared with their peers from schools in the other three poverty concentration categories, teachers from high poverty schools were more likely to perceive teacher absenteeism as a moderate to serious problem (figure 4.23).

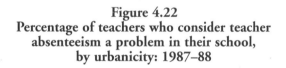

**Figure 4.22
Percentage of teachers who consider teacher absenteeism a problem in their school, by urbanicity: 1987–88**

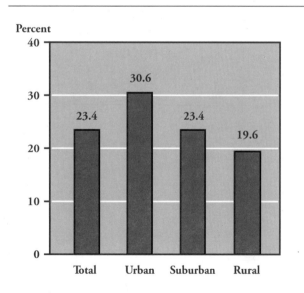

SOURCE: U.S. Department of Education, National Center for Education Statistics, Schools and Staffing Survey, 1987–88, Teacher File.

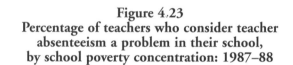

**Figure 4.23
Percentage of teachers who consider teacher absenteeism a problem in their school, by school poverty concentration: 1987–88**

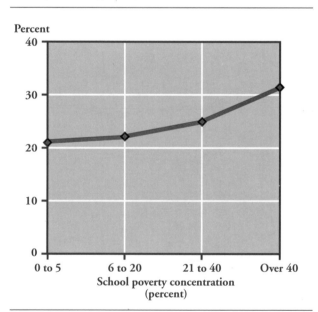

SOURCE: U.S. Department of Education, National Center for Education Statistics, Schools and Staffing Survey, 1987–88, Teacher File.

Are urban schools different after accounting for poverty concentration? After taking into account varying levels of poverty concentration, the responses of teachers in urban schools were still higher than those of teachers in suburban and rural schools.

Was teacher absenteeism more likely to be perceived as a moderate to serious problem in urban high poverty schools than predicted? Teacher absenteeism was perceived to be a problem by a similarly high percentage of teachers in urban and suburban high poverty schools (37 and 35 percent, respectively), but was considered a greater problem in urban than in rural high

poverty schools. However, the responses of teachers in urban high poverty schools were at predicted levels, given their school's location and poverty concentration (figure 4.24).

[24]It is interesting to note that when asked the same question, administrators responded similarly but overall seemed to view the problem of teacher absenteeism as less serious. This is generally true of all responses to opinion questions from the 1987–88 SASS when comparisons were made between teachers and administrators evaluating school problems. Although the responses follow similar patterns by location and poverty concentration in the school (that is, they are usually considered as more serious problems in urban schools and in high poverty schools when compared to other school types), administrators seem less likely to view problems as serious than do teachers.

Figure 4.24
Percentage of teachers who consider teacher absenteeism a problem in their school, by urbanicity and school poverty concentration: 1987–88

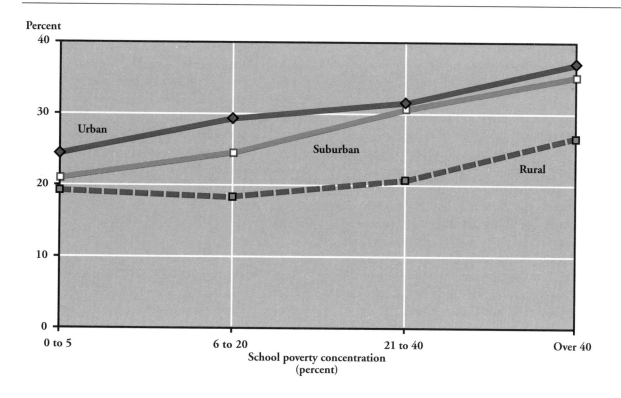

SOURCE: U.S. Department of Education, National Center for Education Statistics, Schools and Staffing Survey, 1987–88, Teacher File.

School Programs and Coursetaking

The programs and courses in which students participate can influence their achievement in school, their opportunities to learn, and their potential experiences after graduating from high school. This section explores student participation in selected public school programs and courses at three levels: preschool, elementary, and secondary. Not all programs and courses could be presented. Those that were selected had varying rates of participation by school location and poverty concentration, and bore important relationships to outcomes.

Many parents elect to send their children to preschool and kindergarten before the age of mandatory schooling. Previous research has suggested a strong relationship between preschool attendance—in particular, high-quality, center-based early childhood programs—and lower participation rates in special education, lower rates of grade retention through the high school years, and higher rates of high school completion and higher earnings in the labor force (Hofferth et al. 1994). This section documents differences in the preschool attendance rates of students in schools with varying concentrations of poverty and in different locations.

Public schools offer programs and services designed to meet students' special needs, such as bilingual education, English as a second language, remedial reading and mathematics, special education, gifted and talented programs, day care, Chapter 1 (now Title 1) and diagnostic services. The availability of these programs is closely related to school size and level (whether a school is elementary or secondary) and each district's policies (Choy et al. 1993b). As part of this study, an analysis of the availability of these programs was undertaken to determine if program offerings varied by school location or level of poverty concentration. It was found that most programs were widely available. As a general rule, urban schools and high poverty schools were as likely to have such programs as suburban schools. More often than not, rural schools appeared less likely to offer a wide range of programs than either urban or suburban schools.

The availability of programs was often found to be related to the nature of the needs addressed by the programs. For example, Chapter 1 (Title 1) programs directed at disadvantaged students were found to be more prevalent in high poverty than low poverty schools in all locales. However, remedial reading and mathematics were found everywhere, as students needing these programs are found everywhere. Such obvious patterns did not warrant further analysis. Gifted and talented programs were selected for additional analysis because gifted and talented children are theoretically found everywhere, but programs serving them are not. Therefore, data on the availability of gifted and talented programs are presented in this section.

Consistent with the findings of chapter 2 and more generally with the findings of education researchers, one would expect students from high poverty schools and urban schools to be more likely to score lower on achievement tests overall and to need remedial programs. Similarly, on average, students from high poverty and urban schools would be less likely to be represented in advanced courses, particularly in science and mathematics, and to be overrepresented in vocational courses. Patterns of coursetaking were examined using transcripts of high school seniors to determine if there were differences between groups of students in their tendency to take vocational education or advanced courses.

Findings

- Urban public school students attended preschool at rates that fell between their suburban and rural peers; however, after accounting for the level of poverty in their schools, their preschool attendance rates differed only from rural students' rates. Students from high poverty schools, regardless of location, were less likely to have attended preschool than students from schools with lower poverty concentrations. Rural students from all but the low poverty schools were also found to be less likely to have attended preschool than students from urban and suburban schools.

- Urban public schools offered fewer gifted and talented programs at the elementary school level than suburban schools, even after accounting for differences in school poverty concentration.

- Neither the likelihood of greater than average participation in vocational education nor taking higher level courses was found to be related to an urban setting apart from poverty concentration. When poverty was taken into account, urban students took vocational education courses and higher level mathematics at rates similar to those of their suburban and rural peers.

- High poverty urban public schools were as likely to offer gifted and talented programs as high poverty suburban schools, but were less likely than predicted to offer these programs than rural schools. Their students were more likely to have attended preschool than those in high poverty rural, but not suburban schools.

- High poverty public schools, in general, offered gifted and talented programs less frequently than low poverty schools. Students were more likely to take vocational education and were less likely to take more advanced courses as the poverty level in their school increased.

Preschool Attendance

As stated above, research has suggested that preschool attendance is related to later school success, particularly for students facing greater disadvantages (Hofferth et al. 1994). Given the importance of preschool and early childhood programs, were students across all locations and poverty concentrations equally likely to have attended preschool? The answer to this question is obtained from the National Education Longitudinal Study of 1988 (NELS:88), which asked parents of 8th graders to report whether or not their child had attended preschool or nursery school programs. Since the students would have attended preschool during the late 1970s, these data do not account for changes in preschool attendance that have occurred since that time.

Are urban schools different? Nationally, according to their parents, 51 percent of public school 8th graders attended preschool, with urban students being less likely than suburban students and more likely than rural students to have attended. Fifty-three percent of students attending urban schools in the 8th grade had attended preschool compared with 58 percent of suburban and only 40 percent of rural students (figure 4.25).

Are high poverty schools different? Rates of preschool attendance varied according to the poverty concentration of the schools the 8th graders attended. Forty percent of the students attending the highest poverty schools had attended preschool compared with 64 percent of students in the lowest poverty schools (figure 4.26).

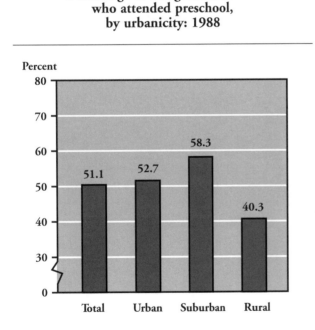

Figure 4.25
**Percentage of 8th-grade students
who attended preschool,
by urbanicity: 1988**

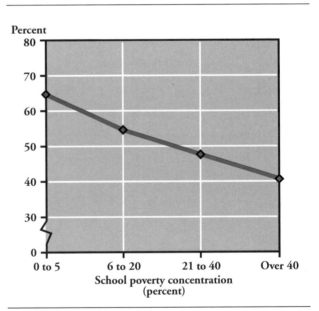

Figure 4.26
**Percentage of 8th-grade students
who attended preschool,
by school poverty concentration: 1988**

SOURCE: U.S. Department of Education, National Center for Education Statistics, National Education Longitudinal Study of 1988, Base Year Parent File.

SOURCE: U.S. Department of Education, National Center for Education Statistics, National Education Longitudinal Study of 1988, Base Year Parent File.

Are urban schools different after accounting for poverty concentration? After accounting for differences in school poverty concentration across school locales, urban students were just as likely to have attended preschool as suburban students, but were still more likely to have attended than rural students. That is, the higher poverty concentration in urban schools seems to account for the differences between students in urban and suburban schools, but not the difference between urban and rural students. Rural students were less likely to have attended preschool than urban students at all levels of school poverty except the lowest.

Were students from urban high poverty schools less likely to have attended preschool than predicted? Urban students from schools with the highest poverty concentration were as likely as one would predict from the combination of their schools' characteristics to have attended preschool (figure 4.27). In fact, 45 percent of the parents of students from urban schools with the highest poverty concentration reported that their children had attended preschool compared with 34 percent of the parents of students attending high poverty rural schools. Students in urban and suburban high poverty schools had about the same levels of preschool attendance.

Figure 4.27
Percentage of 8th-grade students who attended preschool,
by urbanicity and school poverty concentration: 1988

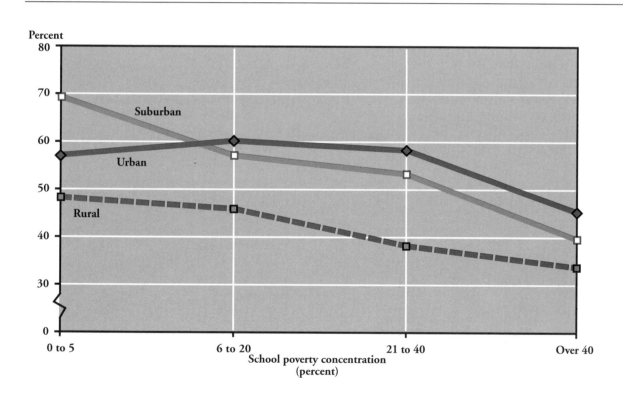

SOURCE: U.S. Department of Education, National Center for Education Statistics, National Education Longitudinal Study of 1988, Base Year Parent File.

Gifted and Talented Programs

Gifted and talented programs provide those students selected by ability with the opportunity to expand their education beyond the basic curriculum. Some researchers have suggested that these programs are not available to all students equally, and that students in inner-city urban public schools are particularly unlikely to be offered or placed in programs for students of high ability (Oakes 1990). If these reports are true, some students who could benefit from more challenging curriculum may be placed at an unnecessary disadvantage when compared with other similar students. Comparisons of the availability of gifted and talented programs between public schools can be made using data from the 1987–88 SASS. Elementary schools were chosen for this analysis because of the importance of early coursework in determining later placement in academic tracks in secondary school, and the greater prevalence of these programs at the elementary level.[25]

Are urban schools different? In 1987–88, 77 percent of public elementary schools offered gifted and talented programs nationally. Urban elementary schools, however, were less likely than suburban schools to offer these programs (figure 4.28). Seventy-three percent of urban elementary schools offered these programs compared with 84 percent of suburban schools. However, urban and rural schools did not differ in the proportions offering gifted and talented programs.

Are high poverty schools different? Schools with high poverty concentrations were less likely than other schools to offer gifted and talented programs. Of schools with the highest poverty concentrations, 70 percent reported offering a gifted and talented program, while 78 to 83 percent of other schools did so (figure 4.29).

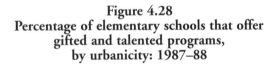

Figure 4.28
Percentage of elementary schools that offer gifted and talented programs, by urbanicity: 1987–88

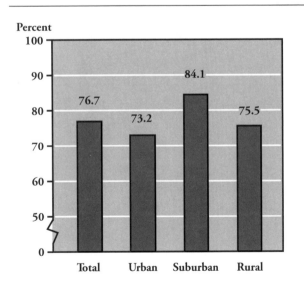

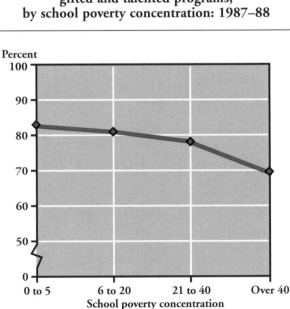

Figure 4.29
Percentage of elementary schools that offer gifted and talented programs, by school poverty concentration: 1987–88

SOURCE: U.S. Department of Education, National Center for Education Statistics, Schools and Staffing Survey, 1987–88, School File.

SOURCE: U.S. Department of Education, National Center for Education Statistics, Schools and Staffing Survey, 1987–88, School File.

Are urban schools different after accounting for poverty concentration? After accounting for school poverty concentration, the differences between urban and suburban schools remained. That is, the higher poverty concentration of urban schools was not the only explanation for the disparity in the rate at which gifted and talented programs were offered in urban and suburban schools.

Were urban high poverty schools less likely to offer gifted and talented programs than predicted? Students in high poverty urban schools are at a disadvantage relative to rural schools in that they are less likely than predicted to have gifted and talented programs in their school. High poverty urban schools offered gifted and talented programs at a lower rate than rural high poverty schools

(figure 4.30). Sixty-six percent of urban high poverty schools offered gifted and talented programs compared with just over 70 percent of rural high poverty schools. Suburban high poverty schools were just as likely as urban high poverty schools to offer these programs; however, urban students at schools with the *lowest* poverty concentration are at a relative disadvantage compared with suburban schools. At the 0–5 percent level of poverty concentration, 80 percent of urban schools had gifted and talented programs compared with 94 percent of suburban schools. The percentages were similar for suburban and urban schools with higher poverty concentrations.

---

[25]The definition of elementary covers schools that include grades from kindergarten through the 6th grade, or ungraded, with no grades higher than the 8th.

Figure 4.30
Percentage of elementary schools that offer gifted and talented programs, by urbanicity and school poverty concentration: 1987–88

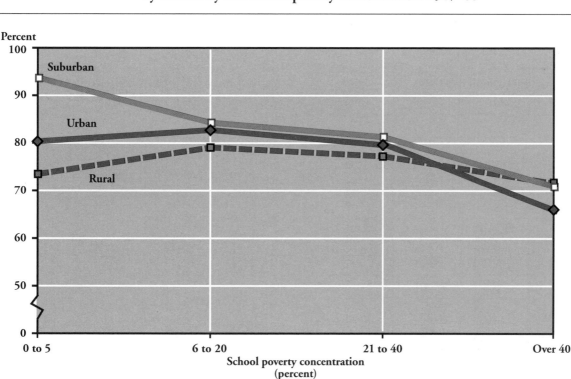

SOURCE: U.S. Department of Education, National Center for Education Statistics, Schools and Staffing Survey, 1987–88, School File.

Vocational Coursetaking

Nearly all students take a vocational course during their high school career. However, some students take considerably more vocational education courses than others. In this analysis, students who take six or more credits of vocational education are considered to be participating in vocational education more than the average high school student (Tuma 1995). The following analysis presents data from the high school transcripts of seniors obtained as part of the 1990 National Assessment of Educational Progress (NAEP) showing that vocational coursetaking varies by school location and poverty concentration. Interestingly, a similar analysis of the total number of academic credits students took did not reveal similar variation by these two school characteristics. This indicates that, although on average some groups of students take more vocational courses than others, academic

coursetaking does not vary when analyzed at the school level. However, research suggests that students who participate more in vocational education courses may take fewer advanced academic courses than their peers (Tuma 1996).

Are urban schools different? In 1990, about 19 percent of all graduating public high school seniors had taken six or more credits in vocational education (figure 4.31).[26] Although it appears that urban students were more likely to take vocational education courses (20 percent) than suburban students (14 percent) and less likely than rural students (25 percent), these differences are not statistically significant. Students in urban schools were just as likely to take six or more credits in vocational education than students in suburban or rural schools. Rural students, however, were more

Figure 4.31
Percentage of graduating high school seniors who took 6 or more credits in vocational education, by urbanicity: 1990

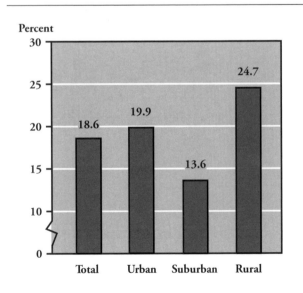

SOURCE: U.S. Department of Education, National Center for Education Statistics, National Assessment of Educational Progress, 1990 High School Transcript Study.

Figure 4.32
Percentage of graduating high school seniors who took 6 or more credits in vocational education, by school poverty concentration: 1990

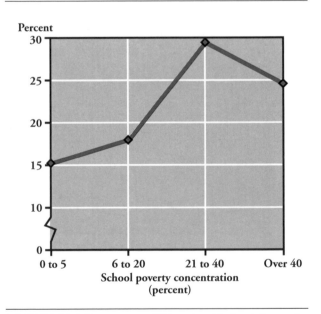

SOURCE: U.S. Department of Education, National Center for Education Statistics, National Assessment of Educational Progress, 1990 High School Transcript Study.

likely than suburban students to take six or more credits of vocational education—about one-fourth of rural students took that many credits compared with suburban students.

Are high poverty schools different? Students in public schools with high poverty concentrations were more likely to take six or more vocational credits than students in low poverty schools (figure 4.32). In the high poverty schools, one-fourth of all graduating seniors had completed six or more credits in vocational education compared with 15 percent of students in the low poverty schools.[27]

Are urban schools different after accounting for poverty concentration? After accounting for differences in school poverty concentration, urban students were still not statistically different in their vocational coursetaking than other students; however, rural students were, again, more likely than suburban students to take six or more vocational education credits.

Were students in urban high poverty schools more likely to have taken six or more vocational credits than predicted? Students in high poverty urban public schools were about as likely to take six or more vocational education credits as one would predict given the location and poverty concentration of their schools. That is, being in a high poverty urban school was not related to a greater than predicted incidence of taking a lot of vocational courses.[28]

---

[26]One credit (or Carnegie Unit) is defined as a 1-year course meeting 1 hour a day.

[27]The categories of poverty concentration used in this section are for illustrative purposes only. The actual statistical test was conducted on a continuous poverty concentration variable. Since the sample sizes for schools by urbanicity and poverty concentration combined were too small to produce reliable estimates, no comparisons were made between urban high poverty and other high poverty schools.

[28]No third figure is presented since the sample sizes for schools by urbanicity and poverty concentration are too small to produce reliable estimates.

Mathematics Coursetaking

A key feature of what constitutes a quality education is the opportunity to take advanced course work. Ideally, a measure of differences in course offerings across school types is desired, since if courses are not offered, students are not able to take them, and differences between schools in student achievement and attainment can result when students are not exposed to the same curricula. However, information on course offerings that schools provide is not a reliable predictor of what classes are actually offered during a school year. Student coursetaking is the best measure available, even though differences in coursetaking reflect students' placement and course selection in addition to differences in course offerings. Further, it is not known precisely how consistently course titles

reflect similar content; however, limited evidence suggests that course titles are reasonably reliable indicators of comparative content (Porter 1994).

The data source for this analysis is the high school transcripts of seniors in the 1990 National Assessment of Educational Progress (NAEP). Since patterns of advanced coursetaking were found to be similar in mathematics, science, and foreign languages, only the results of the analysis of geometry are presented. Geometry was the course chosen because it is the most advanced, yet least specialized, mathematics class that is widely available and that a majority of students take. Also, evidence has shown that successful completion of geometry is related to a greater chance that students

Figure 4.33
Percentage of graduating high school seniors who took geometry, by urbanicity: 1990

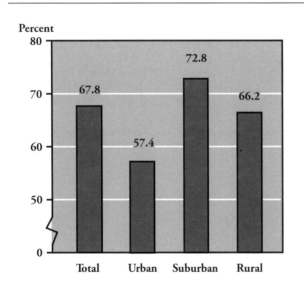

Figure 4.34
Percentage of graduating high school seniors who took geometry, by school poverty concentration: 1990

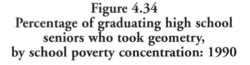
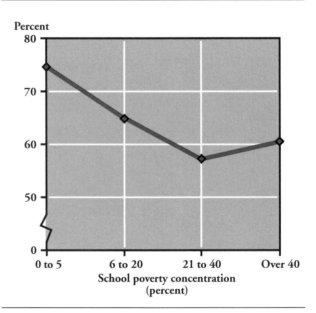

SOURCE: U.S. Department of Education, National Center for Education Statistics, National Assessment of Educational Progress, 1990 High School Transcript Study.

SOURCE: U.S. Department of Education, National Center for Education Statistics, National Assessment of Educational Progress, 1990 High School Transcript Study.

will go on to college when compared with their peers who complete only algebra (Pelavin and Kane 1990).

Are urban schools different? In 1990, a little more than two-thirds (68 percent) of graduating public school seniors had taken geometry in high school (figure 4.33). Urban students were less likely than suburban students to have taken geometry. Fifty-seven percent of urban students had credits in geometry compared with almost 73 percent of suburban students. However, urban and rural students were not statistically different from each other on this measure.

Are high poverty schools different? Students in schools with higher poverty concentrations were less likely to have taken geometry than other students (figure 4.34). Sixty percent of students in the high poverty schools had taken geometry compared with 74 percent of students in the lowest poverty schools.[29]

Are urban schools different after accounting for poverty concentration? When the school poverty

concentration was taken into account, the difference between the proportion of urban and suburban students taking geometry was no longer statistically significant. Rural and suburban students were just as likely to have taken geometry as were urban students.[30]

Were students in urban high poverty schools less likely to have taken geometry than predicted? Students in urban high poverty schools were just as likely to have taken geometry as predicted from the combination of the effects of an urban and high poverty setting. There was no evidence that they were at any additional disadvantage related to the interaction, or compounding effect, of the two.

---

[29]The categories of poverty concentration used in this section are for illustrative purposes only. The actual statistical test was conducted on a continuous poverty concentration variable.

[30]No third figure is presented since the sample sizes for schools by urbanicity and poverty concentration are too small to produce reliable estimates.

Student Behavior

Recently, researchers and policymakers have focused attention on the importance of the school learning environment and the influence of individual and peer behaviors on student performance. Goal six of the National Education Goals states that by the year 2000, "every school in America will be free of drugs and violence and will offer a disciplined environment conducive to learning" (National Education Goals Panel 1992). Because learning is constrained in an atmosphere of fear or disorderliness, student behavior influences school atmosphere and the climate for learning—whether it takes the form of violence and risk-taking activities (such as bringing a weapon to school or using alcohol) or a low commitment to academic effort (such as poor attendance, discipline, or study habits). These student behaviors also play a key role in determining student success in school and beyond. Studies of students considered to be "at risk" for school failure have shown that these students are likely to complete less homework, attend school less frequently, exhibit more aggressive behavior, and use illicit drugs more than their peers who are not at risk (Kaufman and Bradby 1992).

The indicators presented in this section can be broadly grouped into four categories of student behavior. Two indicators of student academic effort are time spent doing homework and watching television. The amount and quality of time spent in the classroom is represented by student absenteeism and time spent on discipline in the classroom. School violence is measured by how safe students feel in school and the extent of weapons possession at school. Finally, data on two student risk-taking behaviors, student alcohol use and pregnancy, are presented. Given the nature of these problems, the analysis is limited to secondary school data, with the exception of 8th-grade teacher reports of time spent maintaining classroom order and discipline.

When considering the results, it is important to emphasize that the actual incidence of a particular student behavior cannot be extrapolated from the data. These data reflect teachers' and students' perceptions of a particular problem. In one sense, teacher and student perceptions are direct measures of classroom and school conditions. However, teachers may have different perceptions of the seriousness of student behavior problems regardless of the frequency with which students engage in these particular behaviors in their schools. Behavior that might be considered intolerable to a teacher in one school may be a more common occurrence and, thus, less problematic to a teacher in another.

Findings

- About half of the student behaviors studied were more likely to be worse in public urban schools than in suburban or rural schools, even after accounting for the higher concentration of poverty in urban schools. More time was spent maintaining classroom discipline in urban schools, and student absenteeism, possession of weapons, and student pregnancy were greater problems.

- For the other half of behaviors studied, urban students were similar to other students after accounting for poverty differences. They spent the same amount of time doing homework and watching television as other students. Although they felt less safe at school than rural students, they were as likely to report feeling safe as suburban students. Urban students were considered by their teachers to be as likely to use alcohol as suburban students, but less likely than rural students.

- Discipline was more likely to be a problem in urban high poverty schools than in any other high poverty schools. Student absenteeism and weapons possession were worse in urban than in rural high poverty schools, but were the same as in suburban schools with a similar poverty concentration.

- Students in urban high poverty schools were similar to students in other high poverty schools in their homework effort, feelings of safety, alcohol use, and problems with pregnancy.

- The hours that students in urban high poverty schools spent watching television were higher than predicted, and cannot be explained by the combination of an urban school location and high poverty concentration alone.

Hours of Television Watched on Weekdays

Time spent watching television limits the number of hours a student has available to complete homework (Mullis et al. 1991). Moreover, spending large amounts of time watching television has been correlated with weaker academic performance in recent national assessments (U.S. Department of Education 1993b). The National Assessment of Educational Progress (NAEP) has documented that students watched more hours of television and spent less time on homework per day in 1990 than in 1982 (U.S. Department of Education 1993b).

Are urban schools different? Nationally, 33 percent of public school 10th graders in 1990 reported watching at least 3 hours of television on weekdays. Urban students (37 percent) were more likely than suburban students (30 percent) to watch this much television.

However, there was no statistical difference between urban and rural students (35 percent) on this measure (figure 4.35).

Are high poverty schools different? Students who attend high poverty schools were more likely to watch 3 or more hours of television per weekday than their peers in schools with lower poverty concentrations. Forty-three percent of students in high poverty schools watched 3 or more hours of television compared with 26 percent of students in low poverty schools, a difference of 17 percentage points (figure 4.36).

Are urban schools different after accounting for poverty concentration? After accounting for school poverty concentration, the difference between students attending urban and suburban schools disappeared.

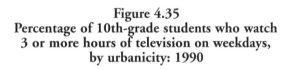

Figure 4.35
Percentage of 10th-grade students who watch 3 or more hours of television on weekdays, by urbanicity: 1990

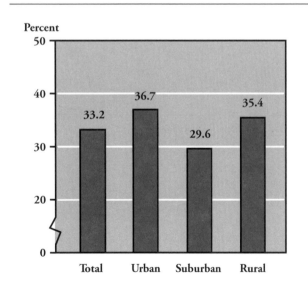

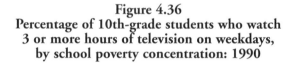

Figure 4.36
Percentage of 10th-grade students who watch 3 or more hours of television on weekdays, by school poverty concentration: 1990

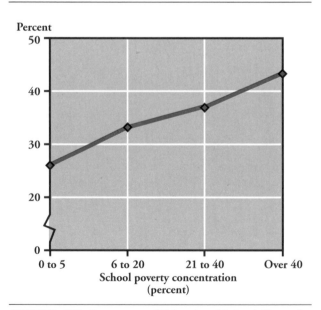

SOURCE: U.S. Department of Education, National Center for Education Statistics, National Education Longitudinal Study of 1988, First Follow-up Student File.

SOURCE: U.S. Department of Education, National Center for Education Statistics, National Education Longitudinal Study of 1988, First Follow-up Student File.

Therefore, the greater percentage of urban students watching a lot of television compared with their suburban counterparts can be explained by the greater likelihood that urban students attend schools with higher poverty concentrations.

Were students in urban high poverty schools likely to view television more frequently than predicted? Nearly one-half of students in urban high poverty schools reported watching television more than 3 hours per day. In fact, the rate for urban high poverty schools was higher than predicted given the overall rates of television

watching for urban students and students in all schools with high poverty concentrations. Although on average, after accounting for poverty, the proportion of urban students watching a lot of television was no different from suburban and rural students, this average masks the differences by level of poverty within urban schools. There was a wider gap between the television viewing habits of urban students in high poverty schools compared with urban students in low poverty schools than there was for either suburban or rural students (figure 4.37). In other words, poverty concentration mattered more in urban schools than in schools in other locations.

Figure 4.37
Percentage of 10th-grade students who watch 3 or more hours of television on weekdays, by urbanicity and school poverty concentration: 1990

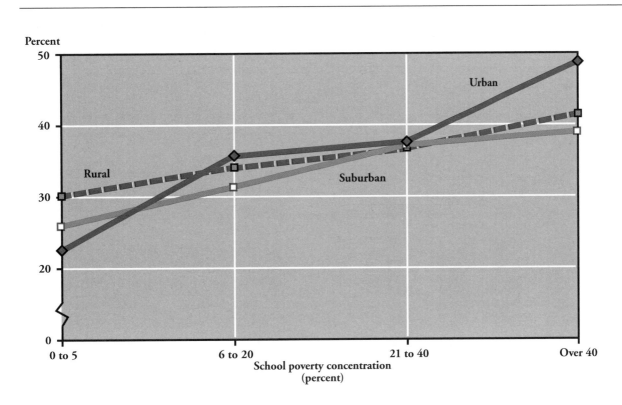

SOURCE: U.S. Department of Education, National Center for Education Statistics, National Education Longitudinal Study of 1988, First Follow-up Student File.

Hours Spent on Homework

The amount of time spent on homework is an important indicator of student effort. Tenth-grade students participating in the 1990 follow-up to the NELS:88 survey were questioned about the amount of time they spent on homework both in and out of school,[31] and these data are presented below.

Are urban schools different? No difference was found in the number of hours students attending public schools in different locations spent doing homework. The average number of hours that urban, suburban, and rural students spent on homework was a little over 7 hours per week (figure 4.38).

Are high poverty schools different? The number of hours of homework completed by students differed according to the poverty concentration of their schools. Students attending high poverty schools completed 6 and a half hours of homework on average during the week, while students in low poverty schools completed almost 8 hours (figure 4.39).

Are urban schools different after accounting for poverty concentration? There were still no differences between students attending urban, suburban, and rural schools after accounting for the varying school poverty concentration.

Figure 4.38
Average number of hours 10th-grade students spend on homework per week, by urbanicity: 1990

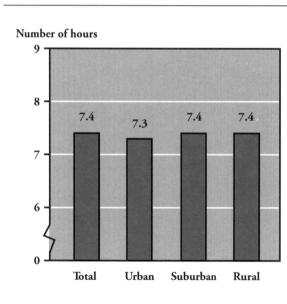

Number of hours

Figure 4.39
Average number of hours 10th-grade students spend on homework per week, by school poverty concentration: 1990

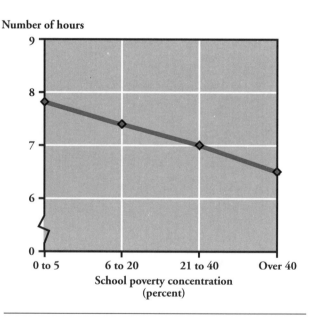

Number of hours

SOURCE: U.S. Department of Education, National Center for Education Statistics, National Education Longitudinal Study of 1988, First Follow-up Student File.

SOURCE: U.S. Department of Education, National Center for Education Statistics, National Education Longitudinal Study of 1988, First Follow-up Student File.

Were students in urban high poverty schools less likely to spend time on homework than predicted? Students from urban high poverty schools did not spend less time doing homework than predicted. In fact, students attending these schools did as much homework as students in schools in other locations with similar poverty concentrations. Thus, despite their unusually high rate of television watching, these students did not appear to spend less time on home-work than students in other high poverty schools (figure 4.40).

---

[31]To create a figure for homework hours completed during the week, data on time spent on homework both in and out of school were combined. In order to combine these data, which were already in discrete categories, a score midway between the range for each category was created; then, an overall score was created by summing the two separate scores for homework completed in and out of school. The analysis was conducted using this overall score.

Figure 4.40
Average number of hours 10th-grade students spend on homework per week, by urbanicity and school poverty concentration: 1990

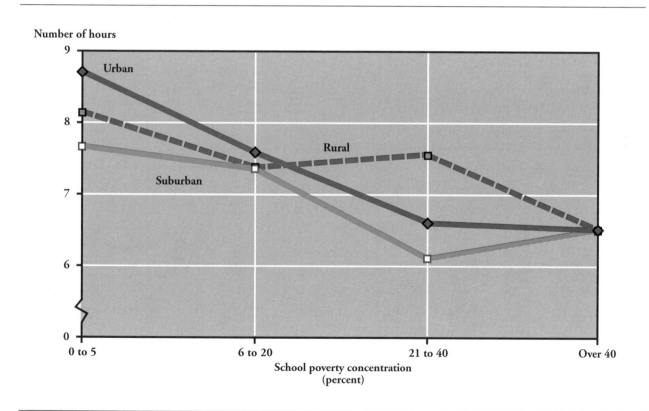

SOURCE: U.S. Department of Education, National Center for Education Statistics, National Education Longitudinal Study of 1988, First Follow-up Student File.

Student Absenteeism

Of all the student behavior problems that teachers were asked about in the 1987–88 SASS, absenteeism was the one rated serious most frequently, regardless of school location and poverty concentration.[32] A related behavior, tardiness, was also frequently rated as a serious problem by teachers, particularly in urban and high poverty schools. Since the patterns for these two indicators were quite similar, only data for student absenteeism are presented below. Teachers who rated absenteeism either as a moderate or serious problem were grouped together to produce a percentage who consider this behavior a problem in their school.

Are urban schools different? Nationally, 68 percent of public school teachers rated student absenteeism as a moderate or serious problem in their schools. Urban teachers were more likely than either suburban or rural teachers to rate this as a problem. Seventy-eight percent of urban teachers considered this a problem in their schools as opposed to 68 percent of suburban and 63 percent of rural teachers (figure 4.41).

Are high poverty schools different? Student absenteeism was most likely to be considered a problem by teachers in high poverty schools. Seventy-four percent of teachers in schools with more than 40 percent poverty concentration considered student absenteeism a moderate or serious problem, while 65 percent of teachers in low poverty schools held the same view (figure 4.42).

Figure 4.41
Percentage of secondary teachers who believe that student absenteeism is a problem in their school, by urbanicity: 1987–88

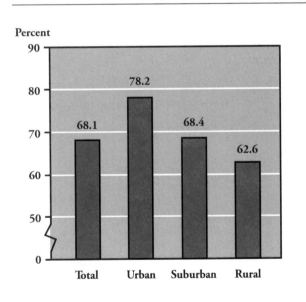

SOURCE: U.S. Department of Education, National Center for Education Statistics, Schools and Staffing Survey, 1987–88, Teacher File.

Figure 4.42
Percentage of secondary teachers who believe that student absenteeism is a problem in their school, by school poverty concentration: 1987–88

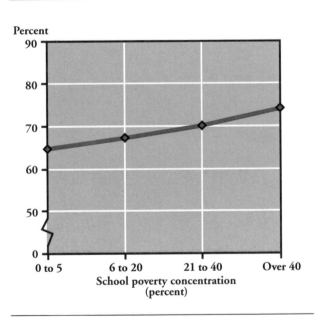

SOURCE: U.S. Department of Education, National Center for Education Statistics, Schools and Staffing Survey, 1987–88, Teacher File.

Are urban schools different after accounting for poverty concentration? Accounting for poverty concentration did not eliminate the differences by school location. Urban teachers were still more likely to consider student absenteeism a moderate or serious problem in their schools when compared with suburban and rural teachers.

Were teachers in urban high poverty schools more likely to consider student absenteeism a problem in their schools than predicted? Teachers in urban high poverty schools were more likely to consider student absenteeism a problem than teachers in rural high poverty schools (84 percent compared with 65 percent). However, this rate was no higher than predicted.

There was little difference between teachers in suburban schools with moderately high to the highest poverty concentrations and their urban counterparts on this measure. Teachers in urban and suburban schools were more likely to consider student absenteeism a problem as school poverty concentration increased. However, the percentage of rural teachers rating student absenteeism a problem was lower than that of teachers in suburban and urban schools, and it did not increase as much with poverty concentration as it did in urban and suburban schools (figure 4.43).

---

[32]Administrators also rated this as a serious problem most frequently.

Figure 4.43
Percentage of secondary teachers who believe that student absenteeism is a problem in their school, by urbanicity and school poverty concentration: 1987–88

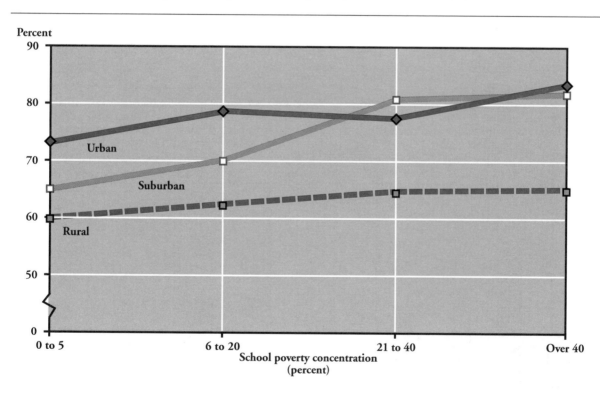

SOURCE: U.S. Department of Education, National Center for Education Statistics, Schools and Staffing Survey, 1987–88, Teacher File.

Time Spent Maintaining Classroom Discipline

Recent studies comparing U.S. and Asian classroom practices have suggested that in the United States, teachers spend a greater proportion of time on activities other than instruction than they do in Japan and China (Stevenson and Stigler 1992). According to Harold Stevenson, American teachers spend proportionately more time disciplining students in the classroom than their Asian peers. Time spent on discipline means less time available for instruction and learning.

> One index of need for discipline is the degree to which American children engage in irrelevant activities in the classroom . . . Such activities as talking to other children and wandering about the classroom diminish the child's own opportunities for learning and are potentially disruptive to other children. This type of irrelevant behavior, in addition to the fidgeting and inattentiveness often described by American teachers, makes maintaining discipline a pervasive and difficult problem in American classrooms (Stevenson and Stigler 1992).

Researchers have also suggested that teachers spend more time disciplining students and maintaining order in schools in poor urban settings than in non-urban and more advantaged schools (Karweit 1992). In this section, data from the base year of the National Education Longitudinal Survey of 1988 (NELS:88) is used to examine this perception. In NELS:88, 8th-grade teachers were asked about the time they spent maintaining order and discipline in their classrooms.[33] Less than 2 percent of these teachers reported that their classes met more than 5 hours per week. Therefore, teachers who spent 1 hour or more per week maintaining classroom order were spending at least one-fifth of their instruction time on discipline.

Are urban schools different? Teachers of 8th-grade students in urban public schools were more likely to spend substantial amounts of time maintaining classroom order and discipline than their suburban and rural counterparts. Urban 8th-grade teachers were almost twice as likely as rural teachers to report that they spend at least 1 hour per week maintaining order in their classes (25 percent compared with 13 percent). Sixteen percent of suburban teachers reported spending this much classroom time on these tasks (figure 4.44).

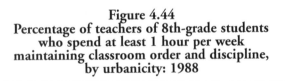

Figure 4.44
Percentage of teachers of 8th-grade students who spend at least 1 hour per week maintaining classroom order and discipline, by urbanicity: 1988

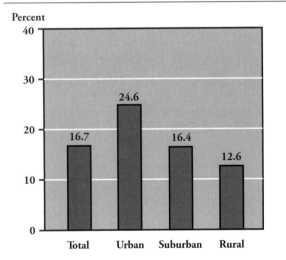

SOURCE: U.S. Department of Education, National Center for Education Statistics, National Education Longitudinal Study of 1988, Base Year Teacher File.

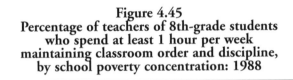

Figure 4.45
Percentage of teachers of 8th-grade students who spend at least 1 hour per week maintaining classroom order and discipline, by school poverty concentration: 1988

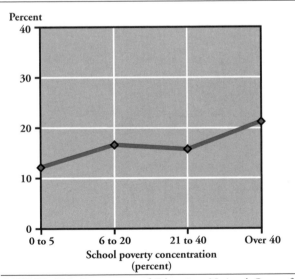

SOURCE: U.S. Department of Education, National Center for Education Statistics, National Education Longitudinal Study of 1988, Base Year Teacher File.

Are high poverty schools different? Teachers of 8th-grade students from the highest poverty schools were generally more likely to spend classroom time maintaining order and discipline than were teachers from schools with lower poverty concentrations (figure 4.45). In particular, 21 percent of 8th-grade teachers from high poverty schools spent at least 1 hour per week in their classes on discipline compared with 12 percent of teachers in low poverty schools.

Are urban schools different after accounting for poverty concentration? After taking poverty concentration into account, urban teachers of 8th-grade students were still more likely to spend at least 1 hour per week maintaining order in their classrooms. The higher proportion of poor students in urban locations is not the only explanation for the fact that teachers in urban schools were likely to spend more time disciplining their students than teachers in rural and suburban schools.

Were teachers in urban high poverty schools more likely to spend at least 1 hour on discipline in their classrooms than predicted? Teachers of 8th-grade stu-

dents in urban high poverty schools were more likely to spend at least 1 hour maintaining classroom order and discipline than 8th-grade teachers in other high poverty schools. However, their responses were no different from teachers in other urban schools with moderate levels of poverty concentration (figure 4.46). Twenty-eight percent of urban 8th-grade teachers spent this amount of time on discipline—at least 10 percentage points higher than 8th-grade teachers in suburban or rural high poverty schools. However, teachers in urban high poverty schools did not spend more time disciplining students than predicted compared with teachers in other schools. This suggests that high poverty concentration and an urban setting do not interact to add to the already larger amounts of time teachers spend on maintaining discipline in these schools.

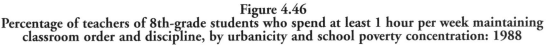

[33]Although the student sample in the NELS:88 survey was designed to represent the student population in the United States, the teacher sample is not nationally representative. This means that one can discuss these data nationally for students, but not teachers. In one of the following combinations of subject areas—math and English, math and social studies, science and English, or science and social studies—two teachers were chosen for each student. (If one teacher taught both subjects to a student, then one teacher was chosen for that student.)

Figure 4.46
Percentage of teachers of 8th-grade students who spend at least 1 hour per week maintaining classroom order and discipline, by urbanicity and school poverty concentration: 1988

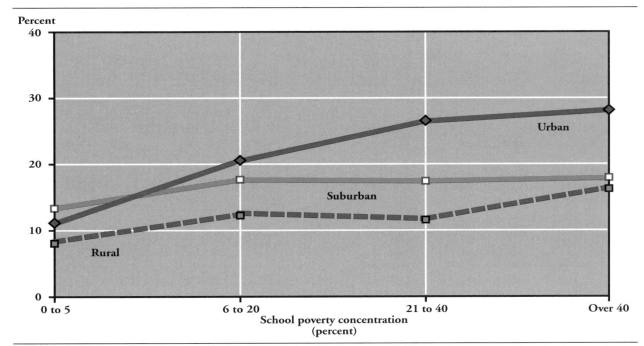

SOURCE: U.S. Department of Education, National Center for Education Statistics, National Education Longitudinal Study of 1988, Base Year Teacher File.

School Safety

Perhaps no other school climate issue has received as much recent media attention as safety in the public schools. Reports surface almost weekly on incidents of weapons possession, drug use, violence, racial conflict and crime on school campuses, particularly in the inner cities. There have even been individual reports of students choosing not to attend their classes out of fear. (Such behavior clearly may exacerbate the problem of student absenteeism discussed earlier in this section.)[34] Despite what appears to be increasing reports of school violence, a recent study comparing sophomores in 1980 and 1990 revealed that in 1990, 10th graders were in general less likely to report that they felt unsafe at school than were students surveyed in 1980 (Rasinski et al. 1993). Whether this suggests a positive change in school safety nationally or simply increased desensitization to violence is unclear. Nevertheless, in 1990 the percentage of students who reported feeling unsafe at school differed by school location and poverty concentration, as presented below.

Are urban schools different? Nationally, approximately 9 percent of 10th graders agreed or strongly agreed that they did not feel safe at school in 1990. Tenth graders attending urban schools were more likely to report that they did not feel safe at school—13 percent compared with 8 percent each of suburban and rural students (figure 4.47).

Are high poverty schools different? Students in high poverty schools were less likely to feel safe than those in schools with the lowest poverty concentrations (figure 4.48). However, students in schools with the highest poverty concentration were just as likely to feel unsafe

Figure 4.47
Percentage of 10th-grade students who do not feel safe at school, by urbanicity: 1990

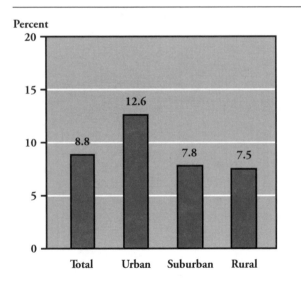

SOURCE: U.S. Department of Education, National Center for Education Statistics, National Education Longitudinal Study of 1988, First Follow-up Student File.

Figure 4.48
Percentage of 10th-grade students who do not feel safe at school, by school poverty concentration: 1990

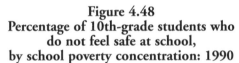
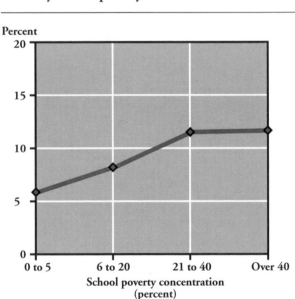

SOURCE: U.S. Department of Education, National Center for Education Statistics, National Education Longitudinal Study of 1988, First Follow-up Student File.

as those in schools with the next to highest concentration of poverty. Approximately 12 percent of students in high poverty schools felt unsafe, compared with 6 to 8 percent in schools with the lowest and next to lowest poverty concentrations.

Are urban schools different after accounting for poverty concentration? Once the higher poverty concentrations in urban schools are considered, urban and suburban students' perception of school safety are similar; but urban students overall still felt less safe than their rural peers.

Were students in urban high poverty schools more likely to feel unsafe at school than predicted? Students in urban high poverty schools were just as likely to feel unsafe as students in high poverty schools in other locations. In fact, the percentage who did not feel safe in urban high poverty schools was not statistically different from the percentages in other urban schools, with the exception of urban students in the lowest poverty schools. Thus, an urban high poverty setting did not present any additional safety risk from the students' perspective. Given the heightened news reports, what seems most surprising is that the magnitude of the problem as reported by students is not high, ranging from 5 percent of students in low poverty rural schools to approximately 16 percent of students in urban and suburban schools with a poverty concentration of 21 to 40 percent (figure 4.49).

---

[34]See, for example, *The New York Times*, October 15, 1993, B3. According to Robert D. McFadden, "20% of New York City Public-School Students Carry Weapons, Study Finds." This statement refers to a study conducted in June 1992 by the Federal Centers for Disease Control and Prevention, the city Health Department, and city school officials, which links school violence to student attitudes.

Figure 4.49
Percentage of 10th-grade students who do not feel safe at school, by urbanicity and school poverty concentration: 1990

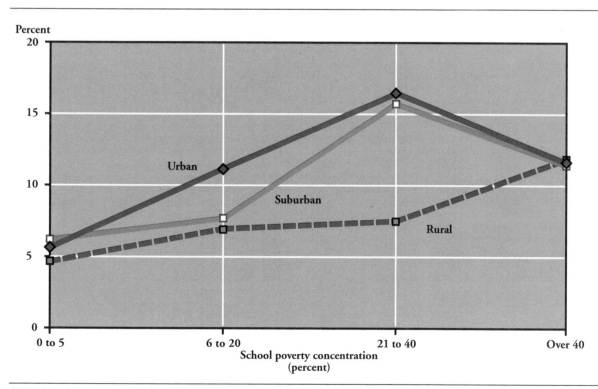

SOURCE: U.S. Department of Education, National Center for Education Statistics, National Education Longitudinal Study of 1988, First Follow-up Student File.

Student Possession of Weapons

The presence of weapons on school campuses poses a serious threat to the school learning environment. Though still rare, shootings and weapon-related violent acts occurring inside or near schools have received much publicity in recent years, and, to the extent they do occur, they interfere with the ability of students and teachers to concentrate on schooling.

Are urban schools different? Nationally, 11 percent of teachers reported that weapons possession by students was a moderate or serious problem in their school in 1987–88. Teachers' responses, however, varied widely by location (figure 4.50). Urban teachers were more than twice as likely as suburban or rural teachers to view weapons possession as a problem in their schools —21 percent compared with 9 percent and 7 percent, respectively. This finding supports the perception that urban students are exposed to more weapons in the school than either suburban or rural students.

Are high poverty schools different? Teachers in high poverty schools were more than twice as likely to report that weapons possession was a problem than teachers in schools with the two lowest concentrations of poverty (figure 4.51). Twenty-one percent of teachers in high poverty schools reported that

Figure 4.50
Percentage of secondary teachers who believe that student weapons possession is a problem in their school, by urbanicity: 1987–88

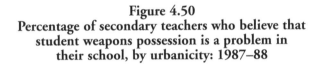

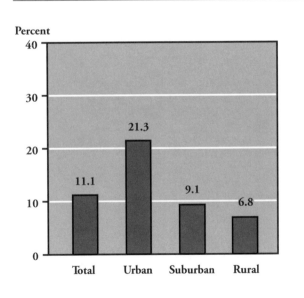

SOURCE: U.S. Department of Education, National Center for Education Statistics, Schools and Staffing Survey, 1987–88, Teacher File.

Figure 4.51
Percentage of secondary teachers who believe that student weapons possession is a problem in their school, by school poverty concentration: 1987–88

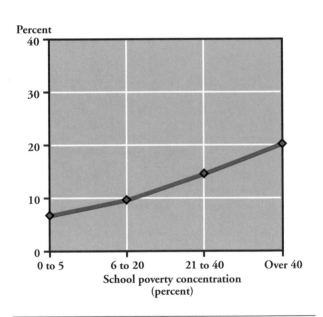

SOURCE: U.S. Department of Education, National Center for Education Statistics, Schools and Staffing Survey, 1987–88, Teacher File.

weapons possession was a problem compared with 6 percent of teachers in the lowest poverty schools and 10 percent of the teachers in schools with a 6–20 percent poverty concentration.

Are urban schools different after accounting for poverty concentration? After accounting for differences in school poverty concentration, school location was still found to be strongly related to teacher responses. Teachers in urban schools were more likely to view student weapons possession as a problem in their schools when compared with either suburban or rural teachers.

Were teachers in urban high poverty schools more likely to view student possession of weapons as a moderate to serious problem in their schools than predicted? Teachers in urban high poverty schools were more likely to report that weapons possession was a problem than teachers in many other school types, but their reports were no different from teachers in urban schools with the next highest poverty concentration and suburban schools with the highest poverty concentrations. The combination of an urban and a high poverty setting did not reveal an additional risk of exposure to weapons (figure 4.52).

Figure 4.52
Percentage of secondary teachers who believe that student weapons possession is a problem in their school, by urbanicity and school poverty concentration: 1987–88

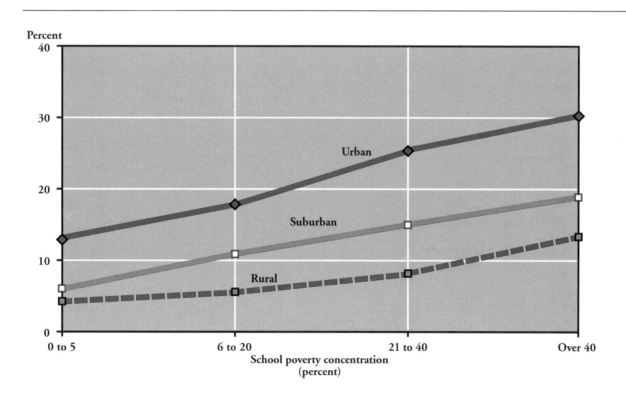

SOURCE: U.S. Department of Education, National Center for Education Statistics, Schools and Staffing Survey, 1987–88, Teacher File.

Student Alcohol Use

Some recent reports on the "at-risk" behaviors of youth have shown that student use of illegal substances has declined over the past two decades (U.S. Department of Education 1993c). Nevertheless, students' use of alcohol and drugs has remained a serious issue for educators and parents, with recent reports indicating that the use of illegal substances by teenagers may be again on the rise (University of Michigan 1994). Even in the late 1980s, alcohol use among students seems to have been of particular concern to teachers who participated in the 1987–88 SASS. Secondary school teachers nationwide rated student use of alcohol as a moderate or serious problem in their schools more frequently than student drug abuse (63 percent compared with 57 percent).

Are urban schools different? Nationwide, 63 percent of teachers considered student alcohol use as a moderate to serious problem in their schools. Teachers in urban schools were *less* likely (58 percent) to consider alcohol use a problem than were teachers from either suburban (63 percent) or rural (65 percent) schools. Of the four student problems presented in this report, this is the only case where urban teachers were less likely to report a student behavior as a problem than teachers in schools in other locations (figure 4.53). However, urban public school teachers view the use of drugs as a serious problem in their schools more frequently than do suburban or rural school teachers, although the percentages who do so are less than for alcohol use (Choy et al. 1992).

Figure 4.53
Percentage of secondary teachers who think that student alcohol use is a problem in their school, by urbanicity: 1987–88

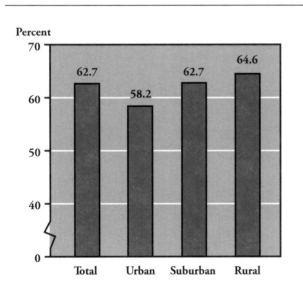

SOURCE: U.S. Department of Education, National Center for Education Statistics, Schools and Staffing Survey, 1987–88, Teacher File.

Figure 4.54
Percentage of secondary teachers who think that student alcohol use is a problem in their school, by school poverty concentration: 1987–88

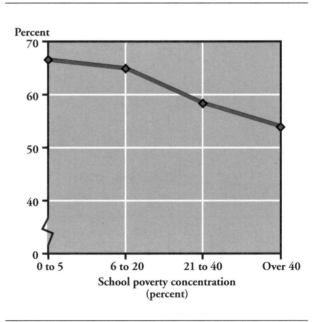

SOURCE: U.S. Department of Education, National Center for Education Statistics, Schools and Staffing Survey, 1987–88, Teacher File.

Are high poverty schools different? Teachers in high poverty schools were *less* likely than teachers in any other school poverty concentration category to report alcohol use as a moderate or serious problem in their schools. Fifty-four percent of teachers in high poverty schools considered student alcohol use a problem compared with 65 to 67 percent of teachers in the two low poverty concentration categories (figure 4.54). In this report, there are no other indicators describing a student behavior negatively related to academic outcomes that is more prevalent in schools with low poverty concentrations.

Are urban schools different after accounting for poverty concentration? When poverty concentration was taken into account, the differences by urbanicity changed. Urban teachers were still less likely than rural teachers to report alcohol use as a moderate to serious problem. Urban teachers, however, no longer differed from their suburban counterparts in their perception of alcohol use as a problem.

Were teachers in urban high poverty schools less likely to think that student alcohol use was a moderate to serious problem in their schools than predicted? Teacher reports that alcohol use was a problem were similar in urban, suburban, and rural high poverty schools (51, 57, and 56 percent respectively), and were no different than predicted in urban high poverty schools (figure 4.55). It is interesting that student alcohol use is considered a problem more often by rural teachers than either urban or suburban teachers for the two middle levels of poverty concentration.

Figure 4.55
Percentage of secondary teachers who think that student alcohol use is a problem in their school, by urbanicity and school poverty concentration: 1987–88

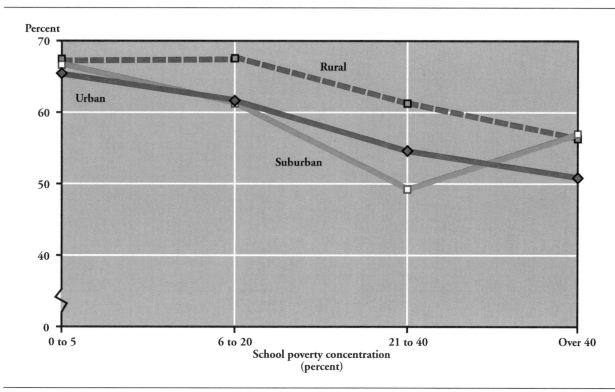

SOURCE: U.S. Department of Education, National Center for Education Statistics, Schools and Staffing Survey, 1987–88, Teacher File.

Student Pregnancy

Teenage pregnancy limits the educational opportunities of many female students, particularly those in poor urban settings. In addition, student pregnancy places significant demands on the social services of both the school and the community (Males 1993; 1994; Caldas 1994). This section examines how teachers perceive the problem in their schools.

Are urban schools different? Nationally, 39 percent of teachers in 1987-88 considered student pregnancy to be a moderate or serious problem in their schools. A much larger percentage of urban teachers (48 percent)

considered this a problem when compared with suburban and rural teachers (30 percent and 38 percent, respectively) (figure 4.56).

Are high poverty schools different? Teachers' perceptions of the problem of pregnancy differed greatly by school poverty concentration. Teachers in high poverty schools were twice as likely to consider student pregnancy a moderate or serious problem than teachers in low poverty schools (52 percent compared with 26 percent) (figure 4.57).

Figure 4.56
Percentage of secondary teachers who think that student pregnancy is a problem in their school, by urbanicity: 1987–88

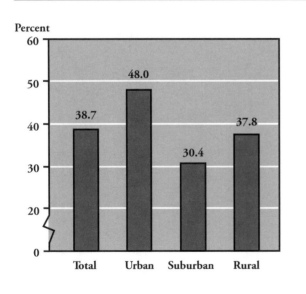

SOURCE: U.S. Department of Education, National Center for Education Statistics, Schools and Staffing Survey, 1987–88, Teacher File.

Figure 4.57
Percentage of secondary teachers who think that student pregnancy is a problem in their school, by school poverty concentration: 1987–88

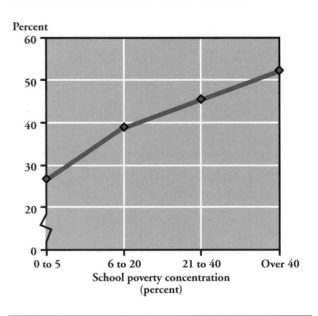

SOURCE: U.S. Department of Education, National Center for Education Statistics, Schools and Staffing Survey, 1987–88, Teacher File.

Are urban schools different after accounting for poverty concentration? After accounting for poverty concentration, urban teachers were still more likely to consider student pregnancy a problem than their counterparts in other locations. The higher concentration of poverty in urban schools is not the only explanation for the greater prevalence of teacher concern about student pregnancy in these schools.

Were teachers in urban high poverty schools more likely to consider student pregnancy a moderate or serious problem in their schools than predicted? Teachers in urban high poverty schools were as likely to consider student pregnancy a moderate or serious problem as predicted, given the poverty concentration and location of their schools. Urban teachers reported this problem more frequently than their counterparts at the middle two levels of school poverty concentration and more frequently than suburban teachers in low poverty schools, but not more frequently than those in high poverty schools (figure 4.58). There is no statistical difference between the proportion of teachers in urban high poverty schools who thought student pregnancy was a problem and the proportion of teachers who thought so in other high poverty schools.

Figure 4.58
Percentage of secondary teachers who think that student pregnancy is a problem in their school, by urbanicity and school poverty concentration: 1987–88

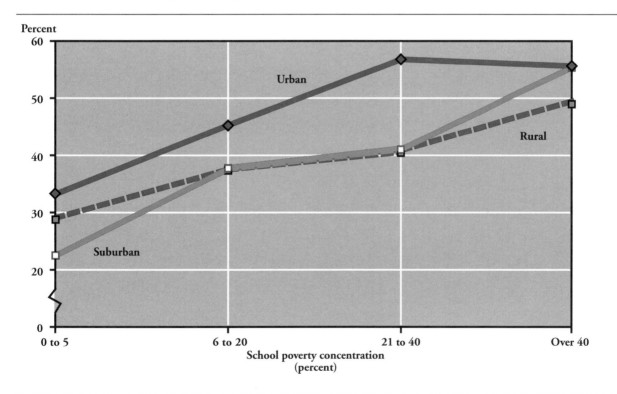

Appendix A

Estimates and Standard Error Tables

Table 1.1—Data and standard errors for figures 1.1 and 1.2: Number and percentage distribution of students enrolled in public schools, by urbanicity: 1980 and 1990

School urbanicity and year	Number (in millions)	Standard error	Percentage distribution	Standard error
Total				
1980	40.4	0.1	100.0	—
1990	37.7	0.1	100.0	—
Urban				
1980	10.6	0.2	26.3	0.4
1990	10.4	0.2	27.6	0.4
Suburban				
1980	16.5	0.2	40.8	0.3
1990	16.8	0.2	44.5	0.2
Rural				
1980	13.3	0.3	32.9	0.2
1990	10.5	0.3	27.9	0.2

— Not applicable.

SOURCE: U.S. Bureau of the Census, Current Population Survey, October 1980 and October 1990.

Table 1.2—Percentage of students in public and private schools, by urbanicity: 1987–88

School urbanicity	Percentage	Standard error
Total		
Public	88.4	0.2
Private	11.6	0.2
Urban		
Public	83.4	0.6
Private	16.6	0.6
Suburban		
Public	86.7	0.7
Private	13.3	0.7
Rural		
Public	92.9	0.3
Private	7.1	0.3

SOURCE: U.S. Department of Education, National Center for Education Statistics, Schools and Staffing Survey, 1987–88.

Table 1.3—Average school size, by urbanicity and level: 1987–88

School urbanicity and level	Average school size	Standard error
Total		
Elementary	424	3.5
Middle/junior high	569	8.3
Secondary	825	10.0
Urban		
Elementary	528	7.9
Middle/junior high	735	17.0
Secondary	1,313	31.0
Suburban		
Elementary	492	7.0
Middle/junior high	662	21.0
Secondary	1,197	30.0
Rural		
Elementary	354	4.2
Middle/junior high	463	11.0
Secondary	577	11.0

SOURCE: U.S. Department of Education, National Center for Education Statistics, Schools and Staffing Survey, 1987–88.

Table 1.4—Data and standard errors for figures 1.3 and 1.8: Poverty rates for children under age 18, by urbanicity: 1980 and 1990, and percentage of students with difficulty speaking English, by urbanicity: 1979 and 1989

Urbanicity and year	Rate or Percentage	Standard error
Total		
Poverty rate		
1980	17.9	0.2
1990	19.9	0.4
Difficulty speaking English		
1979	2.7	0.1
1989	4.6	0.2
Urban		
Poverty rate		
1980	26.2	0.4
1990	30.0	0.9
Difficulty speaking English		
1979	6.2	0.3
1989	9.1	0.5
Suburban		
Poverty rate		
1980	11.2	0.2
1990	12.5	0.5
Difficulty speaking English		
1979	1.9	0.2
1989	3.7	0.2
Rural		
Poverty rate		
1980	19.4	0.3
1990	22.2	0.9
Difficulty speaking English		
1979	1.2	0.2
1989	1.9	0.3

SOURCE: U.S. Bureau of the Census, Current Population Reports, Series P–60, Nos. 181 and 133; and Current Population Survey, November 1979 and 1989.

Table 1.5—Data and standard errors for figure 1.4: Percentage of 8th graders whose family was in the lowest socioeconomic quartile, by urbanicity and school poverty concentration: 1988

School urbanicity and school poverty concentration*	Percentage	Standard error
Total	26.5	0.7
0 to 5%	13.0	1.3
6 to 20%	19.1	1.0
21 to 40%	26.8	1.1
Over 40%	44.3	1.4
Urban—all	32.6	1.6
0 to 5%	17.8	5.9
6 to 20%	18.8	2.0
21 to 40%	26.0	3.2
Over 40%	44.6	2.1
Suburban—all	19.1	1.0
0 to 5%	9.6	1.2
6 to 20%	14.8	1.1
21 to 40%	23.6	1.7
Over 40%	44.4	3.4
Rural—all	31.9	1.1
0 to 5%	22.2	3.1
6 to 20%	27.3	1.9
21 to 40%	29.2	1.4
Over 40%	44.0	2.3

*"School poverty concentration" refers to the percentage of students in the school receiving free and reduced price lunch.

NOTE: Totals may include a small proportion of students for whom school urbanicity and/or poverty concentration are unknown.

SOURCE: U.S. Department of Education, National Center for Education Statistics, National Education Longitudinal Study of 1988, Base Year Survey.

Table 1.6—Data and standard errors for figure 1.5: Percentage of students in poverty-related programs, by urbanicity: 1987–88

School urbanicity	Eligible for free or reduced price lunch		Receiving free or reduced price lunch		Receiving Chapter 1 services	
	Per-centage	Standard error	Per-centage	Standard error	Per-centage	Standard error
Total	31.2	0.3	28.5	0.2	11.1	0.2
Urban	41.8	0.7	37.9	0.6	14.1	0.5
Suburban	17.9	0.4	16.2	0.4	6.8	0.5
Rural	30.6	0.3	28.3	0.3	11.2	0.2

SOURCE: U.S. Department of Education, National Center for Education Statistics, Schools and Staffing Survey, 1987–88.

Table 1.7—Data and standard errors for figure 1.6: Percentage distribution of students by school poverty concentration within urbanicity categories: 1987–88

School urbanicity and school poverty concentration*	Percentage distribution of students	Standard error
Total	100.0	—
0 to 5%	17.2	0.4
6 to 20%	31.8	0.6
21 to 40%	25.0	0.5
Over 40%	26.0	0.5
Urban—all	100.0	—
0 to 5%	12.1	0.8
6 to 20%	25.8	1.2
21 to 40%	22.0	1.1
Over 40%	40.1	1.1
Suburban—all	100.0	—
0 to 5%	35.5	1.1
6 to 20%	38.7	1.1
21 to 40%	15.6	1.2
Over 40%	10.2	0.8
Rural—all	100.0	—
0 to 5%	11.7	0.5
6 to 20%	32.3	0.8
21 to 40%	31.5	0.7
Over 40%	24.5	0.8

—Not applicable.
*"School poverty concentration" refers to the percentage of students in the school receiving free and reduced price lunch.

SOURCE: U.S. Department of Education, National Center for Education Statistics, Schools and Staffing Survey, 1987–88.

Table 1.8—Data and standard errors for figure 1.7: Percentage distribution of students by school poverty concentration deciles, by urbanicity: 1987–88

School urbanicity and school poverty concentration*	Percentage distribution of students	Standard error
Urban—all	100.0	—
0%	2.8	0.5
>0–10%	21.6	1.2
11–20%	13.7	0.8
21–30%	12.4	0.8
31–40%	9.4	0.6
41–50%	9.6	0.7
51–60%	6.3	0.4
61–70%	5.9	0.6
71–80%	5.9	0.6
81–90%	5.4	0.5
91–100%	7.0	0.6
Suburban—all	100.0	—
0%	3.5	0.5
>0–10%	50.0	1.3
11–20%	20.8	1.1
21–30%	9.4	0.9
31–40%	6.2	0.6
41–50%	3.3	0.5
51–60%	3.0	0.5
61–70%	1.7	0.4
71–80%	1.1	0.4
81–90%	0.6	0.2
91–100%	0.4	0.2
Rural—all	100.0	—
0%	2.6	0.3
>0–10%	21.9	0.6
11–20%	19.8	0.6
21–30%	18.2	0.6
31–40%	13.2	0.5
41–50%	9.1	0.6
51–60%	5.9	0.4
61–70%	3.7	0.3
71–80%	2.2	0.3
81–90%	2.0	0.3
91–100%	1.4	0.2

— Not applicable.

*"School poverty concentration" refers to the percentage of students in the school receiving free and reduced price lunch.

SOURCE: U.S. Department of Education, National Center for Education Statistics, Schools and Staffing Survey, 1987–88.

Table 1.9—Data and standard errors for figure 1.9: Trends in the racial-ethnic distribution of urban students: 1980 and 1990

Race-ethnicity	1980		1990	
	Percentage	Standard error	Percentage	Standard error
White	48.5	0.3	42.7	0.4
Black	33.0	0.4	31.9	0.4
Hispanic	15.4	0.9	19.4	1.0
Other	3.1	1.4	6.0	1.3

NOTE: White refers to white, non-Hispanic students. Black refers to black, non-Hispanic students.

SOURCE: U.S. Bureau of the Census, Current Population Survey, October 1980 and October 1990.

Table 1.10—Data and standard errors for figures 1.10 and 1.11: Racial-ethnic distribution of students by urbanicity and school poverty concentration: 1987–88

School urbanicity and school poverty concentration[1]	White		Black		Hispanic		Other	
	Per-centage	Standard error	Per-centage	Standard error	Per-centage	Standard error	Per-centage	Standard error
Total[2]	75.2	0.2	13.8	0.2	7.4	0.2	3.5	0.1
0 to 5%	87.7	0.7	5.4	0.5	3.3	0.3	3.5	0.2
6 to 20%	86.4	0.4	6.8	0.2	4.1	0.3	2.5	0.1
21 to 40%	81.6	0.5	9.8	0.4	5.7	0.3	2.6	0.2
Over 40%	50.9	0.8	29.1	0.7	14.6	0.6	5.5	0.4
Urban—all	50.7	0.7	30.0	0.8	14.8	0.5	4.3	0.2
0 to 5%	73.8	2.3	14.4	2.0	6.8	1.0	4.6	0.7
6 to 20%	68.9	1.3	16.0	1.0	9.8	1.0	4.7	0.4
21 to 40%	60.3	1.3	22.9	1.3	11.3	0.9	4.3	0.4
Over 40%	31.3	0.9	44.3	1.0	20.8	1.0	3.9	0.3
Suburban—all	79.4	0.6	10.3	0.4	6.2	0.4	3.8	0.2
0 to 5%	90.0	0.6	4.1	0.3	2.5	0.2	3.6	0.2
6 to 20%	84.5	0.7	7.2	0.5	4.6	0.4	3.4	0.2
21 to 40%	73.1	1.5	13.9	1.2	8.7	1.2	4.4	0.5
Over 40%	42.9	2.6	32.9	2.6	18.4	2.3	5.1	1.4
Rural—all	83.5	0.4	8.4	0.2	4.9	0.2	3.1	0.2
0 to 5%	90.9	0.9	3.3	0.4	2.8	0.7	3.0	0.5
6 to 20%	92.6	0.4	3.8	0.3	2.2	0.2	1.4	0.1
21 to 40%	88.5	0.4	5.7	0.3	3.8	0.3	1.8	0.2
Over 40%	64.6	1.0	18.8	0.7	10.0	0.8	6.5	0.6

[1]"School poverty concentration" refers to the percentage of students in the school receiving free and reduced price lunch.
[2]Percentages may not add to 100 because of missing or miscoded data.

NOTE: White refers to white, non-Hispanic students. Black refers to black, non-Hispanic students.

SOURCE: U.S. Department of Education, National Center for Education Statistics, Schools and Staffing Survey, 1987–88.

Table 1.11—Percentage of students who belong to a racial-ethnic minority, by urbanicity and school poverty concentration: 1987–88

School urbanicity and school poverty concentration*	Percentage	Standard error
Total	24.7	0.2
0 to 5%	12.2	0.6
6 to 20%	13.4	0.4
21 to 40%	18.1	0.5
Over 40%	49.2	0.8
Urban—all	49.0	0.6
0 to 5%	25.7	2.2
6 to 20%	30.5	1.3
21 to 40%	38.5	1.4
Over 40%	69.0	0.9
Suburban—all	20.4	0.6
0 to 5%	10.1	0.6
6 to 20%	15.2	0.7
21 to 40%	27.0	1.6
Over 40%	56.4	2.6
Rural—all	16.4	0.3
0 to 5%	9.1	0.9
6 to 20%	7.4	0.3
21 to 40%	11.3	0.4
Over 40%	35.4	1.0

*"School poverty concentration" refers to the percentage of students in the school receiving free and reduced price lunch.

SOURCE: U.S. Department of Education, National Center for Education Statistics, Schools and Staffing Survey, 1987–88.

Table 1.12—Data and standard errors for figures 1.12–1.14: Selected measures of victimization and health, by urbanicity: 1988 and 1990

Urbanicity	Rate or percentage	Standard error
Total		
Victimization rate, per 1,000 persons ages 12 and over		
Crimes of violence, 1990	29.6	0.7
Crimes of theft, 1990	63.8	1.0
Infant mortality rate, per 1000 live births, 1990	9.2	+/−0.1*
Regular source of health care is a clinic, health center, or emergency room, ages 17 and under, 1988	15.5	0.4
Covered by health insurance/Medicaid, ages 17 and under, 1988	83.1	0.4
Urban		
Victimization rate, per 1,000 persons ages 12 and over		
Crimes of violence	41.3	1.5
Crimes of theft	81.5	2.1
Infant mortality rate, per 1000 live births, 1990	9.6	+/−0.1*
Regular source of health care is a clinic, health center, or emergency room, ages 17 and under, 1988	23.3	0.9
Covered by health insurance/Medicaid, ages 17 and under, 1988	81.5	0.8
Suburban		
Victimization rate, per 1,000 persons ages 12 and over		
Crimes of violence, 1990	25.2	1.0
Crimes of theft, 1990	64.0	1.6
Infant mortality rate, per 1000 live births, 1990	7.8	+/−0.2*
Regular source of health care is a clinic, health center, or emergency room, ages 17 and under, 1988	10.6	0.5
Covered by health insurance/Medicaid, ages 17 and under, 1988	84.9	0.6
Rural		
Victimization rate, per 1,000 persons ages 12 and over		
Crimes of violence, 1990	23.2	1.2
Crimes of theft, 1990	43.4	1.7
Infant mortality rate, per 1000 live births, 1990	9.2	+/−0.2*
Regular source of health care is a clinic, health center, or emergency room, ages 17 and under, 1988	15.5	0.9
Covered by health insurance/Medicaid, ages 17 and under, 1988	81.7	0.9

*Random variation.

SOURCE: U.S. Department of Justice, Bureau of Justice Statistics, *Criminal Victimization in the United States, 1990.* National Center for Health Statistics, *Vital Statistics of the United States, 1990, Vol. 2, Mortality,* Public Health Service, Washington, D.C., Government Printing Office, 1993. U.S. Department of Health and Human Services, National Center for Health Statistics, Vital and Health Statistics, *Advance Data,* No. 188, Oct. 1, 1990.

Table 1.13—Percentage of girls scheduled to be in 12th grade[1] who have or who are expecting a child, by urbanicity: 1992

School urbanicity and school poverty concentration[2]	Percentage	Standard error
Total	13.6	0.7
Urban	16.5	1.4
Suburban	10.3	1.2
Rural	14.2	1.0

[1]Includes girls who dropped out but would have been in 12th grade had they stayed in school and progressed normally.
[2]"School poverty concentration" refers to the percentage of students in the school receiving free and reduced price lunch.

SOURCE: U.S. Department of Education, National Center for Education Statistics, National Education Longitudinal Survey, Third Follow-up, 1992.

Table 2.1—Data and standard errors for figures 2.1–2.3: Average standardized test composite scores[1] of 8th-grade students, by urbanicity and school poverty concentration: 1988

School urbanicity and school poverty concentration[2]	Composite score	Standard error
Total	49.5	0.2
0 to 5%	52.7	0.4
6 to 20%	51.0	0.3
21 to 40%	49.3	0.3
Over 40%	45.3	0.4
Urban—all	47.0	0.4
0 to 5%	50.8	1.4
6 to 20%	50.8	0.6
21 to 40%	47.6	0.6
Over 40%	44.0	0.4
Suburban—all	50.8	0.3
0 to 5%	51.4	0.4
6 to 20%	51.1	0.4
21 to 40%	49.3	0.4
Over 40%	45.6	0.6
Rural—all	49.4	0.3
0 to 5%	49.4	0.3
6 to 20%	50.9	0.5
21 to 40%	49.8	0.4
Over 40%	46.5	0.7

[1]Standardized scores are transformations of the IRT-Estimated Number Correct scores, rescaled to a mean of 50 and standard deviation of 10. The Standardized Test Composite is the equally weighted mean of the standardized reading and mathematics scores, restandardized to a mean of 50 and standard deviation of 10. Because of missing data, the sample analyzed here has a weighted mean of 49.5.

[2]"School poverty concentration" refers to the percentage of students in the school receiving free and reduced price lunch.

NOTE: Totals may include a small proportion of students for whom school urbanicity is unknown.

SOURCE: U.S. Department of Education, National Center for Education Statistics, National Education Longitudinal Study of 1988, Base Year Survey.

Table 2.2—Data and standard errors for figures 2.4–2.6: Average standardized test composite scores[1] of 10th-grade students, by urbanicity and school poverty concentration: 1990

School urbanicity and school poverty concentration[2]	Composite Score	Standard error
Total	50.0	0.2
0 to 5%	52.8	0.3
6 to 20%	50.6	0.3
21 to 40%	48.7	0.3
Over 40%	45.1	0.3
Urban—all	48.8	0.4
0 to 5%	53.0	0.8
6 to 20%	50.3	0.8
21 to 40%	47.7	0.5
Over 40%	44.7	0.6
Suburban—all	51.2	0.2
0 to 5%	53.0	0.3
6 to 20%	50.9	0.4
21 to 40%	47.4	0.9
Over 40%	45.4	0.7
Rural—all	49.3	0.3
0 to 5%	50.9	1.1
6 to 20%	50.3	0.4
21 to 40%	49.6	0.5
Over 40%	45.2	0.5

[1] Standardized scores are transformations of the IRT-Estimated Number Correct scores, rescaled to a mean of 50 and standard deviation of 10. The Standardized Test Composite is the equally weighted mean of the standardized reading and mathematics scores, restandardized to a mean of 50 and standard deviation of 10.
[2] "School poverty concentration" refers to the percentage of students in the school receiving free and reduced price lunch.

NOTE: Totals may include a small proportion of students for whom school urbanicity and/or poverty concentration are unknown.

SOURCE: U.S. Department of Education, National Center for Education Statistics, National Education Longitudinal Study of 1988, First Follow-up Survey, 1990.

Table 2.3—Data and standard errors for figure 2.7: Average number correct in mathematics for 10th-grade students, by urbanicity: 1980 and 1990, and 1980–1990 change

School urbanicity	1980		1990		1980–1990 change	
	Number correct	Standard error	Number correct	Standard error	Number correct	Standard error
Total	33.2	0.2	35.6	0.2	2.4	0.3
Urban	29.7	0.5	33.9	0.5	4.2	0.7
Suburban	33.7	0.3	37.2	0.3	3.5	0.4
Rural	31.7	0.3	34.9	0.3	3.2	0.4

NOTE: Totals may include a small proportion of students for whom school urbanicity is unknown.

SOURCE: U.S. Department of Education, National Center for Education Statistics, High School and Beyond, Base Year Survey, 1980 and the National Education Longitudinal Study, First Follow-up Survey, 1990.

Table 2.4—Data and standard errors for figures 2.8–2.10: Percentage graduating on time among the sophomore class of 1980, by urbanicity and percent disadvantaged in school

School urbanicity and percent disadvantaged*	Percentage	Standard error
Total	81.8	0.6
0 to 5%	85.5	0.9
6 to 20%	81.6	1.0
21 to 40%	79.7	1.7
Over 40%	72.7	2.3
Urban—all	73.7	1.7
0 to 5%	80.3	3.3
6 to 20%	75.8	2.6
21 to 40%	71.6	3.7
Over 40%	66.1	3.9
Suburban—all	84.3	0.9
0 to 5%	87.1	1.2
6 to 20%	82.6	1.4
21 to 40%	81.8	2.6
Over 40%	74.0	4.1
Rural—all	83.3	0.9
0 to 5%	84.1	1.5
6 to 20%	83.4	1.5
21 to 40%	84.1	1.8
Over 40%	80.1	2.8

*"Percent disadvantaged" refers to the percentage of students identified as disadvantaged by school administrators.

NOTE: Totals may include a small proportion of students for whom school urbanicity and/or percent disadvantaged are unknown.

SOURCE: U.S. Department of Education, National Center for Education Statistics, High School and Beyond Study, Third Follow-up, Spring 1986.

Table 2.5—Data and standard errors for figures 2.11–2.13: Percentage of young adults completing a postsecondary degree by 1990, by high school urbanicity and percent disadvantaged in high school

School urbanicity and percent disadvantaged*	Percentage	Standard error
Total	26.3	1.2
0 to 5%	36.2	2.1
6 to 20%	24.7	1.4
21 to 40%	19.5	2.0
Over 40%	16.8	2.3
Urban—all	23.2	2.2
0 to 5%	26.6	6.7
6 to 20%	25.5	3.8
21 to 40%	23.3	4.3
Over 40%	14.5	2.2
Suburban—all	30.2	1.8
0 to 5%	39.5	2.6
6 to 20%	24.9	2.1
21 to 40%	15.6	3.2
Over 40%	17.1	4.1
Rural—all	21.7	1.7
0 to 5%	24.1	4.7
6 to 20%	24.0	2.2
21 to 40%	20.1	2.7
Over 40%	17.7	3.7

*"Percent disadvantaged" refers to the percentage of students identified as disadvantaged by school administrators.

NOTE: Totals may include a small proportion of students for whom school urbanicity and/or percent disadvantaged are unknown.

SOURCE: U.S. Department of Labor, National Longitudinal Survey of Youth, 1990.

Table 2.6—Data and standard errors for figures 2.14–2.16: Percentage of young adults employed or attending school full time 4 years after high school, by high school urbanicity and percent disadvantaged in high school: 1986

School urbanicity and percent disadvantaged*	Percentage	Standard error
Total	60.9	0.7
0 to5%	64.3	1.2
6 to 20%	62.1	1.1
21 to 40%	59.8	1.8
Over 40%	47.6	2.5
Urban—all	56.6	1.5
0 to 5%	61.3	3.6
6 to 20%	60.6	2.8
21 to 40%	56.9	3.2
Over 40%	46.9	3.2
Suburban—all	64.3	0.9
0 to 5%	66.6	1.4
6 to 20%	64.8	1.6
21 to 40%	57.1	3.9
Over 40%	43.7	2.9
Rural—all	58.9	1.3
0 to 5%	60.5	2.5
6 to 20%	59.0	1.8
21 to 40%	63.2	2.6
Over 40%	50.5	5.3

*"Percent disadvantaged" refers to the percentage of students identified as disadvantaged by school administrators.

NOTE: Totals may include a small proportion of students for whom school urbanicity and/or percent disadvantaged are unknown.

SOURCE: U.S. Department of Education, National Center for Education Statistics, High School and Beyond Study, Third Follow-up Survey, 1986.

Table 2.7—Data and standard errors for figures 2.17–2.19: Percentage of young adults employed or attending school full time, by high school urbanicity and percent disadvantaged in high school: 1990

School urbanicity and percent disadvantaged*	Percentage	Standard error
Total	84.2	0.7
0 to 5%	87.5	1.1
6 to 20%	86.0	1.0
21 to 40%	80.9	1.6
Over 40%	76.1	1.5
Urban—all	81.5	1.4
0 to 5%	87.1	3.0
6 to 20%	85.2	1.8
21 to 40%	79.0	3.0
Over 40%	72.7	2.5
Suburban—all	86.4	0.7
0 to 5%	88.2	1.3
6 to 20%	86.0	1.3
21 to 40%	83.0	2.5
Over 40%	80.8	4.4
Rural—all	82.3	1.3
0 to 5%	84.3	2.6
6 to 20%	86.3	2.2
21 to 40%	80.5	2.6
Over 40%	76.0	1.5

*"Percent disadvantaged" refers to the percentage of students identified as disadvantaged by school administrators.

NOTE: Totals may include a small proportion of students for whom school urbanicity and/or percent disadvantaged are unknown.

SOURCE: U.S. Department of Labor, National Longitudinal Survey of Youth, 1990.

Table 2.8—Data and standard errors for figures 2.20–2.22: Percentage of young adults unemployed, by high school urbanicity and percent disadvantaged in high school: 1990

School urbanicity and percent disadvantaged*	Percentage	Standard error
Total	3.6	0.3
0 to 5%	2.1	0.4
6 to 20%	3.4	0.5
21 to 40%	3.8	0.8
Over 40%	7.6	1.2
Urban—all	5.8	0.8
0 to 5%	3.3	1.9
6 to 20%	4.5	1.1
21 to 40%	5.2	1.6
Over 40%	10.8	1.7
Suburban—all	2.6	0.4
0 to 5%	1.9	0.5
6 to 20%	3.2	0.7
21 to 40%	2.2	1.0
Over 40%	5.1	1.7
Rural—all	4.0	0.6
0 to 5%	2.3	1.0
6 to 20%	2.8	1.0
21 to 40%	4.1	1.2
Over 40%	6.9	1.9

*"Percent disadvantaged" refers to the percentage of students identified as disadvantaged by school administrators.

NOTE: Totals may include a small proportion of students for whom school urbanicity and/or percent disadvantaged are unknown.

SOURCE: U.S. Department of Labor, National Longitudinal Survey of Youth, 1990.

Table 2.9—Data and standard errors for figures 2.23–2.25: Percentage of young adults living in poverty, by high school urbanicity and percent disadvantaged in high school: 1990

School urbanicity and percent disadvantaged*	Percentage	Standard error
Total	8.3	0.5
0 to 5%	4.6	0.6
6 to 20%	8.0	0.7
21 to 40%	10.1	1.3
Over 40%	14.7	2.1
Urban—all	14.5	1.4
0 to 5%	7.9	2.3
6 to 20%	11.3	1.8
21 to 40%	15.6	3.0
Over 40%	25.5	3.0
Suburban—all	6.0	0.5
0 to 5%	3.7	0.8
6 to 20%	6.5	0.9
21 to 40%	9.3	2.4
Over 40%	13.7	3.5
Rural—all	8.6	0.6
0 to 5%	7.6	2.1
6 to 20%	8.4	1.2
21 to 40%	8.2	1.5
Over 40%	10.2	1.8

*"Percent disadvantaged" refers to the percentage of students identified as disadvantaged by school administrators.

NOTE: Totals may include a small proportion of students for whom school urbanicity and/or percent disadvantaged are unknown.

SOURCE: U.S. Department of Labor, National Longitudinal Survey of Youth, 1990.

Table 3.1—Data and standard errors for figures 3.1–3.3: Percentage of 8th-grade students living in a two-parent family, by urbanicity and school poverty concentration: 1988

School urbanicity and school poverty concentration*	Percentage	Standard error
Total	77.5	0.5
0 to 5%	85.0	0.8
6 to 20%	79.5	0.8
21 to 40%	76.6	0.9
Over 40%	71.4	1.2
Urban—all	67.7	1.2
0 to 5%	80.7	3.2
6 to 20%	71.8	2.0
21 to 40%	68.2	2.9
Over 40%	63.6	1.8
Suburban—all	80.7	0.6
0 to 5%	85.3	0.9
6 to 20%	81.2	1.0
21 to 40%	75.9	1.4
Over 40%	77.4	1.7
Rural—all	79.6	0.7
0 to 5%	85.7	1.4
6 to 20%	80.9	1.3
21 to 40%	79.7	1.0
Over 40%	75.8	1.8

*"School poverty concentration" refers to the percentage of students in the school receiving free and reduced price lunch.

NOTE: Totals may include a small proportion of students for whom school urbanicity and/or poverty concentration are unknown.

SOURCE: U.S. Department of Education, National Center for Education Statistics, National Education Longitudinal Study of 1988, Base Year Survey.

Table 3.2—Data and standard errors for figures 3.4–3.6: Percentage of 8th-grade students living in a one-parent family with parent working full time, by urbanicity and school poverty concentration: 1988

School urbanicity and school poverty concentration*	Percentage	Standard error
Total	65.4	1.0
0 to 5%	74.4	2.6
6 to 20%	74.0	1.6
21 to 40%	65.2	1.9
Over 40%	55.0	2.0
Urban—all	59.4	1.9
0 to 5%	60.6	8.5
6 to 20%	72.7	3.0
21 to 40%	64.4	4.3
Over 40%	52.6	2.5
Suburban—all	71.3	1.6
0 to 5%	75.5	2.8
6 to 20%	78.1	2.3
21 to 40%	68.1	2.9
Over 40%	51.7	4.6
Rural—all	64.6	1.9
0 to 5%	76.7	6.3
6 to 20%	67.6	3.3
21 to 40%	63.3	2.9
Over 40%	61.3	4.2

*"School poverty concentration" refers to the percentage of students in the school receiving free and reduced price lunch.

NOTE: Totals may include a small proportion of students for whom school urbanicity and/or poverty concentration are unknown.

SOURCE: U.S. Department of Education, National Center for Education Statistics, National Education Longitudinal Study of 1988, Base Year Survey.

Table 3.3—Data and standard errors for figures 3.7–3.9: Percentage of 8th-grade students living in a two-parent family with at least one parent working full time, by urbanicity and school poverty concentration: 1988

School urbanicity and school poverty concentration*	Percentage	Standard error
Total	93.5	0.3
0 to 5%	97.0	0.4
6 to 20%	95.5	0.4
21 to 40%	93.2	0.5
Over 40%	87.9	0.7
Urban—all	91.7	0.6
0 to 5%	94.0	1.7
6 to 20%	95.0	0.7
21 to 40%	93.5	1.2
Over 40%	88.1	1.1
Suburban—all	95.4	0.4
0 to 5%	98.1	0.4
6 to 20%	96.0	0.6
21 to 40%	94.5	0.7
Over 40%	90.6	1.4
Rural—all	91.7	0.5
0 to 5%	95.0	0.9
6 to 20%	95.0	0.8
21 to 40%	92.3	0.8
Over 40%	86.1	1.3

*"School poverty concentration" refers to the percentage of students in the school receiving free and reduced price lunch.

NOTE: Totals may include a small proportion of students for whom school urbanicity and/or poverty concentration are unknown.

SOURCE: U.S. Department of Education, National Center for Education Statistics, National Education Longitudinal Study of 1988, Base Year Survey.

Table 3.4—Data and standard errors for figures 3.10–3.12: Percentage of 8th-grade students with a parent in the household who had completed 4 years of college, by urbanicity and school poverty concentration: 1988

School urbanicity and school poverty concentration*	Percentage	Standard error
Total	23.7	0.7
0 to 5%	41.5	2.2
6 to 20%	26.4	1.1
21 to 40%	20.1	0.9
Over 40%	11.4	0.8
Urban—all	20.4	1.2
0 to 5%	32.5	6.4
6 to 20%	31.0	2.4
21 to 40%	23.1	2.4
Over 40%	11.9	1.3
Suburban—all	29.5	1.2
0 to 5%	46.4	2.5
6 to 20%	28.5	1.6
21 to 40%	19.2	1.7
Over 40%	10.4	1.4
Rural—all	18.6	0.9
0 to 5%	28.6	4.9
6 to 20%	19.8	1.5
21 to 40%	19.8	1.2
Over 40%	11.6	1.2

*"School poverty concentration" refers to the percentage of students in the school receiving free and reduced price lunch.

NOTE: Totals may include a small proportion of students for whom school urbanicity and/or poverty concentration are unknown.

SOURCE: U.S. Department of Education, National Center for Education Statistics, National Education Longitudinal Study of 1988, Base Year Survey.

Table 3.5—Data and standard errors for figures 3.13–3.15: Percentage of 8th-grade students who have changed schools more than once since first grade, by urbanicity and school poverty concentration: 1988

School urbanicity and school poverty concentration*	Percentage	Standard error
Total	34.2	0.6
0 to 5%	30.5	1.3
6 to 20%	32.7	0.9
21 to 40%	34.6	1.2
Over 40%	37.5	1.3
Urban—all	45.6	1.1
0 to 5%	38.8	2.9
6 to 20%	45.0	2.3
21 to 40%	47.2	2.3
Over 40%	46.1	1.8
Suburban—all	33.6	0.8
0 to 5%	29.6	1.5
6 to 20%	32.2	1.2
21 to 40%	38.7	2.1
Over 40%	37.3	2.5
Rural—all	28.0	0.9
0 to 5%	29.8	3.2
6 to 20%	26.2	1.6
21 to 40%	28.1	1.4
Over 40%	28.9	1.8

*"School poverty concentration" refers to the percentage of students in the school receiving free and reduced price lunch.

NOTE: Totals may include a small proportion of students for whom school urbanicity and/or poverty concentration are unknown.

SOURCE: U.S. Department of Education, National Center for Education Statistics, National Education Longitudinal Study of 1988, Base Year Survey.

Table 3.6—Data and standard errors for figures 3.16–3.18: Percentage of 8th-grade students whose parents expect them to complete 4 years of college, by urbanicity and school poverty concentration: 1988

School urbanicity and school poverty concentration*	Percentage	Standard error
Total	55.3	0.7
0 to 5%	66.2	1.9
6 to 20%	57.8	1.2
21 to 40%	51.3	1.0
Over 40%	48.5	1.2
Urban—all	55.7	1.3
0 to 5%	61.0	7.8
6 to 20%	63.2	2.4
21 to 40%	55.2	1.8
Over 40%	51.3	1.7
Suburban—all	60.2	1.1
0 to 5%	71.0	1.9
6 to 20%	60.6	1.7
21 to 40%	51.7	2.0
Over 40%	47.4	2.3
Rural—all	49.0	1.0
0 to 5%	52.5	4.3
6 to 20%	49.0	1.7
21 to 40%	49.8	1.5
Over 40%	46.2	2.1

*"School poverty concentration" refers to the percentage of students in the school receiving free and reduced price lunch.

NOTE: Totals may include a small proportion of students for whom school urbanicity and/or poverty concentration are unknown.

SOURCE: U.S. Department of Education, National Center for Education Statistics, National Education Longitudinal Study of 1988, Base Year Survey.

Table 3.7—Data and standard errors for figures 3.19–3.21: Percentage of 8th-grade students whose parents rarely talk to them about school, by urbanicity and school poverty concentration: 1988

School urbanicity and school poverty concentration*	Percentage	Standard error
Total	21.7	0.4
0 to 5%	16.6	0.8
6 to 20%	20.0	0.6
21 to 40%	21.4	0.6
Over 40%	27.6	0.9
Urban—all	24.9	0.9
0 to 5%	16.7	1.9
6 to 20%	21.3	1.6
21 to 40%	25.9	1.4
Over 40%	27.6	1.5
Suburban—all	19.6	0.6
0 to 5%	16.0	0.9
6 to 20%	18.1	0.8
21 to 40%	21.1	1.1
Over 40%	28.4	1.9
Rural—all	22.5	0.6
0 to 5%	18.6	1.7
6 to 20%	22.5	1.1
21 to 40%	20.2	0.9
Over 40%	27.1	1.3

*"School poverty concentration" refers to the percentage of students in the school receiving free and reduced price lunch.

NOTE: Totals may include a small proportion of students for whom school urbanicity and/or poverty concentration are unknown.

SOURCE: U.S. Department of Education, National Center for Education Statistics, National Education Longitudinal Study of 1988, Base Year Survey.

Table 3.8—Data and standard errors for figures 3.22–3.24: Average number of sports-related activities offered by the schools attended by 10th-grade students, by urbanicity and school poverty concentration: 1990

School urbanicity and school poverty concentration*	Number of Activities	Standard error
Total	7.3	0.0
0 to 5%	7.8	0.1
6 to 20%	7.4	0.1
21 to 40%	6.9	0.1
Over 40%	6.7	0.1
Urban—all	7.4	0.1
0 to 5%	7.3	0.4
6 to 20%	7.7	0.1
21 to 40%	7.4	0.1
Over 40%	6.9	0.2
Suburban—all	7.7	0.1
0 to 5%	7.9	0.1
6 to 20%	7.7	0.1
21 to 40%	7.1	0.3
Over 40%	7.1	0.2
Rural—all	6.7	0.1
0 to 5%	7.4	0.2
6 to 20%	7.0	0.2
21 to 40%	6.6	0.1
Over 40%	6.2	0.2

*"School poverty concentration" refers to the percentage of students in the school receiving free and reduced price lunch.

NOTE: Totals may include a small proportion of students for whom school urbanicity and/or poverty concentration are unknown.

SOURCE: U.S. Department of Education, National Center for Education Statistics, National Education Longitudinal Study of 1988, First Follow-up Survey.

Table 3.9—Data and standard errors for figures 3.25–3.27: Percentage of 10th-grade students who participated in school sports-related activities, by urbanicity and school poverty concentration: 1990

School urbanicity and school poverty concentration*	Percentage	Standard error
Total	51.6	0.7
0 to 5%	55.5	1.2
6 to 20%	52.1	1.1
21 to 40%	50.5	1.6
Over 40%	43.5	1.8
Urban—all	45.0	1.4
0 to 5%	46.8	3.3
6 to 20%	45.2	2.5
21 to 40%	45.4	2.7
Over 40%	40.1	3.3
Suburban—all	54.4	0.9
0 to 5%	57.1	1.4
6 to 20%	53.3	1.6
21 to 40%	45.1	2.9
Over 40%	46.4	3.3
Rural—all	52.7	1.2
0 to 5%	54.0	3.5
6 to 20%	54.4	1.9
21 to 40%	55.1	2.4
Over 40%	44.7	2.7

*"School poverty concentration" refers to the percentage of students in the school receiving free and reduced price lunch.

NOTE: Totals may include a small proportion of students for whom school urbanicity and/or poverty concentration are unknown.

SOURCE: U.S. Department of Education, National Center for Education Statistics, National Education Longitudinal Study of 1988, First Follow-up Survey.

Table 3.10—Data and standard errors for figures 3.28–3.30: Percentage of 10th-grade students who worked 11 or more hours per week, by urbanicity and school poverty concentration: 1990

School urbanicity and school poverty concentration*	Percentage	Standard error
Total	18.4	0.5
0 to 5%	20.0	1.1
6 to 20%	20.1	0.9
21 to 40%	15.8	1.0
Over 40%	14.4	1.3
Urban—all	18.3	1.1
0 to 5%	14.5	3.3
6 to 20%	21.7	2.2
21 to 40%	17.1	1.7
Over 40%	17.8	2.4
Suburban—all	19.9	0.8
0 to 5%	20.4	1.2
6 to 20%	20.7	1.5
21 to 40%	18.8	2.6
Over 40%	14.4	2.3
Rural—all	16.8	0.8
0 to 5%	22.2	3.1
6 to 20%	18.8	1.2
21 to 40%	14.3	1.3
Over 40%	11.5	1.8

*"School poverty concentration" refers to the percentage of students in the school receiving free and reduced price lunch.

NOTE: Totals may include a small proportion of students for whom school urbanicity and/or poverty concentration are unknown.

SOURCE: U.S. Department of Education, National Center for Education Statistics, National Education Longitudinal Study of 1988, First Follow-up Survey.

Table 4.1—Data and standard errors for figures 4.1–4.3: Percentage of teachers who agreed that necessary materials are available in their school, by urbanicity and school poverty concentration: 1987–88

School urbanicity and school poverty concentration*	Percentage	Standard error
Total	76.3	0.3
0 to 5%	80.0	0.8
6 to 20%	77.7	0.6
21 to 40%	76.6	0.7
Over 40%	71.5	0.6
Urban—all	70.1	0.7
0 to 5%	74.9	1.9
6 to 20%	72.7	1.4
21 to 40%	71.1	1.1
Over 40%	66.9	0.8
Suburban—all	79.3	0.7
0 to 5%	82.9	1.0
6 to 20%	79.9	1.1
21 to 40%	73.8	1.9
Over 40%	70.7	2.5
Rural—all	78.0	0.5
0 to 5%	78.5	1.4
6 to 20%	78.5	0.8
21 to 40%	79.1	0.9
Over 40%	75.8	0.9

*"School poverty concentration" refers to the percentage of students in the school receiving free and reduced price lunch.

NOTE: Totals may include a small proportion of students for whom school urbanicity and/or poverty concentration are unknown.

SOURCE: U.S. Department of Education, National Center for Education Statistics, Schools and Staffing Survey, 1987–88, Teacher File.

Table 4.2—Data and standard errors for figures 4.4–4.6: Average years of teaching experience and average academic base year teacher salary, by urbanicity and school poverty concentration: 1987–88

School urbanicity and school poverty concentration*	Teacher experience		Teacher salary	
	Average years	Standard error	Average dollars	Standard error
Total	14.6	0.0	$25,507	$ 72.4
0 to 5%	15.6	0.1	28,841	141.5
6 to 20%	14.7	0.1	25,896	147.7
21 to 40%	14.4	0.1	24,085	112.2
Over 40%	13.8	0.1	24,179	131.2
Urban—all	15.0	0.1	27,372	150.8
0 to 5%	15.8	0.3	29,087	394.6
6 to 20%	15.0	0.2	27,565	304.6
21 to 40%	15.5	0.2	27,403	241.4
Over 40%	14.5	0.2	26,772	253.4
Suburban—all	15.4	0.1	28,528	185.6
0 to 5%	16.3	0.2	30,470	256.9
6 to 20%	15.3	0.2	27,813	357.4
21 to 40%	14.6	0.3	26,759	379.4
Over 40%	13.7	0.4	26,467	535.1
Rural—all	14.0	0.1	23,293	93.3
0 to 5%	14.6	0.2	26,530	284.9
6 to 20%	14.3	0.1	24,270	154.4
21 to 40%	13.9	0.1	22,426	122.3
Over 40%	13.3	0.1	21,471	143.4

*"School poverty concentration" refers to the percentage of students in the school receiving free and reduced price lunch.

NOTE: Totals may include a small proportion of students for whom school urbanicity and/or poverty concentration are unknown.

SOURCE: U.S. Department of Education, National Center for Education Statistics, Schools and Staffing Survey, 1987–88, Teacher File.

Table 4.3—Data and standard errors for figures 4.7–4.9: Percentage of teachers with 3 years or less teaching experience, by urbanicity and school poverty concentration: 1987–88

School urbanicity and school poverty concentration*	Percentage	Standard error
Total	9.8	0.2
0 to 5%	7.1	0.3
6 to 20%	8.9	0.3
21 to 40%	10.4	0.3
Over 40%	12.2	0.3
Urban—all	9.6	0.4
0 to 5%	6.2	0.8
6 to 20%	8.4	0.7
21 to 40%	9.6	0.7
Over 40%	11.5	0.7
Suburban—all	8.1	0.4
0 to 5%	6.1	0.5
6 to 20%	8.5	0.7
21 to 40%	10.2	1.1
Over 40%	11.3	1.5
Rural—all	10.6	0.3
0 to 5%	8.9	0.5
6 to 20%	9.4	0.4
21 to 40%	10.7	0.4
Over 40%	13.0	0.5

*"School poverty concentration" refers to the percentage of students in the school receiving free and reduced price lunch.

NOTE: Totals may include a small proportion of students for whom school urbanicity and/or poverty concentration are unknown.

SOURCE: U.S. Department of Education, National Center for Education Statistics, Schools and Staffing Survey, 1987–88, Teacher File.

Table 4.4—Data and standard errors for figures 4.10–4.12: Percentage of principals who report difficulty hiring teachers, by urbanicity and school poverty concentration: 1987–88

School urbanicity and school poverty concentration*	Percentage	Standard error
Total	15.7	0.4
0 to 5%	11.4	1.2
6 to 20%	11.6	0.9
21 to 40%	13.1	0.8
Over 40%	24.0	0.9
Urban—all	23.2	1.1
0 to 5%	11.2	2.5
6 to 20%	15.2	2.0
21 to 40%	19.2	2.1
Over 40%	31.1	1.6
Suburban—all	13.2	0.9
0 to 5%	12.0	1.8
6 to 20%	10.9	1.3
21 to 40%	12.9	2.5
Over 40%	25.7	4.0
Rural—all	13.4	0.7
0 to 5%	10.9	1.5
6 to 20%	10.8	1.1
21 to 40%	11.4	0.9
Over 40%	19.1	1.5

*"School poverty concentration" refers to the percentage of students in the school receiving free and reduced price lunch.

NOTE: Totals may include a small proportion of students for whom school urbanicity and/or poverty concentration are unknown.

SOURCE: U.S. Department of Education, National Center for Education Statistics, Schools and Staffing Survey, 1987–88, Administrator File.

Table 4.5—Data and standard errors for figures 4.13–4.15: Percentage of teachers who are minority, by urbanicity and school poverty concentration: 1987–88

School urbanicity and school poverty concentration*	Percentage	Standard error
Total	13.3	0.4
0 to 5%	5.9	0.6
6 to 20%	7.0	0.4
21 to 40%	9.2	0.6
Over 40%	26.8	1.0
Urban—all	28.5	1.4
0 to 5%	16.8	2.8
6 to 20%	17.8	1.5
21 to 40%	23.4	2.7
Over 40%	38.7	2.2
Suburban—all	10.1	0.7
0 to 5%	3.7	0.3
6 to 20%	6.7	0.6
21 to 40%	13.3	1.5
Over 40%	28.5	2.5
Rural—all	8.1	0.3
0 to 5%	3.7	0.7
6 to 20%	3.7	0.4
21 to 40%	4.8	0.3
Over 40%	18.7	0.7

*"School poverty concentration" refers to the percentage of students in the school receiving free and reduced price lunch.

NOTE: Totals may include a small proportion of students for whom school urbanicity and/or poverty concentration are unknown.

SOURCE: U.S. Department of Education, National Center for Education Statistics, Schools and Staffing Survey, 1987–88, Teacher File.

Table 4.6—Data and standard errors for figures 4.16–4.18: Percentage of secondary school teachers who are male, by urbanicity and school poverty concentration: 1987–88

School urbanicity and school poverty concentration*	Percentage	Standard error
Total	47.9	0.4
0 to 5%	50.7	0.9
6 to 20%	48.4	0.6
21 to 40%	45.7	0.8
Over 40%	43.4	1.2
Urban—all	48.4	0.9
0 to 5%	54.0	2.4
6 to 20%	47.3	1.5
21 to 40%	46.0	1.8
Over 40%	48.5	1.9
Suburban—all	48.8	0.9
0 to 5%	50.9	1.2
6 to 20%	47.2	1.4
21 to 40%	45.3	3.1
Over 40%	41.5	4.7
Rural—all	47.1	0.7
0 to 5%	48.8	1.7
6 to 20%	49.2	0.9
21 to 40%	45.7	1.1
Over 40%	39.3	1.8

*"School poverty concentration" refers to the percentage of students in the school receiving free and reduced price lunch.

NOTE: Totals may include a small proportion of students for whom school urbanicity and/or poverty concentration are unknown.

SOURCE: U.S. Department of Education, National Center for Education Statistics, Schools and Staffing Survey, 1987–88, Teacher File.

Table 4.7—Data and standard errors for figures 4.19–4.21: Percentage of teachers who think that teachers have a great deal of influence on establishing curriculum, by urbanicity and school poverty concentration: 1987–88

School urbanicity and school poverty concentration*	Percentage	Standard error
Total	34.9	0.4
0 to 5%	40.5	0.8
6 to 20%	37.5	0.6
21 to 40%	35.1	0.8
Over 40%	27.6	0.6
Urban—all	26.0	0.7
0 to 5%	32.6	1.7
6 to 20%	30.1	1.4
21 to 40%	25.3	1.2
Over 40%	21.9	1.0
Suburban—all	35.6	0.7
0 to 5%	41.0	1.2
6 to 20%	35.5	1.1
21 to 40%	28.4	2.4
Over 40%	25.9	2.0
Rural—all	39.3	0.5
0 to 5%	43.7	1.4
6 to 20%	41.4	1.0
21 to 40%	39.7	0.9
Over 40%	33.0	0.9

*"School poverty concentration" refers to the percentage of students in the school receiving free and reduced price lunch.

NOTE: Totals may include a small proportion of students for whom school urbanicity and/or poverty concentration are unknown.

SOURCE: U.S. Department of Education, National Center for Education Statistics, Schools and Staffing Survey, 1987–88, Teacher File.

Table 4.8—Data and standard errors for figures 4.22–4.24: Percentage of teachers who consider teacher absenteeism a problem in their school, by urbanicity and school poverty concentration: 1987–88

School urbanicity and school poverty concentration*	Percentage	Standard error
Total	23.4	0.4
0 to 5%	20.8	0.9
6 to 20%	22.0	0.7
21 to 40%	25.0	0.9
Over 40%	31.1	1.4
Urban—all	30.6	0.7
0 to 5%	24.3	2.3
6 to 20%	29.5	2.0
21 to 40%	31.7	1.7
Over 40%	37.0	2.4
Suburban—all	23.4	0.9
0 to 5%	20.7	1.1
6 to 20%	24.3	1.3
21 to 40%	30.8	3.5
Over 40%	35.3	4.3
Rural—all	19.6	0.6
0 to 5%	19.1	1.5
6 to 20%	18.2	1.0
21 to 40%	20.4	1.0
Over 40%	25.5	1.8

*"School poverty concentration" refers to the percentage of students in the school receiving free and reduced price lunch.

NOTE: Totals may include a small proportion of students for whom school urbanicity and/or poverty concentration are unknown.

SOURCE: U.S. Department of Education, National Center for Education Statistics, Schools and Staffing Survey, 1987–88, Teacher File.

Table 4.9—Data and standard errors for figures 4.25–4.27: Percentage of 8th-grade students who attended preschool, by urbanicity and school poverty concentration: 1988

School urbanicity and school poverty concentration*	Percentage	Standard error
Total	51.1	0.8
0 to 5%	64.3	1.9
6 to 20%	53.9	1.3
21 to 40%	46.9	1.3
Over 40%	39.8	1.5
Urban—all	52.7	1.4
0 to 5%	56.6	7.1
6 to 20%	59.4	2.1
21 to 40%	57.9	2.2
Over 40%	44.9	2.2
Suburban—all	58.3	1.2
0 to 5%	69.6	1.9
6 to 20%	56.3	1.9
21 to 40%	53.5	2.1
Over 40%	39.9	3.7
Rural—all	40.3	1.3
0 to 5%	48.1	4.6
6 to 20%	45.6	2.5
21 to 40%	38.1	1.9
Over 40%	34.0	2.1

*"School poverty concentration" refers to the percentage of students in the school receiving free and reduced price lunch.

NOTE: Totals may include a small proportion of students for whom school urbanicity and/or poverty concentration are unknown.

SOURCE: U.S. Department of Education, National Center for Education Statistics, National Education Longitudinal Study of 1988, Base Year Parent File.

Table 4.10—Data and standard errors for figures 4.28–4.30: Percentage of elementary schools that offer gifted and talented programs, by urbanicity and school poverty concentration: 1987–88

School urbanicity and school poverty concentration*	Percentage	Standard error
Total	76.7	0.7
0 to 5%	82.9	2.1
6 to 20%	81.1	1.2
21 to 40%	78.3	1.2
Over 40%	69.5	1.1
Urban—all	73.2	1.2
0 to 5%	80.2	3.3
6 to 20%	82.3	2.6
21 to 40%	79.9	3.1
Over 40%	66.1	1.3
Suburban—all	84.1	1.2
0 to 5%	93.5	2.2
6 to 20%	84.2	2.0
21 to 40%	81.0	2.3
Over 40%	70.6	3.8
Rural—all	75.5	1.0
0 to 5%	73.6	4.1
6 to 20%	79.1	1.6
21 to 40%	77.4	1.5
Over 40%	71.8	1.7

*"School poverty concentration" refers to the percentage of students in the school receiving free and reduced price lunch.

NOTE: Totals may include a small proportion of students for whom school urbanicity and/or poverty concentration are unknown.

SOURCE: U.S. Department of Education, National Center for Education Statistics, Schools and Staffing Survey, 1987–88, School File.

Table 4.11—Data and standard errors for figures 4.31–4.32: Percentage of graduating high school seniors who took 6 or more credits in vocational education, by urbanicity and school poverty concentration: 1990

School urbanicity and school poverty concentration*	Percentage	Standard error
Total	18.6	1.3
Urbanicity		
Urban	19.9	3.4
Suburban	13.6	2.0
Rural	24.7	2.3
School poverty concentration		
0 to 5%	15.2	2.8
6 to 20%	18.0	2.3
21 to 40%	29.4	3.1
Over 40%	24.8	10.6

*"School poverty concentration" refers to the percentage of students in the school receiving free and reduced price lunch.

NOTE: Totals may include a small proportion of students for whom school urbanicity and/or poverty concentration are unknown.

SOURCE: U.S. Department of Education, National Center for Education Statistics, National Assessment of Educational Progress, 1990 High School Transcript Study.

Table 4.12—Data and standard errors for figures 4.33–4.34: Percentage of graduating high school seniors who took geometry, by urbanicity and school poverty concentration: 1990

School urbanicity and school poverty concentration*	Percentage	Standard error
Total	67.8	2.1
Urbanicity		
Urban	57.4	4.7
Suburban	72.8	2.4
Rural	66.2	4.5
School poverty concentration		
0 to 5%	74.4	3.2
6 to 20%	64.7	4.7
21 to 40%	57.4	8.2
Over 40%	60.4	6.3

*"School poverty concentration" refers to the percentage of students in the school receiving free and reduced price lunch.

NOTE: Totals may include a small proportion of students for whom school urbanicity and/or poverty concentration are unknown.

SOURCE: U.S. Department of Education, National Center for Education Statistics, National Assessment of Educational Progress, 1990 High School Transcript Study.

Table 4.13—Data and standard errors for figures 4.35–4.37: Percentage of 10th-grade students who watch 3 or more hours of television on weekdays, by urbanicity and school poverty concentration: 1990

School urbanicity and school poverty concentration*	Percentage	Standard error
Total	33.2	0.6
0 to 5%	26.0	1.1
6 to 20%	33.2	1.1
21 to 40%	36.8	1.5
Over 40%	43.2	1.9
Urban—all	36.7	1.6
0 to 5%	22.4	3.3
6 to 20%	35.8	2.6
21 to 40%	37.4	2.4
Over 40%	48.5	3.4
Suburban—all	29.6	0.9
0 to 5%	26.0	1.2
6 to 20%	31.3	1.5
21 to 40%	37.1	3.8
Over 40%	38.7	3.5
Rural—all	35.4	1.1
0 to 5%	30.1	3.1
6 to 20%	34.0	1.9
21 to 40%	36.4	2.2
Over 40%	41.4	2.8

*"School poverty concentration" refers to the percentage of students in the school receiving free and reduced price lunch.

NOTE: Totals may include a small proportion of students for whom school urbanicity and/or poverty concentration are unknown.

SOURCE: U.S. Department of Education, National Center for Education Statistics, National Education Longitudinal Study of 1988, First Follow-up Student File.

Table 4.14—Data and standard errors for figures 4.38–4.40: Average number of hours 10th-grade students spend on homework per week, by urbanicity and school poverty concentration: 1990

School urbanicity and school poverty concentration*	Average number of hours	Standard error
Total	7.4	0.1
0 to 5%	7.8	0.2
6 to 20%	7.4	0.1
21 to 40%	7.0	0.2
Over 40%	6.5	0.2
Urban—all	7.3	0.2
0 to 5%	8.7	0.6
6 to 20%	7.6	0.3
21 to 40%	6.6	0.3
Over 40%	6.5	0.4
Suburban—all	7.4	0.1
0 to 5%	7.7	0.2
6 to 20%	7.4	0.2
21 to 40%	6.1	0.4
Over 40%	6.5	0.3
Rural—all	7.4	0.1
0 to 5%	8.1	0.5
6 to 20%	7.4	0.2
21 to 40%	7.6	0.2
Over 40%	6.5	0.3

*"School poverty concentration" refers to the percentage of students in the school receiving free and reduced price lunch.

NOTE: Totals may include a small proportion of students for whom school urbanicity and/or poverty concentration are unknown.

SOURCE: U.S. Department of Education, National Center for Education Statistics, National Education Longitudinal Study of 1988, First Follow-up Student File.

Table 4.15—Data and standard errors for figures 4.41–4.43: Percentage of secondary teachers who believe that student absenteeism is a problem in their school, by urbanicity and school poverty concentration: 1987–88

School urbanicity and school poverty concentration*	Percentage	Standard error
Total	68.1	0.4
0 to 5%	64.6	1.2
6 to 20%	67.5	1.0
21 to 40%	70.2	0.9
Over 40%	74.2	1.0
Urban—all	78.2	0.8
0 to 5%	73.2	2.7
6 to 20%	78.6	1.5
21 to 40%	77.7	1.7
Over 40%	83.7	1.6
Suburban—all	68.4	1.1
0 to 5%	64.8	1.5
6 to 20%	70.0	1.8
21 to 40%	80.5	3.0
Over 40%	81.7	6.6
Rural—all	62.6	0.7
0 to 5%	60.0	2.0
6 to 20%	62.1	1.4
21 to 40%	64.4	1.4
Over 40%	65.0	1.9

*"School poverty concentration" refers to the percentage of students in the school receiving free and reduced price lunch.

NOTE: Totals may include a small proportion of students for whom school urbanicity and/or poverty concentration are unknown.

SOURCE: U.S. Department of Education, National Center for Education Statistics, Schools and Staffing Survey, 1987–88, Teacher File.

Table 4.16—Data and standard errors for figures 4.44–4.46: Percentage of teachers of 8th-grade students who spend at least 1 hour per week maintaining classroom order and discipline, by urbanicity and school poverty concentration: 1988

School urbanicity and school poverty concentration*	Percentage	Standard error
Total	16.7	0.7
0 to 5%	12.2	1.3
6 to 20%	16.7	1.2
21 to 40%	15.9	1.4
Over 40%	21.1	1.7
Urban—all	24.6	1.5
0 to 5%	11.3	3.1
6 to 20%	20.5	2.5
21 to 40%	26.4	2.8
Over 40%	28.2	2.4
Suburban—all	16.4	1.0
0 to 5%	13.6	1.7
6 to 20%	17.8	1.7
21 to 40%	17.6	2.5
Over 40%	18.0	3.6
Rural—all	12.6	1.2
0 to 5%	8.0	2.0
6 to 20%	12.2	2.2
21 to 40%	11.6	1.9
Over 40%	16.1	2.8

*"School poverty concentration" refers to the percentage of students in the school receiving free and reduced price lunch.

NOTE: Totals may include a small proportion of students for whom school urbanicity and/or poverty concentration are unknown.

SOURCE: U.S. Department of Education, National Center for Education Statistics, National Educational Longitudinal Study of 1988, Teacher File.

Table 4.17—Data and standard errors for figures 4.47–4.49: Percentage of 10th-grade students who do not feel safe at school, by urbanicity and school poverty concentration: 1990

School urbanicity and school poverty concentration*	Percentage	Standard error
Total	8.8	0.4
0 to 5%	5.8	0.5
6 to 20%	8.1	0.5
21 to 40%	11.5	0.9
Over 40%	11.6	1.0
Urban—all	12.6	1.0
0 to 5%	5.6	1.7
6 to 20%	11.2	1.5
21 to 40%	16.4	1.6
Over 40%	11.6	1.8
Suburban—all	7.8	0.5
0 to 5%	6.1	0.6
6 to 20%	7.7	0.8
21 to 40%	15.7	3.4
Over 40%	11.4	1.9
Rural—all	7.5	0.5
0 to 5%	4.7	1.3
6 to 20%	6.8	0.8
21 to 40%	7.4	0.9
Over 40%	11.7	1.6

*"School poverty concentration" refers to the percentage of students in the school receiving free and reduced price lunch.

NOTE: Totals may include a small proportion of students for whom school urbanicity and/or poverty concentration are unknown.

SOURCE: U.S. Department of Education, National Center for Education Statistics, National Education Longitudinal Study of 1988, First Follow-up Student File.

Table 4.18—Data and standard errors for figures 4.50–4.52: Percentage of secondary teachers who believe that student weapons possession is a problem in their school, by urbanicity and school poverty concentration: 1987–88

School urbanicity and school poverty concentration*	Percentage	Standard error
Total	11.1	0.3
0 to 5%	6.4	0.6
6 to 20%	9.5	0.5
21 to 40%	14.4	1.1
Over 40%	20.8	1.4
Urban—all	21.3	0.9
0 to 5%	12.4	1.7
6 to 20%	17.9	1.9
21 to 40%	25.6	2.1
Over 40%	30.1	3.2
Suburban—all	9.1	0.6
0 to 5%	5.9	0.8
6 to 20%	10.9	0.9
21 to 40%	15.1	2.3
Over 40%	18.9	4.6
Rural—all	6.8	0.4
0 to 5%	4.0	0.7
6 to 20%	5.7	0.5
21 to 40%	8.1	1.1
Over 40%	13.0	1.5

*"School poverty concentration" refers to the percentage of students in the school receiving free and reduced price lunch.

NOTE: Totals may include a small proportion of students for whom school urbanicity and/or poverty concentration are unknown.

SOURCE: U.S. Department of Education, National Center for Education Statistics, Schools and Staffing Survey, 1987–88, Teacher File.

Table 4.19—Data and standard errors for figures 4.53–4.55: Percentage of secondary teachers who think that student alcohol use is a problem in their school, by urbanicity and school poverty concentration: 1987–88

School urbanicity and school poverty concentration*	Percentage	Standard error
Total	62.7	0.5
0 to 5%	66.6	0.9
6 to 20%	64.9	0.8
21 to 40%	58.3	1.1
Over 40%	53.9	1.6
Urban—all	58.2	1.2
0 to 5%	65.7	2.1
6 to 20%	61.5	1.6
21 to 40%	54.7	2.2
Over 40%	50.7	3.1
Suburban—all	62.7	1.2
0 to 5%	66.4	1.6
6 to 20%	61.3	1.7
21 to 40%	49.2	3.2
Over 40%	57.1	5.6
Rural—all	64.6	0.5
0 to 5%	67.4	1.7
6 to 20%	67.6	1.0
21 to 40%	61.7	1.1
Over 40%	56.1	2.4

*"School poverty concentration" refers to the percentage of students in the school receiving free and reduced price lunch.

NOTE: Totals may include a small proportion of students for whom school urbanicity and/or poverty concentration are unknown.

SOURCE: U.S. Department of Education, National Center for Education Statistics, Schools and Staffing Survey, 1987–88, Teacher File.

Table 4.20—Data and standard errors for figures 4.56–4.58: Percentage of secondary teachers who think that student pregnancy is a problem in their school, by urbanicity and school poverty concentration: 1987–88

School urbanicity and school poverty concentration*	Percentage	Standard error
Total	38.7	0.6
0 to 5%	26.4	1.2
6 to 20%	39.0	1.0
21 to 40%	45.7	1.5
Over 40%	52.2	1.8
Urban—all	48.0	1.3
0 to 5%	33.5	3.2
6 to 20%	45.0	2.3
21 to 40%	56.4	2.1
Over 40%	55.8	3.0
Suburban—all	30.4	1.2
0 to 5%	22.2	1.4
6 to 20%	37.8	1.8
21 to 40%	40.9	5.0
Over 40%	55.1	6.7
Rural—all	37.8	0.8
0 to 5%	29.0	1.7
6 to 20%	37.0	1.3
21 to 40%	40.4	1.6
Over 40%	48.7	2.3

*"School poverty concentration" refers to the percentage of students in the school receiving free and reduced price lunch.

NOTE: Totals may include a small proportion of students for whom school urbanicity and/or poverty concentration are unknown.

SOURCE: U.S. Department of Education, National Center for Education Statistics, Schools and Staffing Survey, 1987–88, Teacher File.

Methodology of Analysis

There are four basic steps to the analysis for this report. Each answers a specific question:

1) Are urban schools different?

2) Are high poverty schools different?

3) Are urban schools different after taking into account the poverty concentration of the school?

4) Are urban high poverty schools different than predicted? Is there something about these schools that puts the students at particular risk for poor educational outcomes and experiences?

Four models that correspond to these four questions can be calculated. Each of the models uses the following notation:

Y_i = the score on a particular outcome measure for the ith student

$X1_i$ and $X2_i$ = a set of contrast-coded variables representing the urbanicity of the ith student's school where:

$X1_i$ = 2 if suburban and -1 otherwise

$X2_i$ = 2 if rural and -1 otherwise

$X3_i$, $X4_i$, and $X5_i$ = a set of contrast-coded variables representing the poverty concentration of the ith student's school where:

$X3_i$ = 3 if the school has 0 to 5 percent poverty concentration and -1 otherwise

$X4_i$ = 3 if the school has 6 to 20 percent poverty concentration and -1 otherwise

$X5_i$ = 3 if the school has 21 to 40 percent poverty concentration and -1 otherwise

$X6_i$, $X7_i$, $X8_i$, $X9_i$, $X10_i$, and $X11_i$ = a set of variables representing various aspects of the interaction between urbanicity and poverty concentration where:

$$X6_i = X1_i * X3_i$$
$$X7_i = X1_i * X4_i$$
$$X8_i = X1_i * X5_i$$
$$X9_i = X2_i * X3_i$$
$$X10_i = X2_i * X4_i$$
$$X11_i = X2_i * X5_i$$

Model 1 estimates:

$$\hat{Y}_i = \beta_0 + \beta_1 X_1 + \beta_2 X_2$$

A joint test of $\beta_1 + \beta_2$ tests the overall effect of urbanicity. If the overall test is significant, then a test that $\beta_1 = 0$ tests the difference between students in rural and urban schools on Y, while the test that $\beta2 = 0$ tests the contrast between students in suburban and urban schools.

Model 2 estimates:

$$\hat{Y}_i = \beta_0 + \beta_3 X_3 + \beta_4 X_4 + \beta_5 X_5$$

A joint test of $\beta_3 + \beta_4 + \beta_5$ tests the overall effect of poverty concentration. If the overall test is significant, then a test that $\beta_3 = 0$ tests the difference on Y between students in schools with 0 to 5 percent poverty concentration and students in schools with over 40 percent poverty concentration; a test that $\beta_4 = 0$ tests the difference on Y between students in schools with 6 to 20 percent poverty concentration and students in schools with over 40 percent poverty concentration; and a test that $\beta_5 = 0$ tests the difference on Y between students in schools with 21 to 40 percent poverty concentration and students in schools with over 40 percent poverty concentration.

Model 3 estimates:

$$\hat{Y}_i = \beta_0 + \beta_1 X_1 + \beta_2 X_2 + \beta_3 X_3 + \beta_4 X_4 + \beta_5 X_5$$

A joint test of $\beta_1+\beta_2$ tests the overall effect of urbanicity (controlling for poverty concentration). If the overall test is significant, then a test that $\beta_1=0$ tests the difference between students in rural and urban schools on Y (controlling for poverty concentration), while the test that $\beta_2=0$ tests the contrast between students in suburban and urban schools (controlling for poverty concentration). Model 3 tests whether figure 1 or figure 2 holds for the data.

Figure 1 indicates an effect of poverty concentration but not of urbanicity when poverty concentration is held constant. That is, the differences between urban and other schools are explained by the higher concentration of poor students in urban schools. The difference between urban and other schools with high poverty concentrations is the same as it is at schools

Figure 1

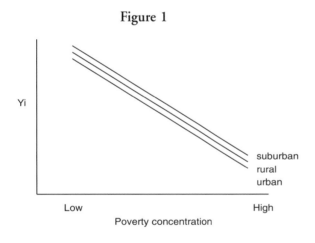

with low poverty concentrations; therefore, urban high poverty schools are no different than predicted.

Figure 2 indicates both an effect of poverty concentration and of urbanicity above and beyond the effect of poverty concentration. That is, significant differences between urban and other schools remain after accounting for the higher concentration of poverty in urban schools. Since the difference between urban and other schools with high poverty concentrations is the same as it is at low poverty concentrations, urban high poverty schools are no different than predicted.

Figure 2

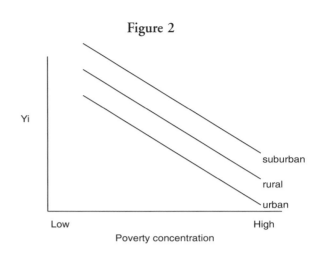

Model 4 estimates:

$$\hat{Y}_i=\beta_0+\beta_1X_1+\beta_2X_2+\beta_3X_3+\beta_4X_4+\beta_5X_5+\beta_6X_6+\beta_7X_7+\beta_8X_8+\beta_9X_9+\beta_{10}X_{10}+\beta_{11}X_{11}$$

A joint test that $\beta_6+\beta_7+\beta_8+\beta_9+\beta_{10}+\beta_{11}=0$ tests the overall effect of the interaction between urbanicity and poverty concentration. If the overall test is significant, each term in the interaction tests a different aspect of the interaction. Specifically, the test of $\beta_6=0$ tests whether the difference between rural and urban schools with 0 to 5 percent poverty concentration is the same as the difference between rural and urban schools with over 40 percent poverty concentration. The test of $\beta_9=0$ tests whether the difference between suburban and urban schools with 0 to 5 percent poverty concentration is larger or smaller than the difference between suburban and urban schools with over 40 percent poverty concentration. And this pattern continues for β_7 and β_8 through β_{10} and β_{11}.

Figure 3 displays an instance in which students in urban schools with a high poverty concentration are at particular risk for less desirable experiences or outcomes. The difference between urban and other schools with high poverty concentrations is greater than it is at schools with low poverty concentrations; therefore, urban high poverty schools are different than predicted. The combination of an urban and high poverty setting interact so that the outcomes and experiences of

Figure 3

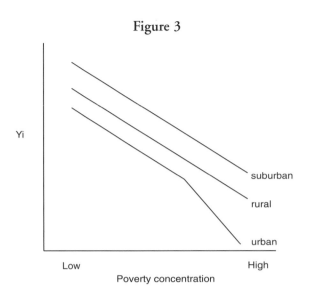

Yi

suburban

rural

urban

Low   High
Poverty concentration

Figure 4

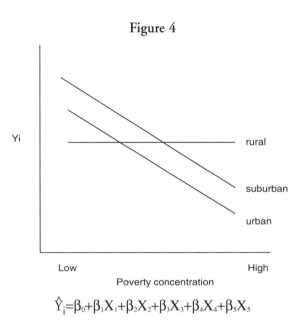

Yi

rural

suburban

urban

Low   High
Poverty concentration

$$\hat{Y}_i = \beta_0 + \beta_1 X_1 + \beta_2 X_2 + \beta_3 X_3 + \beta_4 X_4 + \beta_5 X_5$$

students in those settings are different than predicted. Also, students in urban high poverty schools are different from students in other high poverty schools.

Of course, the actual data do not behave as simply as the data in figures 1, 2, and 3, and the patterns can be quite complicated. In fact, sometimes the atypical group is the advantaged urban students.

In addition, there is another simple pattern that occurs in the data—one that is not explicitly tested in models 1 through 4. This pattern is shown in figure 4.

In this case, there is an interaction between urbanicity and poverty concentration, but not the one explicitly looked for in model 4. In fact, what is interesting is the lack of an overall effect of poverty concentration on rural schools as compared with a quite marked effect for urban and suburban schools. That is, what is of interest here is the overall effect of poverty concentration for rural schools, rather than the simple contrast between high poverty concentration and low poverty concentration schools. One can hypothesize that the slopes of the lines defining the poverty concentration are different for students in urban, suburban, and rural schools and that the slope for the students in rural schools is, in fact, not different from zero. For example, assume we ran the following model:

where:

$X1_i$ and $X2_i$ = a set of contrast-coded variables representing the urbanicity of the ith student's school

where:

> $X1_i$ = 2 if suburban and -1 otherwise
> $X2_i$ = 2 if rural and -1 otherwise
> $X3_i$ = poverty concentration expressed as a continuous variable (in most cases percent of free and reduced price lunch);

$X4_i$ and $X5_i$ = a set of variables representing the interaction of urbanicity and poverty concentration with:

> $X4_i = X1_i * X3_i$
> $X5_i = X2_i * X3_i$

A joint test of $\beta_4 + \beta_5$ is now an overall test of the interaction. Simple substitution of appropriate values for X_1 through X_5 results in the following simple regression equations for students in urban, rural, and suburban schools:

$$\hat{Y}_{urban} = \beta_0 + \beta_1(-1) + \beta_2(-1) + \beta_3(PCLNCH) + \beta_4$$
$$(-1*PCLNCH) + \beta_5(-1*PCLNCH)$$

where:

$(\beta_3 - \beta_4 - \beta_5)$*PCLNCH represents the poverty concentration slope for urban schools;

$$\hat{Y}_{rural} = \beta_0 + \beta_1(2) + \beta_2(-1) + \beta_3(PCLNCH) + \beta_4(2*PCLNCH) + \beta_5(-1*PCLNCH)$$

where:

$(\beta_3 + 2\beta_4 - \beta_5)$*PCLNCH represents the poverty concentration slope for rural schools; and

$$\hat{Y}_{suburban} = \beta_0 + \beta_1(-1) + \beta_2(2) + \beta_3(PCLNCH) + \beta_4(-1*PCLNCH) + \beta_5(2*PCLNCH)$$

where:

$(\beta_3 - \beta_4 + 2\beta_5)$*PCLNCH represents the poverty concentration slope for suburban schools.

After calculating the appropriate standard errors (combining terms from the coefficients' variance/covariance matrix), one can test whether the simple slopes for urban, rural, and suburban schools differ from one another, or whether they differ from zero.

Appendix C

Technical Notes

I. SIGNIFICANCE

All comparisons made in the text were tested using two-tailed tests for significance at the .05 level unless otherwise specified. When multiple comparisons were made, a Bonferroni adjustment to the significance level was used.

II. SELECTION OF INDICATORS FOR CHAPTER 4 ON SCHOOL EXPERIENCES

Indicators that were plausibly related to the differences in education outcomes in chapter 2 were chosen based on their important relationship to education outcomes as expressed in the research and policy communities. Indicators that were relevant to the school experience were examined for schools by urbanicity, poverty concentration, and urbanicity and poverty concentration combined. The final list of indicators was paired down by eliminating indicators for one or more of the following reasons:

1. No significant differences in the extreme categories of urbanicity or poverty concentration were revealed. Data for the extreme categories were compared using *t*-tests. "No differences" means that these variables could not contribute to the differences observed in the chapter 2 outcomes. The lack of variation for some of these variables is discussed in the text.

2. Significant differences were found in the extreme categories of urbanicity and poverty concentration; however, given the constraints of this report, indicators that were considered less important than others, after reviewing the recent literature, were excluded. These indicators are sometimes discussed in the text, particularly when they show similar patterns as those for which data are presented. The strongest indicator of a group relative to the same phenomenon was chosen to represent what the data showed about that area of inquiry.

3. The data available for an indicator would not support the analysis of variance methodology used in this report. Sample sizes were too small and/or the standard errors were too large when estimates were produced for urbanicity and poverty concentration combined.

The report examined data in three broad categories of the school experience: characteristics of schools, characteristics of teachers and staff, and student behavior. Some of the data that were initially examined to determine variations in the characteristics of schools but not shown in this report include the following:

- School facilities—types available

- School policies—graduation requirements, testing, control of decision-making, ability grouping of students

- Curriculum offerings and special programs available

- School climate—opinion data from students, teachers, and administrators on overall school climate, rules and discipline, the learning atmosphere, teacher morale

The following characteristics of teachers and staff examined for variation were not included in chapter 4:

- Pupil/teacher and pupil/staff ratios

- Teacher turnover rate

- School staffing patterns

- Number of years teaching in same school

- Highest degree earned by teachers

- Number of courses taken by teachers in primary and secondary field

- Certification in primary and secondary field

- Teacher benefits and pay incentives

- Professional development of teachers

- Instructional practices

- Teacher expectations for student achievement

- Ratings of teacher quality by students and administrators

In the area of student behavior, the following issues were analyzed in addition to those presented in the indicators section of this report:

- Average daily attendance/tardiness

- Student course selection

- Student effort on schoolwork and their ratings on difficulty of subject matter taught

- Outside reading

- Students' perceived locus of control and self-concept indicators

- Students' expectations for completing high school and for attending college

- Delinquency

- Illegal substance abuse

- Physical conflicts/abuse of teachers

- Theft and robbery in school

Data for indicators that are not presented in the text can be made available on request.

Appendix D

Data Sources and Definitions

I. DATA SOURCES

National Education Longitudinal Study

The National Education Longitudinal Study of 1988 (NELS:88) is a longitudinal survey that began in the spring of 1988 with a cohort of 24,599 8th graders. A two-stage stratified probability design was used to select a nationally representative sample of schools and students. In the first stage, 1,734 schools were selected, of which 1,052 (61 percent) participated—815 public and 237 private schools. From these participating schools, 26,599 students (93 percent) participated in the survey. On average, each of the participating schools was represented by 23 students. The student, who filled out a background questionnaire and completed an assessment test, is the basic unit of analysis in the NELS:88. All other components of the study—school, teacher, and parent questionnaires—are primarily intended to supplement the student data set.

NCES has been conducting NELS follow-up surveys every 2 years. This report uses data from the NELS Base Year Survey and the First Follow-up Survey, which was conducted in 1990 (when the students were generally in the 10th grade). For the First Follow-up Survey, several components were added, including a dropout study.

Schools and Staffing Survey

The Schools and Staffing Survey (SASS) is an integrated survey of schools, school districts, school administrators, and teachers designed to explore the major issues concerning the school work force and workplace. A sample of more than 9,300 public and 3,500 private schools was drawn for the SASS that the National Center for Education Statistics (NCES) conducted in the 1987–88 school year. From these schools, a sample of 56,000 public and 11,000 private school teachers

were selected. For this report, data from the 1987–88 survey were used to construct several indicators. In addition to the 1987–88 survey, NCES also conducted the SASS in the 1990–91 school year. Since SASS does not survey students, information on the students enrolled in a particular school is only available through the items directed at the schools, school administrators, and teachers concerning the characteristics of teachers and schools.

National Assessment of Educational Progress (NAEP) and NAEP High School Transcript Study

The National Assessment of Educational Progress (NAEP) is a federally funded periodic assessment of the educational achievement of students in various subject areas. The school and student samples for the 1990 NAEP were selected using a complex multistage sampling design. The four stages included 1) selection of geographically based Primary Sampling Units (PSUs); 2) selection of schools within sampling units; 3) assignment of session types (these are based on assessment subjects) to schools; and 4) selection of students for session types within schools. The resulting samples were nationally representative of schools and students. The High School Transcript Study (HSTS), which was linked to the 1990 NAEP survey, included a representative sample of high school seniors who graduated in the 1990 calendar year. The file includes high school transcripts of approximately 21,500 students from 330 schools; 16,456 of these students were from public schools. To increase the reliability of estimates, private schools and public schools with high enrollments of Hispanic or black students were oversampled.

The schools included in the sample for the 1990 HSTS included all schools with 12th grades that were selected to participate in the 1990 NAEP assessment whether they participated or not. The students chosen, when possible, were the same students who participated in the 1990 NAEP assessment. When this was not possible, such as cases where schools had not participated in the NAEP, a sample of students from those schools was drawn specifically for the HSTS.

High School and Beyond

High School and Beyond (HS&B) is a national longitudinal survey of high school sophomores and seniors conducted by NCES. HS&B is a stratified national probability sample of students. For the first stage of the HS&B, a sample of public and private high schools was selected. In the second stage, 36 seniors and 36 sophomores were selected in each school. (In schools with fewer than 36 students in either of these groups, all eligible students were included.) Certain types of schools were oversampled to make the study more useful for policy analysis: public schools with a high percentage of Hispanic students, Catholic schools with a high percentage of minority students, alternative public schools, and private schools with high achieving students. In 1980, more than 30,000 sophomores and 28,000 seniors enrolled in 1,015 public and private high schools participated in the Base Year Survey. The survey instruments used in the Base Year Survey included a sophomore questionnaire, a senior questionnaire, a school questionnaire, a teacher comment checklist, and a parent questionnaire. HS&B participants have been followed through the 1980s (1982, 1984, and 1986) and into the 1990s, with the Fourth Follow-up of the 1980 sophomores taking place in 1992.

Technical Note

The weight (panelwt4) applied to the data reported here is the weight used for cases with data from all of the HS&B surveys: the Base Year, First Follow-up, Second Follow-up and Third Follow-up. This is necessary because the samples drawn for the follow-up surveys were not the same as the original base year sample. The base year sample included 28,000 sophomores from 1,015 schools with a target number of 36 students from each school. For the First Follow-up, 30,000 people who were 1980 sophomores were selected. The Second and Third Follow-up sophomore

cohort samples were the same, totaling 15,000. The response rate for the 1984 survey was 92 percent, and for the 1986 survey, it was 91 percent.

National Longitudinal Survey of Youth

The National Longitudinal Survey of Youth (NLSY), conducted by the Bureau of Labor Statistics, is a longitudinal survey of a representative sample of the noninstitutionalized civilian and military population born between the years of January 1, 1957, through December 31, 1964. They have been interviewed on an annual basis since 1979, with the most recent interview year being 1996. Two special subsamples of the survey are 1) a supplemental sample that overrepresents the civilian Hispanic, black, and economically disadvantaged non-black/non-Hispanic youth living in the United States; and 2) a military sample representing the youth population serving in the armed forces as of September 30, 1978, and born January 1, 1957, through December 31, 1961. Although a subsample of the original military sample has been surveyed, the military sample was dropped in 1985 as a complete subsample.

In order to categorize respondents by the community type of the high school they attended, a separate file was used that included an item for urbanicity derived from the HS&B survey. This file contains data only for respondents who attended public high schools.

II. DEFINITION OF URBANICITY AND POVERTY CONCENTRATION IN SURVEYS

Although every effort was made to categorize schools by the same criteria for location and poverty concentration across all of the surveys used in this report, the way in which these two variables were defined in each of the data sources does vary. Below is a brief description of the definition of these two variables for each data source analyzed.

National Education Longitudinal Study

School urbanicity, either urban, suburban, or rural, for the Base Year Survey of NELS was based on urbanicity assigned to schools in the frame used to create the NELS sample, and corresponds to U.S. Bureau of the Census classifications. For this survey, the Quality Education Data (QED), a universe database of public and private parochial and nonparochial schools in the United States, was used. When urbanicity data were unavailable from the QED, Bureau of the Census data were used. For the NELS 10th-grade Follow-up Survey, the same source for school location data was used to ensure comparability with the 1988 survey. Schools classified as urban are located in central cities of Metropolitan Statistical Areas (MSAs); schools classified as suburban are located within the area surrounding a central city within a county constituting the MSA; and schools classified as rural are outside of an MSA.

For poverty concentration, the 1988 base year school administrators were asked to report the *number of students* receiving free or reduced price lunches. For the analysis in this report, the number reported was divided by the total school enrollment to get the percentage of students receiving free or reduced price lunch. This resulted in school poverty concentrations that were similar in distribution to those produced by the SASS. However, for the 10th-grade follow-up, school administrators were asked to list the *percentage of students* receiving free or reduced price lunch. The resulting distribution of schools matches more closely the data on the percentage of disadvantaged students reported for the HS&B and the NLSY databases.

Schools and Staffing Survey

Respondents reported on the urbanicity of schools in the school questionnaire administered as part of the 1987–88 SASS, while in the other surveys (NELS, NAEP, HS&B, and NLSY) school urbanicity was assigned to the school based upon the address. All subsequent administrations of the SASS survey have used a locale code assigned to the school based upon its address. As of the publication of this report, these codes have been added to the 1987–88 data to enable comparisons between the different administrations of SASS. In 1987–88, the SASS respondents chose from 10 residence categories, ranging in size from a rural or farming community to a very large city of more than

500,000 people. For this report, the 10 categories have been collapsed into the same three urbanicity categories (urban, suburban, and rural) as were used in the other data sets. Three city sizes in SASS—ranging from a medium-sized city of 50,000 to 100,000 people, a large city of 100,000 to 500,000 people, or a very large city of more than 500,000 people—have been collapsed into one urban group comprised of cities of 50,000 people or more. The suburbs of each of these cities have been collapsed into one suburban category, with military bases or stations added to this group. One rural category has been created from the following three groups: a rural or farming community, a small city or town of fewer than 50,000 people that is not a suburb of a larger city, or an Indian reservation.

The self-reported urbanicity in the 1987–88 SASS results in noticeable differences in how schools are categorized when compared with data on school location from other sources. Although the number of urban schools appears to be roughly comparable between the 1987–88 SASS and other data sources, the number of schools classified as rural is higher, and consequently, the number of suburban schools is lower, when compared with Bureau of the Census location data. For example, according to 1990 Bureau of the Census data presented in appendix table 1.1, 28 percent of public school students attended urban schools, 45 percent attended suburban, and 28 percent attended rural schools. However, according to the comparable SASS enrollment data for 1987–88 using the school-reported location, 30 percent of public school enrollment is in urban schools, 23 percent in suburban, and 47 percent in rural.

Poverty concentration for the SASS survey was defined as "the percentage of students in the school receiving free or reduced price lunch." This figure was calculated by using the number of students receiving lunches divided by the total enrollment.

National Assessment of Educational Progress (NAEP) and NAEP High School Transcript Study

The urbanicity of schools in the National Assessment of Educational Progress (NAEP) High School Transcript Study (HSTS) survey was assigned to schools based on school address using 1980 Bureau of Census data and definitions of urban, suburban, and rural areas. Schools classified as urban are located in central cities of Metropolitan Statistical Areas (MSAs); schools classified as suburban are located within the area surrounding a central city within a county constituting the MSA; and schools classified as rural are outside of an MSA.

The definition of poverty concentration used for the NAEP survey, which was linked to the HSTS, was the percentage of students in a school receiving free or reduced price lunch which was derived from estimates by the school administrator who filled out the questionnaire.

High School and Beyond

School urbanicity was assigned to schools in the High School and Beyond (HS&B) survey based on 1980 Bureau of the Census data and definitions for urban, suburban, and rural areas. Schools classified as urban are located in central cities of Metropolitan Statistical Areas (MSAs); schools classified as suburban are located within the area surrounding a central city within a county constituting the MSA; and schools classified as rural are outside of an MSA.

School poverty concentration was derived from school administrator responses to a school questionnaire item asking first what criteria, whether federal, state, or other guidelines, were used to classify students as disadvantaged. Then the responding school official was asked to estimate the percentage of "disadvantaged"

students in the school, according to the guidelines of Chapter 1 of the Elementary and Secondary Education Act. This figure was used to classify schools into the poverty concentration categories used in this report.

National Longitudinal Survey of Youth

School urbanicity was not a variable on the public release file of the National Longitudinal Survey of Youth (NLSY) survey. However, urbanicity codes were matched to the respondent's high school by the Center for Human Resource Research at Ohio State University using the original HS&B sampling frame. School urbanicity was assigned to schools in the HS&B survey based on 1980 Bureau of the Census data and definitions for urban, suburban, and rural areas. Schools classified as urban are located in central cities of Metropolitan Statistical Areas (MSAs); schools classified as suburban are located within the area surrounding a central city within a county constituting the MSA; and schools classified as rural are outside of an MSA. For the purpose of this report, urbanicity codes for respondents in the nonmilitary sample who attended public high schools were made available.

Poverty concentration was defined in the same manner as it was for the HS&B survey, as discussed above. School administrators were asked what percentage of the students in their school were classified as "disadvantaged" according to the guidelines of Chapter 1 of the Elementary and Secondary Education Act.

Appendix E

Bibliography

Abt Associates. 1993. Prospects: *The Congressionally Mandated Study of Educational Growth and Opportunity*. Washington, D.C.: U.S. Department of Education.

Anderson, J.; Hollinger, D.; and Conaty, J. 1992. "Poverty and Achievement: Re-examining the Relationship Between School Poverty and Student Achievement." Paper presented at the Annual Meeting of the American Educational Research Association.

Armor, D. J. 1972. "School and Family Effects on Black and White Achievement: A Re-examination of the USOE Data." In *On Equality of Educational Opportunity*. Frederick Mosteller and Daniel P. Moynihan, eds. New York: Vintage Books.

Ascher, C.; Burnett, G. 1993. *Current Trends and Issues in Urban Education*, 1993. Trends and Issues No. 19. New York: ERIC Clearinghouse on Urban Education.

Barro, S.; Kolstad, A. 1987. *Who Drops Out of High School? Findings from High School and Beyond*. Washington, D.C.: National Center for Education Statistics (CS 87-397c).

Bastian, L. D.; Taylor, B.M. 1991. *School Crime: A National Crime Victimization Survey Report*. Washington, D.C.: Bureau of Justice Statistics (NCJ-131645).

Berliner, D. 1993. "Mythology and the American System of Education," *Phi Delta Kappan*, 74,(8), 632,634–40.

Bianchi, S. 1993. "Change in the Educational Performance of U.S. Children in the 1980s." *Working Papers from the Education Analysis Staff*. Paper No. 93–2. Washington, D.C.: Bureau of the Census and National Center for Education Statistics.

Bianchi, S.; McArthur, E. 1991. "Family Disruption and Economic Hardship: the Short-Run Picture for Children." *Current Population Reports*, Series P-70, Report No. 23.

Bobbitt, S. A.; Faupel, E.; and Burns, S. 1991. *Stayers, Movers, and Leavers: Results of the 1988–89 Teacher Followup Survey*, 1991. Washington, D.C.: National Center for Education Statistics (NCES 91–128).

Bobbitt, S. A.; Quinn, P.; and Dabbs, P. 1992. *Filling the Gaps: An Overview of Data on Education in Grades K Through 12*. Washington, D.C.: National Center for Education Statistics (NCES 92–132).

Braddock, J. H., II; et al. 1991. "Bouncing Back: Sports and Academic Resilience Among African-American Males." *Education and Urban Society*, 24 (1), 113–131.

Brooks-Gunn, J.; Duncan, G.; Klebanov, P.; and Sealand, N. 1993. "Do Neighborhoods Influence Child and Adolescent Development?" *American Journal of Sociology*, 99 (2), 353–395.

Caldas, S. J. 1994. "Teen Pregnancy: Why It Remains a Serious Social, Economic and Educational Problem in the U.S." *Phi Delta Kappan*, 75 (5), 402–406.

Carnegie Foundation for the Advancement of Teaching. 1988. *An Imperiled Generation: Saving Urban Schools.* Princeton, NJ: The Carnegie Foundation.

Choy, S. P.; Bobbitt, S. A.; Henke, R. R.; Medrich, E. A.; Horn, L. J.; and Lieberman, J. 1993a. *America's Teachers: Profile of a Profession.* Washington, D.C.: National Center for Education Statistics (NCES 93-025).

Choy, S. P.; Henke, R. R.; Alt, M. N.; Medrich, E. A.; and Bobbitt, S. A. 1993b. *Schools and Staffing in the United States: A Statistical Profile, 1990–91.* Washington, D.C.: National Center for Education Statistics (NCES 93-146).

Choy, S. P.; Medrich, E. A.; Henke, R. R.; and Bobbitt, S. A. 1992. *Schools and Staffing in the United States: A Statistical Profile, 1987–88.* Washington, D.C.: National Center for Education Statistics (NCES 92-120).

Clarke, R. L. 1992. "The Neighborhood Effects of Dropping Out of School among Teenage Boys." Washington, D.C.: The Urban Institute.

Coleman, J. S.; Cambell, E. Q.; Hobson, C. S.; McPartland, J.; Mood, A. M.; Weinfeld, F. D.; York, R. L.; 1966. *Equality of Educational Opportunity.* Washington, D.C.: U.S. Department of Health, Education and Welfare.

Coulton, C. J.; and Pandey, S. 1992. "Geographic Concentration of Poverty and Risk for Children in Urban Neighborhoods." *American Behavioral Scientist*, 25 (3), 238–257.

Council of the Great City Schools. 1994. *National Urban Education Goals: 1992–93 Indicators Report.* Washington, D.C.

Council of the Great City Schools. 1992. *National Urban Education Goals: 1990–91 Indicators Report.* Washington, D.C.

Crane, J. 1991. "The Epidemic Theory of Ghettos and Neighborhood Effects on Dropping Out and Teenage Childbearing." *American Journal of Sociology*, 96 (5), 1226–1259.

Duncan, G. J.; Brooks-Gunn, J.; Klebanov, P. K. 1993. "Economic Deprivation and Early-Childhood Development." *Child Development*, 65 (2), 296–318.

Ellwood, D. 1988. *Poor Support: Poverty in the American Family.* New York: Basic Books.

Entwistle, D. Unpublished paper. 1990. "Recommendations for the NCES Longitudinal Study of Early Childhood Education." Baltimore: *The Johns Hopkins University.*

Finn, J. D. 1993. *School Engagement and Students at Risk.* Washington, D.C.: National Center for Education Statistics (NCES 93-470).

Fordham, S.; Ogbu, J. 1986. "Black Students' School Success: Coping with the Burden of Acting White." *Urban Review*, 18 (3), 176–206.

Freeman, R. 1991. "Employment and Earnings of Disadvantaged Youth in a Labor Shortage Economy." In C. Jencks and P. Peterson, eds., *The Urban Underclass*. Washington, D.C.: Brookings Institution.

Gamoran, A. 1987. "The Stratification of High School Learning Opportunities." *Sociology of Education*, 60 (3), 135–155.

Glazer, N. 1992. "The Real World of Urban Education." *Public Interest*, 106, 57–75.

Greenberger, E.; Steinberg, L. 1986. *When Teenagers Work: The Psychological and Social Costs of Adolescent Employment*. New York, NY: Basic Books, Inc.

Hanushek, E. A. 1994. "Money Might Matter Somewhere: A Response to Hedges, Laine and Greenwald." *Educational Researcher*, 23 (4), 5–8.

Hanushek, E. A. 1989. "The Impact of Differential Expenditures on School Performance." *Educational Researcher*, 18 (4), 45–52.

Hartman, W. T. 1988. "District Spending Disparities: What Do the Dollars Buy?" *Journal of Education Finance*, 13 (4), 436–458.

Haveman, R.; Wolfe, B. L.; Spaulding, J. 1991. "Childhood Events and Circumstances Influencing High School Completion." *Demography*, 28 (2), 133–157.

Hedges, L. V.; Laine, R. D.; Greenwald, R. 1994. "Does Money Matter? A Meta Analysis of Studies of the Effects of Differential School Inputs on Student Outcomes." *Educational Researcher*, 23 (3), 5–14.

Hedges, L. V.; Laine, R. D.; Greenwald, R. 1994. "Money Does Matter Somewhere: A Reply to Hanushek." *Educational Researcher*, 23 (4), 9–10.

Hodgkinson, H. 1989. *The Same Client: The Demographics of Education and Service Delivery Systems*. Washington, D.C.: Institute for Educational Leadership and Center for Demographic Policy.

Hofferth, S. L.; West, J.; Henke, R.; and Kaufman, P. 1994. *Access to Early Childhood Programs for Children at Risk*. Washington, D.C.: National Center For Education Statistics (NCES 93-372).

Horn, L.; West, J. 1992. *A Profile of Parents of Eighth Graders*. Washington, D.C.: National Center for Education Statistics (NCES 92-488).

Jencks, C.; Mayer, S. E. 1990. "Social Consequences of Growing Up in a Poor Neighborhood." *In Inner City Poverty in the U.S.* L. E. Lynn, Jr. and M. G. H. McGeary, eds. Washington, D.C.: National Academy Press.

Jones, L. K. 1992. *The Encyclopedia of Career Change and Work Issues*. Phoenix: Oryx Press.

Jordan, M. July 7, 1992. "Shortage of Minority Male Teachers Reported." *The Washington Post*, A4.

Karweit, N. Unpublished paper. 1992. "Improving the Capacity of the National Education Statistical Database to Address Equity Issues." Baltimore: *Center for the Organization of Schools*. The Johns Hopkins University.

Kaufman, P.; Bradby, D. 1992. *Characteristics of At-Risk Students in NELS:88*. Washington, D.C.: National Center for Education Statistics (NCES 92-042).

Kennedy, M. M.; Jung, R. K.; and Orland, M.E. 1986. *Poverty, Achievement and the Distribution of Compensatory Education Services*. Washington, D.C.: U.S. Department of Education.

King, S. H. 1993. "The Limited Presence of African-American Teachers." *Review of Educational Research*, 63 (2), 115–149.

Kirsch, I. S.; Jungeblut, A. 1986. *Literacy: Profiles of America's Young Adults*. Princeton: National Assessment of Educational Progress. Educational Testing Service. Report No. 16-PL-02.

Knepper, P. 1990. *Trends in Postsecondary Credit Production, 1972 and 1980 High School Graduates*. Washington, D.C.: National Center for Education Statistics (NCES 90-351).

Kozol, J. 1991. *Savage Inequalities: Children in America's Schools*. New York: Crown Publishers.

Lewin-Epstein, N. 1981. *Youth Employment During High School: An Analysis of High School and Beyond, a National Longitudinal Study for the 1980s*. Washington, D.C.: National Center for Education Statistics (NCES 81-249).

Long, L. H. 1975. "Does Migration Interfere with Children's Progress in School?" *Sociology of Education*, 48 (3), 369–381.

Louis, K. S.; Miles, M. B. 1990. *Improving the Urban High School: What Works and Why*. New York, NY: Teachers College Press.

Males, M. 1994. "Poverty, Rape, Adult/Teen Sex." *Phi Delta Kappan*, 75 (5), 407–410.

Males, M. 1993. "Schools, Society and 'Teen' Pregnancy." *Phi Delta Kappan*, 74 (7), 566–68.

Mangum, G. L. 1988. "Youth Transition from Adolescence to the World of Work." prepared for *Youth and America's Future: The William T. Grant Foundation Commission on Work, Family and Citizenship*, 1988.

Massey, D.; Gross, A. B.; and Shibuya, K. 1994. "Migration, Segregation, and the Concentration of Poverty." *American Sociological Review*, 59 (3), 425–445.

Mayer, S.E.; Jencks, C. 1989. "Growing Up in Poor Neighborhoods: How Much Does it Matter?" *Science*, 243 (4897), 1441–1445.

McArthur, E. 1993. *Language Characteristics and Schooling in the United States: A Changing Picture: 1979 and 1989*. Washington D.C.: National Center for Education Statistics (NCES 93-699).

McFadden, R. D. October 15, 1993. "Twenty Percent of New York City Public-School Students Carry Weapons, Study Finds." *The New York Times*, B3.

Mulkey, L. M.; Crain, R. L.; Harrington, A. J. C. 1992. "One-Parent Households and Achievement: Economic and Behavioral Explanations of a Small Effect." *Sociology of Education*, 65 (1), 48-65.

Mullis, I. V. S.; Dossey, J. A.; Foretsch, M. A.; Jones, L. R.; and Gentile, C. A. 1991. *Trends in Academic Progress: Achievement of U.S. Students in Science 1969–70 to 1990; Mathematics, 1973–1990; Reading, 1971 to 1990; and Writing, 1984–1990*. Washington, D.C.: National Center for Education Statistics (ETS-21-T-01).

Myers, D. E. 1985. *The Relationship between School Poverty Concentration and Students' Reading and Math Achievement and Learning*. Washington, D.C.: Decision Resources, Inc.

The National Education Goals Panel. 1992. *The National Education Goals Report: Building a Nation of Learners*. Washington, D.C.

Natriello, G.; McDill, E.; Pallas, A. 1990. *Schooling Disadvantaged Children: Racing Against Catastrophe*. New York: Teachers College Press.

Newmann, F. M., ed. 1992. *Student Engagement and Achievement in American Secondary Schools*. New York: Teachers College Press.

Oakes, J. 1990. *Multiplying Inequalities: The Effects of Race, Social Class, and Tracking on Opportunities to Learn Mathematics and Science*. Santa Monica: The RAND Corporation.

Orland, M. E. 1990. "Demographics of Disadvantage." In *Access to Knowledge: An Agenda for Our Nation's Schools*. J. I. Goodlad and P. Keating, eds. New York: The College Board.

Panel on High-Risk Youth, Commission on Behavioral and Social Sciences and Education, National Research Council. 1993. *Losing Generations: Adolescents in High-Risk Settings*. Washington, D.C.: National Academy Press.

Pelavin, S. H.; Kane, M. 1990. *Changing the Odds: Factors Increasing Access to College*. New York: College Entrance Examination Board.

Peng, S.; Wang, M.; and Walberg, H. 1992. "Demographic Disparities of Inner-City Eighth Graders." *Urban Education*, 26 (4), 441–59.

Porter, A. 1994. "National Standards and School Improvement in the 1990s: Issues and Promise." *American Journal of Education*, 102 (4), 421–449.

Porter, A. C.; Kirst, M. W.; Osthoff, E. J.; Smithson, J. L.; and Schneider, S. A. 1993. *Reform Up Close: An Analysis of High School Mathematics and Science Classrooms. Final Report*. Madison: University of Wisconsin–Madison, Wisconsin Center for Education Research.

Ralph, J. 1992. "Identifying the Problems and Trends of Educationally Disadvantaged Students." In *Effective Schooling of Economically Disadvantaged Students: School Based Strategies for Diverse Student Populations.* J. H. Johnson, ed. Norwood, NJ: Ablex Press.

Ralph, J. 1990. "A Research Agenda on Effective Schooling for Disadvantaged Students." In *Readings on Equal Education, Vol 10: Critical Issues for a New Administration and Congress.* S.S. Goldberg, ed. New York: AMS Press.

Rasinski, K. A.; Ingels, S. J.; Rock, D. A.; Pollack, J. M.; and Wu, S. 1993. *America's High School Sophomores: A Ten Year Comparison.* Washington, D.C.: National Center for Education Statistics (NCES 93-087).

Rotberg, I. June 11, 1993. "Sure-Fire School Reform: You Can Solve a Problem by Throwing Money at It." The Washington Post, A21.

Rowen, B. 1990. "Commitment and Control: Alternative Strategies for the Organizational Design of Schools." In *Review of Research in Education,* Vol 16. Washington, D.C: American Educational Research Association.

Sawhill, I.; O'Connor, A.; Jensen, L.; and Coulton, C. 1992. "Families in Poverty: Patterns, Contexts, and Implications for Policy." *Background Briefing Report.* Washington, D.C.: Family Impact Seminar.

Special Study Panel on Education Indicators. 1991. *Education Counts: An Indicator System to Monitor the Nation's Educational Health.* Washington, D.C.: National Center for Education Statistics (NCES 91-634).

Stevenson, H. and Stigler, J. 1992. *The Learning Gap.* New York: Summit Books.

Straits, B. C. 1987. "Residence, Migration, and School Progress." *Sociology of Education,* 60 (1), 34–43.

Tuma, J. 1996. *Trends in Participation in Secondary Vocational Education, 1982–1992.* Washington, D.C.: National Center for Education Statistics (NCES 96-004).

U.S. Bureau of the Census. 1993. "Poverty in the United States: March 1992." *Current Population Reports,* Series P-60. Report No. 185. Washington, D.C.

U.S. Bureau of the Census. 1992. "Poverty in the United States, 1991." *Current Population Reports,* Series P-60. Report No. 181. Washington, D.C.

U.S. Bureau of the Census. 1992. "Educational Attainment in the United States: March 1991 and 1990." *Current Population Reports,* Series P-20. Report No. 462. Washington, D.C.

U.S. Bureau of the Census. 1981. "Characteristics of the Population Below the Poverty Level: 1980." *Current Population Reports,* Series P-60. Report No. 133. Washington, D.C.

U.S. Bureau of the Census. 1980 and 1990. *Current Population Survey.* Unpublished tabulations.

U.S. Bureau of the Census. 1979 and 1989. *Current Population Survey.* Unpublished tabulations.

U.S. Department of Education. Office of Education Research and Improvement. National Center for Education Statistics. 1994. *Digest of Education Statistics, 1994.* Washington, D.C. (NCES 94-115).

U.S. Department of Education. Office of Education Research and Improvement. National Center for Education Statistics. 1993a. *The Condition of Education, 1993.* Washington, D.C. (NCES 93-290).

U.S. Department of Education. Office of Education Research and Improvement. National Center for Education Statistics. 1993b. *NAEP 1992 Reading Report Card for the Nation and States.* Washington, D.C. (NAEP 23-ST06).

U.S. Department of Education. Office of Education Research and Improvement. National Center for Education Statistics. 1993c. *Youth Indicators 1993: Trends in the Well-Being of American Youth.* Washington, D.C. (NCES 93-242).

U.S. Department of Education. Office of Education Research and Improvement. National Center for Education Statistics. 1992. *The Condition of Education,* 1992. Washington, D.C. (NCES 92-096).

U.S. Department of Education. Office of Education Research and Improvement. National Center for Education Statistics. 1987–88 Schools and Staffing Survey. Unpublished tabulations.

U.S. Department of Education. Office of Education Research and Improvement. National Center for Education Statistics. National Education Longitudinal Study of 1988, Base Year Survey. Unpublished tabulations.

U.S. Department of Education. Office of Education Research and Improvement. Office of Research. 1987. *The Current Operation of the Chapter 1 Program.* Washington, D.C.

U.S. Department of Health and Human Services. National Center for Health Statistics. 1993. *Vital Statistics of the United States, 1990, Volume 2, Mortality.* Public Health Service: Washington, D.C.

U.S. Department of Health and Human Services. National Center for Health Statistics. 1990. *Vital and Health Statistics,* Advance Data. Report No. 188. Washington, D.C.

U.S. Department of Justice. Bureau of Justice Statistics. 1990. *Criminal Victimization in the United States, 1990.* Washington, D.C.

U.S. House of Representatives, Committee on Ways and Means. 1985. *Children in Poverty.* Washington, D.C.: U.S. Government Printing Office.

University of Michigan. January 27, 1994. "Drug Use Rises Among American Teenagers," *News and Information Services.* Ann Arbor, MI.

Walker, L. J. 1989. "Testimony to the House Subcommittee on Select Education on Educational Research and Development Applications to Urban Schools, March 9, 1989."

Waggoner, D. 1991. *Undereducation in America.* New York: Auburn House.

Wilson, W. J. 1987. *The Truly Disadvantaged.* Chicago: University of Chicago Press.

ISBN 0-16-048669-6